SEX IN CRISIS

SEX
IN CRISIS

THE NEW SEXUAL REVOLUTION
and the Future of American Politics

DAGMAR HERZOG

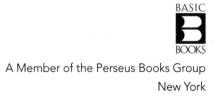

BASIC
BOOKS

A Member of the Perseus Books Group
New York

Books published by Basic Books are available at special discounts for bulk purchases
in the United States by corporations, institutions, and other organizations. For more
information, please contact the Special Markets Department at the Perseus Books
Group, 2300 Chestnut Street, Suite 200, Philadelphia, PA 19103, or call
(800) 810-4145 ext. 5000, or e-mail special.markets@perseusbooks.com.

Designed by Jeff Williams
Set in 12-point Garamond 3 by the Perseus Books Group

Library of Congress Cataloging-in-Publication Data
Herzog, Dagmar, 1961-
Sex in crisis : the new sexual revolution and the future of American politics /
Dagmar Herzog.
        p. cm.
    Includes bibliographical references and index.
    ISBN 978-0-465-00214-6
    1. Sex—United States—History—20th century. 2. Sex customs—United
States—History—20th century. 3. Religious right—United States—History—20th
century. 4. Religion and politics—United States—History—20th century.
5. Homosexuality—United States—History—20th century. I. Title.

HQ18.U5H455 2008
306.70973'0904—dc22

                                                          2008005941

10 9 8 7 6 5 4 3 2 1

For Michael

CONTENTS

PREFACE

THIS BOOK WAS AN AGONY TO WRITE. This was true for several reasons, but I will focus here on only two.

First, during the several years I researched and wrote this book, I found myself inescapably inhabiting the psychic and sexual universe of the Religious Right—a landscape I found consistently disturbing as well as exceptionally disorienting. The sexual rhetoric of right-wing evangelicalism should not have affected me as deeply as it did; I understood this intellectually. After all, I was a university professor who had been teaching a history of sexuality course at a large midwestern university for more than a decade. I considered myself hard to shock.

Yet what I most profoundly felt as I read (and read and reread) right-wing evangelical pronouncements on sex written since the mid–1990s was unnerved. I was shaken in ways I could not shrug off. The rhetoric was graphically explicit and mean and manipulative at once. It was intrusive and insidious. And it got under my skin.

Certainly, though, this anguish had everything to do with the feelings I have about my own Christian faith. This is the second reason this book was so tough on me. Raised in a deeply Christian household—my father and both grandfathers were all three Protestant pastors—I attended church every Sunday until I was well into my early thirties. Christianity was the air I breathed. (The nonbelievers I knew growing up I could count on the fingers of one hand.) I knew nothing else, and sought or needed little else.

Coming of age in the American South during the 1970s and 1980s, I witnessed firsthand how fluid and adaptable sexual choices were for evangelicals and non-evangelicals alike. Throughout these years, I knew evangelicals who experienced not the slightest shame or personal remorse if they engaged in premarital sex, and I also knew non-evangelical Protestants who chose to remain "pure" (if only technically so) until their wedding night. The Bible Belt of my high school and college years was a sensual and beautiful place; the churches left their congregants alone when it came to sexual issues. They were not sex-obsessed, and when (on rare occasion) Sunday school teachers I knew did choose to offer guidance on matters relating to sex, they did so in the most generous manner imaginable. There was no judgment, no shaming, no guilt-inducing diatribe. They either advocated premarital sex as unproblematic or shared the opinion that there were lots of other fun things to do besides have intercourse. Faith was about a relationship with God and about struggling to be a good and kind person, locally and in the world at large.

But the world in which I came of age as a Christian is not a world that exists any longer. Things began to change—and change dramatically—over the course of the last fifteen years and have continued to change ever more drastically since the turn of the new century. As a historian of sexuality, I witnessed this shift most profoundly in the attitudes and ideas expressed by my students at Michigan State University; in 1992 they were remarkably comfortable and forthright, sassy and self-confident, knowledgeable and open-minded. By the time I left the Midwest in 2005, the students appeared far more hesitant and insecure; they communicated an astonishing lack of self-ownership and understanding when it came to sexual matters. What had happened? Writing this book was my way of answering that question too.

OUR NATIONAL CONVERSATION about sex now suffers from a tremendous impoverishment. It is fairly easy to find information about how to have sex or techniques for how to improve sex. It is simple to find near-frenzied talk about adolescents' exposure to sexual imagery on the Internet or alarm over teens' potentially risky behavior. It is far tougher to find frank and open dialogue about our hopes and fears for our children's—and our own—sexual health and happiness. There is much titillating talk about sex in America, yet there is very little talk about sex that is morally engaged and affirmative.

In dozens of variations, Americans are told these days that sex strengthens an individual's sense of self-worth only when it occurs within very narrow boundaries—not just within a monogamous and preferably heterosexual partnership, ideally a marriage, but also one suffused with daily emotional intimacy. Everything else—the sex of teens and of the unmarried of all ages, homosexuality, extramarital sex, emotionally uninvolved sex, porn use, even masturbation—is now recurrently discussed as evidence of "low self-esteem." No matter what the topic, arguments for greater sexual conservatism today invariably come wrapped in the language not just of physical health but especially also of psychological well-being.

The Religious Right, in fifteen years of steady effort, has succeeded, above all, by advancing its cause on secularized and psychologizing grounds. Repression has been repackaged as promotion of mental health. That which used to be deemed immoral is now presented as likely to induce depressive feelings of self-loathing.

I do not lay the blame for the retrenchment with respect to sexuality entirely at the feet of the evangelical Right, however. Liberals also deserve their share of responsibility. For liberals, sex has become the problem that has no name; one simply does not hear liberals articulate a defense of sexual rights. Instead, what we have witnessed is a coalescing of conservative evangelical and mainstream secular perspectives on sex. The conversation on sex in America—when sex is discussed in a serious and earnest way at all—tends largely to adopt the parameters set by the Religious Right. This book will analyze how this development came about as well.

Perhaps it is no surprise that sex has ruled so much in American politics. Sex is an easy means to politically manipulate people precisely because it is so ambiguous and complex. Sex can so often be existentially intense. It can touch the core of our egos, our souls, our (often conflicted) longings.

This book, then, is above all intended as a history of the recent past. The evangelical movement in America has never been monolithic, and there are clear signs in the last couple of years that evangelicals are taking an increased interest in issues long associated with the Left—such as the environment, economic justice, and global health—and that a new leadership is emerging that no longer makes culture war issues like abortion or same-sex marriage its top priorities. Many commentators are hopeful that we are now moving into a post–Religious Right era. But this does not change the fact that over the last fifteen years we have experienced a fundamental shift in how we think about sex.

The Religious Right succeeded in setting the terms of conversation about sex in the United States not least because it creatively adapted aspects of the old sexual revolution, as well as of the feminist and men's movements of the 1960s to 1980s, for its own sexually conservative ends. But another crucial piece of the puzzle lies in the dramatic changes that took place in the sexual landscape of the United States around the turn of the millennium—changes that unleashed an avalanche of insecurities.

My subtitle is *The New Sexual Revolution and the Future of American Politics*. "Revolution" is a strong word, and it's meant to be. We witnessed a revolution in values and attitudes toward sex in the 1960s and 1970s—no one doubts this. There was a seismic shift in perspective and morals when it came to a vast array of sexual choices and behaviors. And these were, for the most part, welcomed by individuals from all walks of life, exhausted as they were by the hypocrisies foisted upon them by the puritanical restrictiveness of the 1950s.

Americans experienced a comparable revolution in attitudes toward sex and sexuality in the last fifteen years. Under the triple impact of Internet porn, sexual pharmacology, and the hypersexualization of popular culture and fashion, confusions about the relationships between bodies and emotions, fantasies and physical sensations, proliferated exponentially. During the same period of time, there was a war on sex in this country—a war the Religious Right in large part won. From the highest court in the land to the Congress and state legislatures to countless local school boards, from news venues to fashion magazines: American political and popular culture alike absorbed the conservative arguments presented in the name of psychological health.

Almost no one is immune from anxiety about being desired, or from worries about the connections (or lack thereof) between sex and love. Anomie and emotional alienation within couples have become major topics of national concern. The proliferation of confusions about these matters created an opening into which the Religious Right stepped with vigor. Whether the moves of the Religious Right were intentional or just intuitive, they certainly worked brilliantly. And it is these confusions that also placed liberals so thoroughly on the defensive.

At the same time, we may now be at a critical moment when change for the better is again possible. The potential for reversing the damage done to our sexual well-being as a nation and a people by the Christian Right and its secular allies has seldom if ever been stronger. There is a chance now to rewrite the script yet again. But before we can chart a new future for our national conversation about sexual politics, we must more fully understand how we allowed ourselves to get to this devastating point in the first place, and also how it became so difficult for those who would prefer a more liberal sexual politics to respond effectively.

SEX IN CRISIS

Chapter 1

ANXIETY NATION

AMERICANS THESE DAYS express remarkable amounts of anxiety about sex. Few topics are as likely to turn otherwise capable adults into sophomoric adolescents. We obsess over sex, but we articulate increasing concern about it as well. Discussions about sex in America center less and less on joy, pleasure, and self-determination and more and more on peril and danger.

Look. Americans are drowning in a daily dose of sexual imagery and information. Padded and push-up bras are practically obligatory for females from fifteen (or younger) to well past sixty. Photographic blow-ups in the display window of Victoria's Secret make the shopping mall experience a soft-core feast. Cable TV and high-speed Internet deliver full frontal nudity and hard-core scenes into a vast number of American homes, while at work and play the Internet provides near-constant opportunity for arousing chats with strangers, acquaintances, and coworkers. Meanwhile, men's magazines like *Stuff, Maxim,* and *FHM,* as well as women's magazines like *Cosmopolitan* and *Glamour,* keep extending the limits of what can be purchased at the neighborhood drug or grocery store. Looking for fresh advice on gentle testicle-tugging, G-spot-locating, perineum-stroking, or nipple-licking sex? Read all about it while in line to buy milk and orange juice or aspirin.

But don't touch. That's the contradiction. *Maxim* publishes endless photographs of young women it likes to call "hotties," but the magazine's imagined audience often has nothing better to do than surf the Web or leaf through *Maxim*. *FHM* reminds young men to put down their beers or turn off the boob tube and touch their girlfriend's actual breasts for a change. Do young men now need to be *reminded* that they might want to have real sex, not just simulated or fantasy sex? Apparently so. Meanwhile, the message to young women is far more direct: "Be sexy. It doesn't mean you have to have sex."[1] *Look—but don't touch.* It has become the national anthem of the new sexual revolution.

We still know that sex can be blissful. Sex can be fun. Sex can be amazing. But we have also gotten the message that sex can be emotionally messy. Sex can be frustrating and boring—or lousy. What we have not adequately registered, however, is how much sex can change—and has changed, even in the last fifteen years. At this moment, sex is continuing to change—dramatically so.

The changes have in part been due to the paradigm-shifting psychopharmacologization of human emotions. Mental state–altering drugs like Zoloft, Paxil, Klonopin, and Ritalin have chemically transformed people's relationships with one another (and with themselves). American culture in the early twenty-first century is also extraordinarily frenetic and competitive, generating wellsprings of insecurity for a whole jumble of economic and social reasons that include, but are certainly not limited to, the consequences of economic downsizing, the fatigue that results from working longer and longer hours, and the rising pressures on both men and women to be perfect parents. Time for sex is getting scarcer, and lack of confidence about financial security makes home life stressful. At the same time, we are incessantly encouraged to monitor what *other* people have, as well as what other people *do*—not least of all what other people do in bed. If we are increasingly an Anxiety Nation, we have also become a Voyeur Nation. The pervasive effect of a "somewhere someone is having better sex than you" syndrome has not been healthful or beneficial, but it does help explain why sex has become such a problem for so many.

Meanwhile, the expectations we place on sex are often astronomically high. How did things get to be this way? Why are people so desperate to be desired—and so dissatisfied with the love they do have? Where did our love go?

In short, we are experiencing sex in crisis. And it is a condition that now applies not only to premarital but also (and even more) to postmarital sex—its quality, its quantity, its improvability, indeed, its very existence. As the cultural flames of sexual confusion and dissatisfaction get fanned daily, never before have so many Americans worried so much about whether they really even want sex at all.

TWO PHENOMENA have been crucial in spurring our new sexual revolution. The first was the discovery of Viagra in 1998. The second was the exponential growth of Internet pornography. In both cases, however, it is less the phenomenon itself that requires close examination and more its unanticipated consequences. Each has changed how we think about sex. And surprisingly, each has caused perplexity about the nature of desire.

This is the last thing we might have expected to follow in the wake of the discovery of Viagra. The drug seemed like it was going to be nothing short of marvelous. Its discovery, after all, was a matter of serendipity—even as, ultimately, it won several researchers the Nobel Prize. Rarely do scientists get so fortunate.

In 1997 the Food and Drug Administration (FDA) lifted its prohibition on the direct-to-consumer (DTC) advertising of prescription medicine. This made the United States one of only two nations in the developed world to permit such advertising. (The other is New Zealand.) The FDA argued that DTC advertising produces more informed consumers and improves the quality of their lives by putting them in a better position to make educated medical choices. No longer would they be wholly dependent on members of the medical profession for their knowledge of pharmaceutical products. Now consumers would get that information from pharmaceutical companies themselves through advertising. And then these consumers could ask their doctors for the drugs they considered best for them. Which is pretty much what happened. Since 1997, pharmaceutical companies have spent more than $2 billion a year promoting prescription medications directly to the public. The number of prescriptions written has increased dramatically, and sales of the more expensive (and most advertised) medications have grown at the fastest rates.[2]

In this heady climate, the first anti-impotence pill appeared on the market in March 1998. The British division of Pfizer had been running trials for men on an experimental drug to treat angina. The drug failed to alleviate chest pain, but trial subjects reported the most excellent erections. Once the trials ended, subjects refused to return their remaining pills. Thus, a new era in impotence treatment was born. As a forty-three-year-old accountant from Springfield, Massachusetts, said about (Viagra-assisted) sex with his wife: "Not only is the frequency of our sex greater, but for me it is much more intense. . . . The orgasm is much more explosive."[3]

Not that promised cures for impotence were anything new. Several anti-impotence treatments predated Viagra, but these could be rather unpleasant. After 1998, no longer would men have to contemplate penile implants (an inflatable prosthesis surgically placed inside the penis). Gone were the days of the vacuum pump. (Attached to the end of the penis, the pump created a vacuum that drew blood into the penis. Once engorged, a band around the lower end of the penis kept the penis erect.) At last there was an alternative to a drug injected with a needle directly into the base of the penis. (Immediately afterwards, the penis became hard.) Now men popped a pill that blocked an enzyme that inhibited blood flow; this alone facilitated engorgement of the penis.

What has been less well understood is that the discovery and dissemination of Viagra represented the culmination of a fundamental and decade-long shift in thinking about male sexuality. Not all that long ago, a man's difficulties with sex and sexual satisfaction had been treated principally as a problem originating in his head, with psychoanalysis or other kinds of counseling the recommended remedy (or in the relationship, with couples counseling the logical path to pursue). It could take months, even years, before he felt improvements—if he ever did. And there were no guarantees. Since the early 1990s, fresh thinking in the medical world had sought to streamline this process and hasten recovery. In 1990 the American Urological Association had changed the script on impotence when it discounted the tired old view that erection difficulties were 80 percent emotional and declared decisively that "sexual dysfunction in the male is a disease entity."[4] By the early 1990s, the National Institutes of Health (NIH) officially agreed and moved to define impotence as preeminently a biological—not a psychological—difficulty.[5] Additionally, the NIH reconceived impotence in far broader and more subjective terms. No longer did it technically mean the inability to get an erection; now it meant the inability to achieve "satisfactory sexual performance." This definition resulted in "a tripling of the number of men estimated to be impotent in this country—some 30 million according to the NIH, half of whom are thought to be under the age of 65."[6] From this point on, male difficulties would be treated first and foremost as a problem originating in the body. Forget your unhappy childhood or unhappy prior relationships. Sex was about *now*.

Male sexuality was increasingly interpreted as something mechanical, as though, at least for the purposes of performance, emotions played only a minor role.[7] No one did more to advance the techno-scientific view than Dr. Irwin Goldstein of the Department of Urology at Boston University School of Medicine, best known as urologist to the stars (including former senator and presidential candidate Bob Dole). With research projects on such topics as "penile tissue mechanical properties," "penile geometry," "the relationship between radial and axial rigidity values," and "axial penile buckling testing as a primary efficacy variable of erection quality" in co-authored scientific journal articles such as "Engineering Analysis of Penile Hemodynamic and Structural-Dynamic Relationships," and in collaboration with Boston University's Department of Aerospace Engineering, Goldstein and his colleagues viewed sexual intercourse in these terms: "Penile rigidity, the ability of the erect penis to overcome vaginally-mediated axial compressive forces during coitus, occurs when corporal smooth muscle relaxation induces increased arterial inflow and restricted venous outflow resulting in constrained, increased blood volume within the stretched penile tunical envelope."[8] As Goldstein acknowledged to a journalist: "I can apply the principles of hydraulics to these problems":

Not to discount psychological aspects, but at a certain point all sex is mechanical. The man needs a sufficient axial rigidity so his penis can penetrate through labia, and he has to sustain that in order to have sex. This is a mechanical structure, and mechanical structures follow scientific principles.

To emphasize his point, Goldstein "poked his forefinger into the palm of his hand and explained that the 'typical resistance' posed by the average vagina is a measurable two pounds. The key is to create an erection that doesn't 'deform' or collapse when engaging that resistance."[9]

Viagra solved this mechanical dilemma. Never mind the endlessly reported news that the majority of women were not all that delighted with coitus in the first place and would have been more than happy to engage in other mutually orgasm-inducing practices. Popular magazines regularly announced that, "as amazing as it sounds, intercourse just doesn't do it"; "more than 70 percent of women don't have an orgasm through intercourse alone"; and "keep in mind that only about 20 percent of women have an orgasm from intercourse alone."[10] Or as *Men's Health* conceded, after running through a long list of possible techniques for "synchronized schwinging," "she's not likely to orgasm with any of these."[11] All that was apparently irrelevant. "Normal" sex was here to stay. If the discovery of Viagra not only facilitated the restoration of men's ability to achieve erection and release but also reinforced a particular model of sexual interaction, then so be it.

Before offering Viagra to the masses, Pfizer worried that men might feel too ashamed to seek professional help for impotence. To tackle the problem, the company promoted an odd little new acronym—ED, or "erectile dysfunction." In hindsight, this was a stroke of genius. After Viagra appeared, no one appeared the slightest bit embarrassed to "admit" to erectile dysfunction. As one urologist noted, "The prevalence [of ED] is stunning."[12] Older men, Pfizer's initial target audience, lined up in droves for their prescriptions at a rate of forty thousand a day—at ten dollars a pill.[13]

The Viagra revolution had begun, and heavily promoted through DTC advertising, the revolution would be televised. Viagra became an overnight sensation. Men who had avoided visiting a doctor's office for years now clamored for their Viagra prescriptions. Satisfied Viagra-takers described the experience as something like a gift from heaven. As one retired packaging foreman for Budweiser put it: "I couldn't perform as a man. My wife and I would be at each other's throats for no reason. This Viagra has brought me back 20 years. I can't praise it enough. I love sex—no ifs, ands or buts. It's back." Some men faked medical emergencies to jump the queue. A doctor in Florida reported, "Pain in the kidney. Blood in the urine. But when they get in here, they just want to ask us about Viagra."[14]

Did those who asked for Viagra really need Viagra? It quickly ceased to matter. As the *New York Times* reported in 1998, among the men who sought out the drug it was difficult to distinguish "the line between real need and sexual enhancement." The *Times* cited this example: "Reached at his Manhattan office, Dr. Steven Lamm took time away from examining a 52-year-old man who wanted Viagra as 'insurance' in his relationship with a 24-year-old woman. His goal was repeated orgasms, though he also inquired about a drug to deal with his baldness."[15] In its first year on the market, Viagra sales topped $1 billion. Within three years, Pfizer became the largest and most powerful drug company in the world, and the fifth most profitable company in the United States.[16]

By 2000, Pfizer's DTC ads had begun also to target men in their thirties. An ad in 2001 announced: "VIAGRA. It works for older guys. Younger guys. Even skeptical guys." And the smaller print elaborated:

> Think you're too young for Viagra? Do you figure "It only happens once in a while, so I'll just live with it"? Then nothing's going to change, especially your sex life. . . . In fact, 1 out of 3 men of all ages have ED (erectile dysfunction) to some degree.

Indeed, "more than 9 million men have turned to VIAGRA to treat their ED." Pfizer's candid advice? Ask your doctor about how you can "join the millions."[17] Pfizer further expanded its potential consumer base by noting that not only "erectile dysfunction" but also "erectile dysphoria" could be treated. What was "erectile dysphoria"? It was defined as "a vague sense of dissatisfaction" with one's erection.[18] Reports circulated that erectile dysphoria afflicted fully 50 percent of the male population between the ages of forty and seventy. Taglines in Pfizer ads targeted any man "not satisfied with your sex life due to poor erections during recent months." *Not satisfied with your sex life?* As one commentator quipped, "Now there's a market segment."[19] By 2003, Pfizer boasted that nine men around the world were ingesting a Viagra pill *every second*.[20] By 2006, it was common knowledge that perfectly healthy men were using Viagra just "to jazz things up."[21]

On the one hand, Viagra actually worked for many, many people. Millions of men experienced a restored ability to perform and enjoy sex. Millions of couples for whom sex had become difficult no longer had to worry about whether there might be some psychological dynamic between them that was inhibiting the man. The problem was mechanical, and it was chemically curable.

On the other hand, Viagra changed how everyone thought about sex. While male impotence had long been considered a psychological issue and now had been redefined as largely mechanical, the mass availability of Viagra and the tremendous enthusiasm for it created unprecedented bewilderment about the link (or lack thereof) between the capacity to perform and the experience of desire. As one seventy-three-year-old man pointed out about his peers in 1998: "'They'll take a pill and get a —,' he grumbled, using a crude word for an erection. 'So what are they going to do with it? They'll take one look at the woman they've been married to for 50 years and immediately lose it,' he commented dourly. 'What these guys need is not a pill but an 18-year-old girl.'"[22] In other words, the appearance of Viagra hauled into the light of day a delicate matter that had long been in the shadows, namely, the degree to which men actually desired the women with whom they were partnered.

EVERYTHING GOT MORE COMPLICATED with the drug companies' search for a female equivalent of Viagra. Tackling women's sexual issues was not easy for the pharmaceutical companies, although this was not due to a lack of effort. So far, the demonstrable success has been the official medicalization of female sexual dissatisfaction. Whereas in the twentieth century the problem had no name—except the unfortunate and politically incorrect "frigidity"—since 2000, when the Food and Drug Administration issued draft guidelines for drug trials to treat it, female sexual dysfunction (FSD) has been a genuine diagnosable disease entity.[23] And while the search for a "pink Viagra" and the official FDA endorsement of the notion of FSD have both been presented as items on a women's rights agenda, in fact the effects of these efforts have been far more ambiguous—even more ambiguous than the effects of Viagra.

Like impotence, FSD was really nothing new. Treatments for it have been available for some time. For decades, popular magazines and feminist health activists sought to help women overcome their difficulties in climaxing. Critics of this "new" diagnosis liked to remind women that there has always been one excellent solution for an unfulfilling sex life. Note the cartoon in which a woman confides to another woman: "I was on hormone replacement for two years before I realized that what I really needed was Steve replacement."[24]

Still, FSD as a conceptual category has been very difficult to dislodge. As "erectile dysfunction" was expanded to include "erectile dysphoria," so too FSD is an intentionally broad and subjectively defined disease, more so even than ED ever was. FSD breaks down a woman's potential troubles with sex into four subsets. First, FSD can mean a low level of desire: a woman lacks sexual thoughts and fantasies or lacks interest in the prospect of sexual contact. Second, it encompasses low levels of physiological arousal in a woman: she experiences an absence of sensations and changes in the body like blood flow to the genital area or lubrication in anticipation of further sexual contact. Third, FSD includes the time-honored difficulty achieving orgasm. And finally, FSD can mean pain and discomfort during intercourse. Furthermore, FSD can be extended to include the condition of a woman's dissatisfaction with the *quality* of her orgasms. Women who have "muffled" orgasms may be candidates for FSD treatment as well.[25]

For the first year or so, researchers targeted the disease's second subset: physiological arousal difficulties in women—the perceived parallel to ED in men. One early effort involved trying the little blue pills on women, to see what would happen. And indeed, some women did experience Viagra as a pleasure-enhancer. A few brave and curious female journalists tried it and liked it. So did some women who convinced their doctors to prescribe it for them "off-label" and others who participated in the experimental clinical trials that Pfizer officially conducted. However, neither Viagra nor Viagra-related pills pharmaceutically struck the bull's-eye in women. In women Viagra turned out to be about as effective, or ineffective, as placebos. Also, despite measurable increases in blood flow to the genital area, some women simply felt no improvements in sensation at all.

This failure to raise arousal levels with pharmaceuticals raised a host of questions. Did women have less of the enzyme that Viagra blocked? Or, since women have lower levels of testosterone than men, would offering them testosterone work more effectively? Or was it that the process of lubrication is so different from erection that the whole enterprise of female arousal demanded a fresh perspective entirely?

The scale of the problem has not deterred researchers. All through the years since the introduction of FSD as a concept, scientists and pharmaceutical companies have kept busy. Dozens of pills, creams, gels, and nasal sprays have been developed and dispensed to trial subjects. Each potential remedy addressed some aspect of FSD; none has officially been announced as a cure. What does exist is a nonpharmacological device. Approved by the FDA in 2000 and called the Eros-CTD (clitoral therapy device), this hand-held device effectively bridged the gap between science and sex toy, providing "gentle suction" to the female genital area and promoting blood flow. Labeling it "an answer to FSD" in its promotional materials, the maker of Eros-CTD thus acknowledged that *the cure* for FSD remained to be discovered.[26]

To MARKET THE CONCEPT OF FSD, a little set of statistics has been extraordinarily useful. These statistics were derived from an analysis of data in the National Health and Social Life Survey (NHSLS) conducted by researchers from the University of Chicago in 1992 and led by Dr. Edward O. Laumann. This was the first comprehensive survey of American sexual attitudes and practices since the Kinsey Reports appeared in 1948 and 1953. The NHSLS results were published in 1994 in two books, *Sex in America* (for popular audiences) and *The Social Organization of Sexuality* (for professionals).

In their study, Laumann and his colleagues found that as many as 43 percent of their female sample and 31 percent of their male sample experienced some form of sexual dysfunction, and that one in three women and one in six men experienced lack of desire for sex. These numbers were included in the academic book; however, back in 1994 no one paid them much mind. In 1999 the authors returned to these findings and published a more detailed analysis in the *Journal of the American Medical Association*. Crucially, the authors found a strong correlation between social class and sexual dysfunction. Individuals who were in overall poor physical and emotional health or had less education—all indicators of lower-class status—were identified as experiencing far greater risk of sexual difficulties. The report in *JAMA* concluded: "With the strong association between sexual dysfunction and impaired quality of life, this problem warrants recognition as a significant public health concern."[27]

Recognition, though not necessarily the kind the academic authors of this professional medical journal article might have preferred, was certainly what the 1999 article received. Once the results crossed over into the klieg-lit mainstream, they were transformed. A lot had apparently changed since 1994. Was it only the shift in thinking that had accompanied the discovery of Viagra? Or were Americans in a more fragile and vulnerable mood? Panic replaced sobriety, and a tempered tone was supplanted by near-hysteria.

Reading popularized accounts of the *JAMA* article, we might be forgiven for concluding that life—or at least sex—as we knew it in the United States had neared the end of days. While some accounts appeared based on no actual empirical evidence at all, others were clearly based on the *JAMA* article of 1999. The numbers 43 and 31 were repeated everywhere from *Psychology Today* to *Ms. Magazine*.[28] The statistics on women were taken as a major cause for alarm. *Newsweek* summarized the news this way in 2000: "As many as four in 10 American women experience some form of sexual dissatisfaction."[29] By 2001, the 43 percent figure was gently getting rounded up: "Nearly half the women in America have trouble enjoying sex."[30]

As the twentieth century receded into history, the news got even worse. Sometime in 2003 the bottom fell out of sex in America. It was no longer enough to state that Americans were experiencing difficulty with sex. Certainly this was bad. Now there was news that the real problem was that Americans no longer desired sex at all.

Turning to numbers from the old 1992 NHSLS survey (though not stating that this was the source), the *New York Times* in 2003 informed its readership that experts estimated that "about one adult man in six and one adult woman in three have little desire for sex or none at all."[31] What had been a matter of minor academic concern when the survey results were first publicized in 1994 had in less than a decade become the diagnosis of a national condition.

So there it was: Americans had lost their libidos. Also in 2003, *Cosmopolitan* announced that 20 percent of married couples had sex less than once a month.[32] Books with attention-getting titles like *Resurrecting Sex*, *The Sex-Starved Marriage*, *Rekindling Desire*, and *In the Mood, Again* started making the rounds.[33] Jokes about DINKs (double income no kids) were regarded as so twentieth-century and were replaced with jokes about DINS (double income no sex).[34] Articles with titles like "Generation Sexless" and "Why My Wife Won't Sleep with Me" found their way into print.[35] At least one study authoritatively claimed that "more than 40 million Americans [are] stuck in a low-sex or no-sex marriage."[36] One headline summarized the conflict between a Viagra-enhanced husband and his disinterested wife: "A Quest for Better Sex Meets 'Not Now, Dear.'"[37] Television talk-show host and renowned marriage adviser Dr. Phil McGraw captured the new millennium's zeitgeist when he said that "sexless marriages are an undeniable epidemic."[38] Americans in the early twenty-first century were told they were having sex less often, and having more difficulties with the sex they were having, than ever before. Sexual frustration was rampant and approaching pandemic proportions.

Reports that couples were no longer into sex were simply assumed to be true, and discussion shifted to trying to identify what might be at the root of the new lustlessness. Arguments overlapped and contradicted one another, as did possible solutions. Over and over, readers were informed that it could be one of the three As: antidepressants, antihistamines, or anger (at your partner). Or it could be a B: body image. Some thought it was the result of the natural aging process of the baby boom generation. Others declared the problem to be the result of the widespread use of the birth control pill, which was now suddenly, after four decades of use (and considerable refinement), obsessively identified as reducing a woman's desire.[39] Yet others proposed that the crisis had emerged because more wives were working more hours outside the home, and this understandably left them dispirited and uninterested by bedtime.[40]

But then, some commentators suggested, the impasse might be the fault of men. "Millions of American marriages involve little or no sex," the *New York Times* announced, "often because husbands are not interested."[41] One study found that in "60 percent of married couples frustrated with their sex lives—it was *the men* who were too tired or otherwise distracted."[42] Younger unmarried men were also said to have a decreased appetite for sex. *Cosmopolitan* jumped in to advise its young female readership what to do "When His Sex Drive Takes a Nosedive."[43] Back in 1996, *Details* magazine had proposed to its male readership that, "if you want to be a real man in bed, maybe you should learn to make love like a lesbian."[44] Less than a decade later, *Details* had dropped that idea like a hot potato. No longer were men urged to become more adept and creative. As of 2003, *Details*—like everyone else it seemed—was reporting on the phenomenon of guys who simply were "too tired to have sex."[45]

By the middle of the first decade of the twenty-first century, the idea that desire was dying across America had a headlock on the national imagination. It is indicative of the escalated obsession with the decline of desire that the book *I'd Rather Eat Chocolate: Learning to Love My Low Libido* caused the stir it did in 2007.[46]

Women's magazines were especially busy getting out the news that lack of interest in sex was a chemical disorder with a pharmaceutical solution. The newest acronym to be bandied about was HSDD, or "hypoactive sexual desire disorder," defined as a "decreased interest in sex," which was "what clinicians say is by far the most common disorder."[47] Here the proposed solution was to give male hormones to women.

However, the effect so far has been felt more in the terms of discussion than in actual product placement. Only Procter and

Gamble's Intrinsa testosterone patch for women has been formally considered by the FDA, but in December 2004 an FDA panel rejected it. There was, according to the panel, not enough data to quell concerns about long-term potential negative side effects. The hesitation may have been the result of scares caused by teen suicides ascribed to selective serotonin reuptake inhibitors, or SSRIs, a class of antidepressants, as well as health problems potentially caused by postmenopausal estrogen supplementation and the thousands of cardiac deaths linked to the blockbuster arthritic drug Vioxx. But the hesitation may also have been due to concern that testosterone can cause facial hair growth, weight gain, and acne in women, as well as liver damage and increased risk of heart disease. And there is some worry that testosterone may heighten the chances of breast cancer.[48] Meanwhile, there are scientific studies that show that there is actually no correlation between low levels of desire and low levels of testosterone.[49]

Nonetheless, testosterone has been given to women off-label. It is available as patches and creams to be applied to the abdomen (like Intrinsa) or directly to the genitals. Doctors and patients say that they have achieved positive results. Testosterone has helped some women relocate their lost libido; some women say it has brought on their orgasms. Some claim that it's saved their marriage postmenopause, or post-hysterectomy.[50] Still others declare that it's made them more energetic and happy. Irwin Goldstein thinks that a whole cluster of women who had been put on antidepressants (and who had as a result lowered their libidos even further) were actually misdiagnosed: they should have been given testosterone all along.[51]

Despite the FDA's rejection of a testosterone patch for women, *Good Housekeeping*, under the heading "Bring Back That Lovin' Feeling," encourages its readers to ask their doctors about a testosterone prescription, while noting that "one in three women has no interest in sex."[52] *Health* magazine agrees, urging women, in an essay on orgasms—under the heading "O, Yes!"—to consider that they might be suffering from "low testosterone."[53] And the numbers game keeps getting scarier. A pro-Intrinsa website declares that there are "nearly 40 million sexually distressed women in the United States alone."[54] Similarly, a company that offers herbal remedies to enhance female sexual function announces that "studies have shown that 82% of sexually active women feel their sex life could be better."[55] Significantly, moreover, it is not just those with an obvious immediate stake in pharmaceutical or herbal product sales or those who are ostensibly reporting on the availability of testosterone who are stoking the sense that American sex lives are filled with frustration. *U.S. News and World Report* declares that "low libido" is the "most common sexual complaint" among women, and that "up to half of all women report that their sex drive could use a boost."[56] *Shape* magazine says that of the twelve thousand of its female readers who participated in a survey, a mere 17 percent describe themselves as satisfied with their sex lives.[57]

A remarkable amount of effort is also now going into telling women to have sex even if they feel no desire. *Self* magazine advises that women should give sex with their partners a whirl even if they don't think they want it, because the very act of doing it might actually get arousal going.[58] *Redbook* makes the same point: "Have sex—even when you don't want to! . . . Once you get going, you'll probably find yourself enjoying it."[59] And *Family Circle* too advises wives to stop saying no and to "surrender" in the bedroom even when they are not in the mood themselves.[60]

FSD—like so many other conditions that straddle biochemistry and psychology and are situated at the blurry boundary between normality and dysfunction—could be understood as an utterly hallucinatory invention, even as many women have come to experience it as real.[61] But even if the condition is, or was, nonexistent, the search to "cure" it has certainly reconfigured how we make sense of female sexuality—as it has also further spiked anxiety levels.

Expectations have been exponentially raised; life in all its ordinariness no longer feels good enough. It is indicative that *Glamour* rhetorically poses the question: "How normal is your orgasm?"[62] Because now, in the ante-upped twenty-first century, women are told that they should refuse to experience only "tiny blips" and instead learn "to transform feeble orgasms into fabulous ones." Furthermore, the challenge is no longer just whether you are getting to an orgasm—or even getting to a great orgasm—but also "whether you're actually going to feel good about the one you have."[63]

FEELING GOOD HAS NEVER FELT THIS BAD. The crisis surrounding sex in the last several years has not just been about encouraging people to feel inadequate about the physiological aspects of sex. It has just as much been about the systematic exacerbation of fears about the potential death of love. The emotional aspects of sex have also received tremendous scrutiny in the mass media of late, and this news has not been uplifting either.

A big trend in the new sexual revolution has been to reintroduce a fifties-style culture of shame into some of the most private and complicated aspects of sexual desire and pleasure: self-touching, fantasy, emotional dissociation during sex, attractions to people other than one's partner. Viagra had already raised destabilizing questions about the connections between bodies and emotions: what exactly was turning the man on—the drug or the woman? And we might ask the same question about the use of testosterone for women: was it the chemicals or the man? Meanwhile, the pervasiveness of Internet porn—its accessibility, affordability, and anonymity, but also its immense popularity—has pushed the possibility of emotionally dissociative sexual pleasure even more into the public eye. Articles circulate in the media about men so jacked on porn that they have no interest in making love to their wives or girlfriends. The headlines say it all: "Not Tonight, Honey. I'm Logging On."[64] Or: "Not Tonight, Darling. I'm Online."[65] No longer is it women feigning headaches to avoid sex.

Antiporn activists have jumped at the opportunity to make new arguments about the evils of nonmutuality in sexual relations. At their most extreme, they present porn as a public health hazard. Much of this new argumentation turns on the idea that porn is chemically addictive. For Dr. Judith Reisman, president of the Institute for Media Education and probably best known for her long-standing campaign to discredit the sex researcher Alfred Kinsey as a pedophilic pervert whose science was fraudulent, "pornography triggers a myriad of endogenous, internal, natural drugs that mimic the 'high' from a street drug." These "erototoxins" (her invented terminology) are "mind-altering drugs produced by the viewer's own brain." Pornography, she asserts, causes "brain sabotage."[66] For Dr. Jeffrey Satinover, a psychologist best known for his campaign to "cure" homosexuality, "an addiction to pornography is chemically nearly identical to a heroin addiction." Satinover further states, "Pornography really does, unlike other addictions, biologically cause direct release of the most perfect addictive substance. . . . That is, it causes masturbation, which causes release of the naturally occurring opioids. It does what heroin can't do, in effect."[67]

Others believe the more pertinent comparison is with cocaine. Dr. Mary Ann Layden, codirector of the Sexual Trauma and Psychopathology Program at the University of Pennsylvania, has said, "Research indicates that even non-sex-addicts will show brain reactions on PET scans while viewing pornography similar to cocaine addicts looking at images of people taking cocaine. This material is potent, addictive and permanently implanted in the brain." In fact, Layden says that "pornography addicts have a more difficult time recovering from their addiction than cocaine addicts, since coke users can get the drug out of their system, but pornographic images stay in the brain forever." Moreover, she declares, a husband who uses porn is "masturbating inside [his wife's] body while he is having sex with the women on the screen." Not only does a husband's porn use damage his wife's self-esteem (Layden argues that spouses of porn addicts tend toward not just depression but also breast implants and suicide), but a porn-using man, she contends, also damages himself. According to Layden, "pornography viewers tend to have problems with premature ejaculation and erectile dysfunction."[68]

The mainstream media have absorbed so many of these formulations that a new kind of cultural common sense has evolved about the purported emotional harm done by porn. Subtler variations on these extreme arguments are now a certifiable piece of a much wider trend. Pamela Paul, a journalist for *Time* and the author of the 2005 antiporn manifesto *Pornified*, stresses the damage done to the self-esteem of female partners of porn users: "I began feeling very insecure about my body image, and I had never been self-conscious before in my life," one woman whose man was now "addicted" to porn told Paul. "I started feeling like I was fat. Like I wasn't sexy enough." But Paul also points to the new American obsession with the mind-body gulf, with what she calls "intimacy disorders," and with the idea that sex between two people has deteriorated into nothing more than sex with oneself. Men, she says, no longer know how to make love to their wives, whom they have come to view solely as "a masturbatory accessory." One man tells Paul that he "used to view porn online, but I began to find it more difficult to stay aroused when having sex with a real woman." Another confides that he went through a phase of difficulty having sex with his wife "without playing an internal movie screen of pornographic images," and he remorsefully says, "During that period of my life, sex had nothing to do with expressing love or affection." More ominously, another man asserts, "I don't see how any male who likes porn can think actual sex is better, at least if it involves all the crap that comes with having a real live female in your life." And finally, in a move complementary to Layden's warning about incipient male sexual dysfunction, Paul argues that porn users have low self-esteem. Men who use porn may think they are manly, but they are sadly mistaken; their use "denotes a lack of confidence in one's manhood and insecurity in one's sexuality."[69]

Journalist Naomi Wolf argues that, far from encouraging sexual aggression toward women (as critics of porn argued in prior decades), porn actually encourages a "deadening" of "male libido in relation to real women." She reminisces about times now long past when, if "there was nothing actively alarming about you, you could get a pretty enthusiastic response by just showing up. Your boyfriend may have seen *Playboy*, but hey, you could move, you were warm, you were real." Pointedly, she too identifies the demise of love even when physical contact occurs. On her visits to colleges, Wolf says, she queries expectant crowds about whether "loneliness" is a big concern on campus. Immediately, she observes how "a deep, sad silence descends on audiences of young men and young women alike. They know they are lonely together, even when conjoined."[70]

While in the 1980s and 1990s antiporn feminists and conservatives tended to argue that pornography encourages violence against women ("pornography is the theory, rape is the practice"), or that porn is itself a form of aggression against women, or that it purveys outlandishly unrealistic body images and notions of how sex works and especially of what women actually enjoy, these older arguments began to run into difficulty in the face of increasing numbers of female users openly admitting that they too enjoyed looking at pornography—both alone and with a partner.[71] A typical recent female pro-porn advice manual, Kim Cattrall's *Satisfaction: The Art of the Female Orgasm*, cowritten with her husband, enthusiastically recommends that a man manually and/or orally pleasure his woman while *she* lounges in a chair watching a porn film.[72] Porn directed at women and couples remains the largest and fastest-growing segment of the pornographic film industry.[73]

There is considerable evidence that women have long made up a sizable percentage of those individuals who like to watch porn. Already in 1987 women accounted for about 40 percent of the approximately 100 million X-rated tapes rented annually.[74] (Though, as feminist scholar Linda Williams quipped at the time, perhaps this was simply because "women still do most of the shopping."[75]) Likewise, a *Redbook* survey that same year among twenty-six thousand women found that almost 50 percent of them regularly watched pornographic films.[76] In the 1990s, the most frequent female question about porn was not why it existed, but why it wasn't better—why wasn't it more arousing and more interesting for women? Even those who didn't particularly like porn films—or who got bored or turned off after watching a few—still confessed to liking some kinds of sexually explicit materials. More recently, there have been reports that one in three users of Internet porn are female.[77]

By 2004, porn film rental revenues in the United States topped $800 million; as of 2005, 40 million Americans regularly viewed Internet pornography, and one-quarter of all search engine requests were for pornographic materials.[78] Industry insiders noted that the so-called red states like their porn even more than so-called blue states.[79] Other commentators observed that across America "pot and porn net more than corn."[80]

The antiporn cause has now aggressively adjusted its arguments. These days the key contentions are that pornography damages its users' sexual performance abilities, or that it destroys the ability to love. In other words, the antiporn cause now insinuates itself precisely into two of the biggest private anxieties currently riling Americans.

In the process, a new ambivalence about masturbation has surfaced, in addition to a novel insistence that if someone is not wholly focused on his (or her) partner during a sexual encounter, he or she is actually engaging in masturbation (even though another body is in the bed)—or even committing adultery. Human beings who fantasize are not connecting with their partner even when they are most intimately together.

Incessantly monitoring ourselves and the ones we love is the latest mantra in relationship and sex advice. Only a decade ago, the core aim was to banish guilt about whatever gave you and your partner more pleasure. The grandmother of American sex advice, Dr. Ruth Westheimer, counseled in 1995: "There is no such thing as a wrong fantasy." And she meant that in a gender-neutral way. "Remember," Dr. Ruth advised, "if your man stops looking at other women, it probably means he's also stopped looking at you. It may mean that he has lost all interest in sex, and that idea's certainly not a bonus."[81]

The 1990s were also all about women banishing their guilt about their own sexual pleasure and the stigma associated with it. Women's magazines playfully encouraged the trifecta of the way to go: masturbation, fantasy, and self-acceptance. Sex experts agreed: women should drop whatever shame they might have picked up from a dysfunctional culture suspicious of female sexual agency. Fantasies set the most awesome orgasms in motion. They were the best antidote to dull routine and a cost-free cure for depression. They were the magic ingredient that kept both your self-esteem and your relationship in excellent form. *New Woman* defined "easily orgasmic women" in 1996: "They like their bodies; they use fantasy to stimulate their love-making; they're able to be fully present in the act."[82] Nor was this advice considered contradictory: fantasy was the means by which a woman *could* feel more fully present in her own body and in the sexual encounter with her lover. Or: "Work up your erotic appetite by doing a little 'window shopping,'" urged a sex therapist in 1998. "Notice attractive men [at work, on the street, in the supermarket], then retain those racy thoughts for later."[83] Again and again, the message was: women who enjoy fantasy and masturbation also enjoy the happiest, most fulfilling sex with a partner.[84]

And it was the late 1990s when best-selling author and psychologist Harriet Lerner responded to the anxious inquiry of a happily married wife who loved her husband deeply but could not "get sexually aroused without thinking of other men. . . . It's making me sick with guilt." She added: "My husband is the only man I want, so why do I fantasize like this?" Lerner's response:

> Sexual fantasies are as far-ranging as the human imagination— and they may have little to do with what we desire in real life. I

have a friend who claims to enjoy wonderful sex with her husband, yet at the moment of orgasm she almost always envisions two red cars crashing head-on.

Lerner's bottom line: "Fire those sex cops in your head." [85]

All this soon changed. Popular sex experts since the turn of the millennium have addressed Americans' confusions and fears about the decline of desire for sex with real bodies by targeting hearts and minds as well. This is an ironic outcome, not least because pornography's attractiveness has only been enhanced by the growing worry about sexually transmitted diseases.

Another trend in the new sexual revolution has been a deliberate promotion of paranoia about who your lover might lust for besides you. Mainstream news venues report on the latest digital technology for catching adulterous spouses in the act and go out of their way to note that it's dual-career couples with long days and exhausting commutes who might be most vulnerable.[86] But Americans are constantly guided as well these days to the use of Internet filters and spousal e-mail prying. "Cheaters Beware!" blares the cover of *O* magazine: "True Stories of Betrayal and Cybersleuthing." And inside, under the title "You Got Nailed!" the magazine describes "some women who caught their husbands with their virtual pants down."[87] Snooping on a partner is now encouraged even when physical contact is not the issue.

The term "emotional infidelity," a condition that scarcely existed before 2000, includes emotionally intense friendships with members of the opposite sex—often forged at work—even when they involve no sexual touching at all. The invention of emotional infidelity is not least an insidious form of backlash against the reality of women's increasing economic independence and equal power in the workplace. The term also connotes flirtations with or fantasies about individuals other than the partner. This could be a coworker, an old flame, someone at the bus stop or su-permarket, or someone met over the Internet. Or it could refer to sexual fantasies of any kind—whether anonymous pornographic scenarios or a focus on one or more particular individuals—during sex with one's partner.

Licensed mental health counselor and family mediator Rabbi M. Gary Neuman writes in his 2001 book *Emotional Infidelity*: "You don't have to have sex with anyone else to be unfaithful. *Emotional infidelity* is just as—and at times even more—destructive to your marriage." Neuman's advice is brutal: "Avoiding friend-ships with members of the opposite sex" is "the single most impor-tant thing you can do for your marriage."[88]

In the years since 2001, numerous sex and marriage experts have talked about the catastrophic implications of this "new kind of adultery." As psychiatrist Gail Saltz writes, it is pre-cisely because emotional infidelity "steers clear of physical inti-macy . . . [that] people enmeshed in nonsexual affairs preserve their 'deniability,' convincing themselves they don't have to change anything." She adds sternly: "That's where they're wrong."[89] Likewise, the news from *Ladies' Home Journal*: don't think that "if you're not having sex, there's nothing wrong with it," because "there's plenty wrong."[90] Or as relationship expert Peggy Vaughan, author of *The Monogamy Myth*, puts it: "You wind up depending on the other person more for daily peaks and perks, and that sucks the love away from you and your partner."[91]

And while some of the new thought-policing media discus-sion is directed at men, the bulk of it is—remarkably—directed at women.

When a letter writer confides to Dr. Phil McGraw that she's become reacquainted with a high school crush after many years, and that now "I can't stop thinking about him"—including when she's in bed with her husband—Dr. Phil's advice is curt and to the point:

> Sure, it's fun to fantasize about someone else. But you're playing with fire here. . . . Of course he makes you feel good—it's easy to be charming for an hour every few years, but you don't really know anything about this man. . . . Never fix problems in a relationship by turning away from your partner. Fix them inside your marriage. You can't improve the situation by inviting in an interloper.[92]

And what's so wrong about fantasy exactly? Research shows that while women do not fantasize quite as much as men (80 percent of women, as compared with 98 percent of men), fantasizing is close to a universal human behavior. Strikingly, in the one study on gender differences in fantasies, researchers found that while many heterosexual women dreamed of being serviced and pleasured (whether by a man, by a woman, or by more than one person at a time), above all they fantasized that they did not need to take responsibility for pleasing their partner. Heterosexual men, by contrast, fantasized that they were making a woman come—and gloriously so.[93] What this finding tells us about the actual state of affairs among and between heterosexuals is anybody's guess.

When we take into account the additional scientific studies on sexual arousal and satisfaction during porn viewing, the evidence gets even messier. Homophobic heterosexual men are aroused by gay male porn.[94] Lesbian and straight women alike enjoy watching woman-on-woman action; many straight men swear by it as well. Some bisexual men are more aroused by gay porn, others by hetero scenes.[95] But rather than marveling at the rich and complicated ways in which the human imagination is stimulated—or shrugging their shoulders at the utter banality and ridiculousness of most fantasies—self-styled experts are calling for moral panic.

Emotional infidelity has been deemed *more* dangerous than physical adultery. "Deep emotional bonds can be much more compelling than a simple sexual attraction."[96] "Mind games are always more dangerous. . . . From what we know now about emotional versus physical intimacy, emotional intimacy is much more threatening to committed relationships than physical intimacy."[97] We hear that three out of every four women apparently consider emotional infidelity "more harmful" than physical infidelity.[98] Or as psychologist Shirley Glass, popularly known as the "godmother of infidelity research," once said: "Sometimes the greatest betrayals happen without touching."[99] Now minds suddenly matter more than bodies. It really is the thought that counts.

What is going on is an ideological assault on something pretty fundamental: the most intimate and personal aspects of sex. It worms its way into the core of the psyche by playing on the imperfections and emotional confusion that so often accompany sex. Rather than helping people get comfortable with the unruliness of desire, the current trendy idea is to freak people out. And freak out we do. This is not least because the state of conversation has been riddled with contradictions.

People understandably yearn to be cherished, to be thought of as unique and extraordinary. Among other things, they long to be the objects of freely and joyfully given fidelity, to love another person both durably and passionately, and—over and over—to experience intense, even overwhelming pleasure. These desires frequently go unmet. Life turns out often to be much more ambiguous and much more ordinary.

People don't always want their partners, or don't always feel wanted by their partners. People are frightened and ashamed both about desires they have that are not normative and about feelings of emptiness they sometimes have even when they do normative things. This is the landscape in which the Religious Right in the United States staked its claim.

The Religious Right recognized that there is a keen and powerful relationship between emotional matters and American politics. Psychological conditions have political consequences. Disorientation about how to deal with the new confusion about the connections between people and their partners, and between people and themselves, left Americans intimidated and vulnerable on a whole range of issues, from sex education for adolescents and the conservative obsession with premarital abstinence to HIV prevention strategies domestically and globally, from women's right to access contraception and abortion to the right for homosexuals to marry.

Over the past fifteen years, religious conservatives succeeded in taking over the terms of conversation about sex and love in the United States by working the contradictions of sex and love and heightening the very anxieties they claimed they could alleviate. And liberals and progressives did not—or chose not to—respond. This was not least because religious conservatives used a strategy that caught liberals and progressives utterly off guard: they bragged boldly and loudly that Christian sex was the most amazing sex on God's green earth.

Chapter 2

SOULGASM

WHEN IT COMES TO SEX, observers have routinely gotten the Religious Right wrong. The general consensus has been that right-wing evangelical Christians are anti-sex. They are an uptight and unforgiving bunch who would rather make war than love.

This assessment of evangelical Christianity is thoroughly misleading. Yes, right-wing evangelicals have been bluntly hostile to homosexuality and abortion rights. And religious conservatives have also been tremendously restrictive about adolescent and premarital sex, even as they have regularly admitted the prevalence of both. But the Religious Right is also hugely sex-affirmative with respect to marital sex. Since at least the mid–1970s, evangelical Christians have been pushing the good word that evangelicals have more fun—that godly sex is the most fabulous sex—and that evangelicals respect women. The still pervasive popular notion that evangelical Christians do not like sex, or do not revel in the joys of breathtaking orgasms (within marriage), is nonsense.

Open any Christian sex advice book published within the last several years and you will read comments like this: "Some people have the mistaken notion that God is anti-sex . . . in fact, he's outspokenly pro-sex! He invented it. What an incredible thought! Passionate sex was God's idea."[1] And there is this: "Orgasm is an integral part of God's design for sex."[2] And in one of the earliest, most admired, and most often recommended evangelical sex advice texts, Clifford and Joyce Penner's *The Gift of Sex* (1981), the emphasis is on "the Bible's loud prosexual message."[3] The Religious Right promises that if its rules are followed, magnificent sex can be yours forever.

Writing about sex has been hugely successful for the evangelical movement. Evangelical author Timothy LaHaye, best known for the "Left Behind" series, his science fiction about Armageddon, was ahead of the curve when in 1976 he published, together with his wife Beverly (now head of the right-wing lobby Concerned Women for America), *The Act of Marriage*. In it, the LaHayes describe sex as *"life's most exciting experience."* For a man, "the titanic emotional and physical explosion that culminates the act of marriage for the husband is easily the most exciting experience he ever enjoys, at least on a repeatable basis." The LaHayes did not hesitate to describe the way a wife's vaginal area becomes "very moist" and her labia "swell to two or three times their normal thickness" under the impact of "gentle stroking" by the husband's fingers. The LaHayes declared that, as long as everything was done correctly, "modern research indicates that a woman's orgasmic experience is every bit as titanic as a man's."[4] They expressed an uncomplicated confidence that evangelical marital sex is the happiest sex, and they assumed that evangelical men naturally cherish their wives.

By the turn of the new century, however, this latter assumption was almost universally understood as outdated. Evangelical sex advice responded with a wholly original analysis of how to promote the joys of marital sex, while recognizing its inevitable discontents as well. The tipping point came in 2000 with the publication of *Every Man's Battle: Winning the War on Sexual Temptation One Victory at a Time* by Stephen Arterburn and Fred Stoeker. Arterburn and Stoeker's strategic asides about "a jaw-dropping beauty in a thong bikini" or a woman with "long legs in heels, and full breasts crowning a silky-thin, miniskirt sundress" are integral to their new, and surprisingly aggressive, assault *against* masturbation and fantasy.[5] Arterburn and Stoeker recognize that they could denounce masturbation at the same time they give their male reader something to masturbate about. In this way, the evangelical sex industry can occasionally linger on descriptions of erotic fantasies—the wilder the better—but it douses those fantasies with the ominous warning that they lead directly to sexual dysfunction and marital unhappiness.

Since 2000, the best-selling evangelical writings on sex have been as titillating as the soft-core stuff any adolescent boy used to keep stashed under his mattress (and now keeps bookmarked on his laptop). Evangelical sex advice lures and tempts and arouses—all in the name of Christ. It has done so in order to argue that not only nonmarital sex but also masturbation and fantasy stunt emotional growth, destroy souls, and devastate marriages. This has been its overt message, but to get that message out there as forcefully as possible, evangelical sex experts now engage in their own variation of Christian pornography.

Here is an example from Arterburn and Stoeker's *Every Man's Battle*:

> Alex remembers the time he was watching TV with his sister-in-law. The rest of the family was at the mall. "She was lying flat

on her stomach on the floor in front of me, wearing tight shorts, and she'd fallen asleep watching TV. I was on the chair, and I happened to look down and see her upper thigh and a trace of her underwear. I tried to ignore it, but my heart started racing a little, and my eyes kept looking at the back of her upper thigh. It got so exciting that I began to stare and really lust. I had to release it somehow. I masturbated while she slept, right out in the open."

Every Man's Battle offers a template for an entirely new genre in evangelical sex advice, which starts from the premise that all husbands fantasize about the sexiness of women they see around them, both in real life and in everything from cable TV movies to Sunday newspaper insert lingerie ads. In the face of such perpetual temptation, Arterburn and Stoeker propose this simple solution:

> To attain sexual purity as we defined it, we must starve our eyes of the bowls of sexual gratification that comes from outside our marriage. When you starve your eyes and eliminate "junk sex" from your life, you'll deeply crave "real food"—your wife.[6]

Every Man's Battle sold more than four hundred thousand copies within two years, and it has gone on to sell many more in the years since.[7] It quickly spawned an entire series of "Every Man" books as well as audiotapes, workbooks, and other spinoffs (including *Every Woman's Battle*, *Every Young Woman's Battle*, *Every Woman's Desire*, *Every Young Man's Battle*, *Every Man's Marriage*, *Every Heart Restored*, *Preparing Your Daughter for Every Woman's Battle*, *Preparing Your Son for Every Man's Battle*, and so on), which have together sold close to three million copies. Arterburn also found funding to mail complimentary copies of his antimasturbation guidebooks to twenty thousand male and female soldiers serving in Afghanistan and Iraq.[8]

On the surface, the argument is straightforward. Arterburn takes the view that masturbation is a "quagmire."[9] He describes it as "an implosion of sexual pleasure that focuses a guy further and further into himself." While "loneliness, insecurity, and broken family relationships are often the stepping-stones to masturbation," he concedes, masturbation "just adds to your loneliness": "It's like slaking your parched thirst with salt water." And while presenting himself as someone able to sympathize with a young man "emptying jar after jar of Vaseline," Arterburn reassures readers that God will provide for nocturnal emissions if they only trust God enough. For those who are anxious about their ability to stay the course, he has two different recommendations. First, "if the idea of never masturbating again produces so much anxiety in you that you're compelled to do it just to prove that it is still an option, then . . . just decide to go one day without masturbating. If that one day is all you ever experience without masturbating, then you're better off to have experienced that one day." Arterburn also advises that a young man find a well-respected older man in his church to be his "accountability partner"—"a person who can encourage you in the heat of battle and ask probing questions like, 'What are you feeling when you're most tempted to masturbate?'"[10] In offering suggestions for breaking the habit, Arterburn turns masturbation into a much more dramatic and meaning-filled practice than it might be otherwise, and he turns the challenge of quitting into a test of both faith and manhood.

While some of the "Every Man" books directed at women are designed to help wives whose husbands crave porn or extramarital encounters, others are directed at wives and single women who have active fantasy lives themselves. Here too there are sexy scenes interspersed with the shame-inducing assertions that fantasizing about anything or anyone other than one's spouse is a recipe for marital disaster.

One excerpt from an interview with "Kelly" that appears in Shannon Ethridge's *Every Woman's Battle: Discovering God's Plan for Sexual and Emotional Fulfillment*, published in 2003, reads:

> As a freshman in college, I began dating Sam, an older man who was far more sexually experienced than I was. I fell head over heels in love with him, and within a few months, we were sleeping together. Within a year, we were living together. That was when I stumbled upon his vast array of videos hidden on the top shelf of his closet. I'm embarrassed to say that at the time, I wasn't offended by his pornography collection, but curious. I began watching the videos with him, just to see what was on them. It wasn't long until I was asking to watch particular ones while we were having sex together. I don't understand why, but the ones that really turned me on were the ones that included a threesome (a guy and two girls) or the ones that had just two women together.

Kelly confessed that even after she broke up with Sam, she masturbated to those videos over and over (Sam had allowed her to keep the videos that had been "her favorites"). She subsequently married a Christian man and threw the videos away, but despite claims that "my husband is a good lover," the memories lingered, and "I think about all those old scenes when I'm trying to orgasm just because that is what really seems to do it for me." Kelly, the text goes on to suggest, has definitely "crossed the line when it comes to sexual integrity." Indeed, as the book warns at another point, "*don't cave in* to the idea that it's okay to entertain any inappropriate thought so you can reach orgasm more quickly. Just because it takes most women approximately five to ten times longer to orgasm as it does men doesn't mean we should just throw caution to the wind and get it over with for the sake of time. . . . Retrain your brain." Over and over, readers are assured that marital sex will be truly spectacular only if their fantasies are completely banished. Ethridge tells women: "Remind yourself frequently: 'This is my husband. Pleasuring him sexually is an act of worship to God.'"[11]

Meanwhile, however, the new evangelical sex advisers openly admit that they are no saints. Evangelical sex advice–writers discuss in loving detail their own and their brethren's sins and peccadilloes. Evangelical abstinence and antimasturbation guru Arterburn, now chairman of New Life Ministries, the largest Christian counseling network in America, and host of the *New Life Live!* daily radio program broadcast on more than 180 stations nationwide, openly acknowledges he got a girlfriend pregnant while still a teenager. He admits he insisted she have an abortion, and she complied. He reveals that he once had an affair with a married woman after a nasty breakup with another woman, that he had a "promiscuous period," and that he used to get off watching porn. After he was married, he grooved on ogling the bouncing breasts of pretty girls as they jogged along the Pacific Coast Highway—until one day he wrecked his Mercedes 450SL near Malibu while doing so. He makes no secret of the fact that he's been married three times, or that he had premarital sex with his first two wives. Only with Misty, his current wife—a curvaceous beauty nearly twenty years his junior—does Arterburn say he adhered to his own principles of no intercourse until matrimony. Then again, Arterburn concedes that he kept his engagement to Misty as brief as possible.[12]

Fred Stoeker typed out the original manuscript for *Every Man's Battle*, although the final product bears the strong imprint of Arterburn's distinctive style (already evident in prior Arterburn books like the classic *Addicted to "Love"*). However, it would be an error to underestimate how much Stoeker contributed to the text's success. With a degree in sociology from Stanford (with honors) and a prior career as an investment adviser, Stoeker brought his own considerable insights and experience to the table when he and Arterburn sat down to reinvent the evangelical sex advice movement. Just like his compadre in the evangelical sex business, Stoeker has been quite open about the details of his own wild and crazy sexual history.

Stoeker talks about his former "ruggedly promiscuous lifestyle" and swaggers a bit when he discusses his success with females: "Eventually, I had sex with anyone at any time. After five years in California, I found myself with four 'steady' girlfriends simultaneously. I was sleeping with three of them and was essentially engaged to marry two of them. None knew of the others."[13]

Nor does *Every Woman's Battle* author and Teen Mania Ministries instructor Shannon Ethridge steer clear of discussing her past sexual encounters.[14] Her first sex was at fourteen with a boy of eighteen, and she had sex with quite a few men while a young single woman. She does point out how unhappy she was and how awful it was that she used sex to get men to like her. Nonetheless, Ethridge admits that she racked up rather a long list of men she slept with or pursued during those years before her marriage. Even during the years of her marriage, Ethridge says, she continued to flirt with other men (because of her low self-esteem, she contends). When one of these guys fell in love with her and asked her to leave her husband and run away with him, Ethridge realized that she had gone too far and needed to gain more control over her life—through prayer and worship. When God intervened and told Shannon to move with her husband far away from Dallas (and temptation) to another town in Texas, she did. Her marriage was saved.[15]

Far from being rigid, leading spokespersons for the Religious Right emphasize the movement's recuperative and therapeutic aspects, using their own biographies as evidence. Instead of ejecting the wayward from the fold, the movement welcomes them and even validates them for their prior failings. Evangelical advice-writers clearly revel in telling stories of their prior promiscuities and sinful misdeeds and mistakes. The conversion narratives that have been part of evangelical tradition for centuries have been given a postmodern twist.

Evangelicals incessantly—even obsessively—admit that they are drawn to the very things they say they despise. Fifty percent of evangelical pastors have confessed that they look at Internet porn, while a recent poll conducted among one thousand evangelicals found that "50% of all Christian men and 20% of all Christian women are addicted to pornography"; that "60% of the women who answered the survey confessed having 'significant struggles with lust'"; and that "40% admitted to being 'involved in sexual sin' in the past year." The sponsor, ChristiaNet.com, concluded from its findings that "no one is immunized against the vice-grip clutches of sexual addictive behaviors" and that the "people who struggle with the repeated pursuit of sexual gratification include church members, deacons, staff, and yes, even clergy."[16] Along related lines, the opening anecdotes in Marsha Means's *Living with Your Husband's Secret Wars* feature the porn usage and extramarital affairs of pastors, church youth leaders, and ordinary Christians warming the pews on a typical Sunday.[17] Or consider the GodMen conference held in Nashville, Tennessee, in 2006. (GodMen have been called "Promise Keepers with an edge.") One speaker, a former pastor, opened his presentation by mentioning that he picked up his first prostitute on the way to a Christmas Eve service.[18] The continual self-castigation, among its many functions, also preempts in advance any attempt on the part of critics to engage in the traditional liberal strategy of muckraking exposé of conservative hypocrisy. For there's nothing anymore to expose. The sins have all long since been confessed.

Preemptive (and simultaneously tantalizing) self-criticism of evangelicals is a tactic Arterburn wields with vigor. Arterburn makes a point of documenting how often Christians fail to live up to Christian standards. It is one of the most frequent themes in his texts: "Look at the statistics for the church, friend. Our divorce rates are no different from the world's." And: "We have countless churches filled with countless men encumbered by sexual sin." *Every Man's Battle* is chock-full of tales like these: The youth minister who needs to look at *Playboy* and *Penthouse* "to stimulate him" before he has sex with his wife. The young pastor whose "tears turned to wrenching sobs as he spoke of his bondage to pornography." The adult singles group at church filled with "players"—that is, men and women just looking for sex partners. The youth group full of kids "actually taking drugs, drinking, partying, and having sex." The congregation member who insists he has a "biblical right to sexual fulfillment" so that when his wife doesn't give it to him, he's driven to have an affair. The nationally known pastor who tells an audience of tens of thousands at a Promise Keepers conference about his powerful impulse to masturbate in his car after "a banking transaction with a lovely bank teller."[19]

And in yet other books authored by Arterburn, or by Arterburn and Stoeker together, there are scenarios ranging from the banal to the disturbing: a husband who gets off on wearing his wife's lingerie; a father sexually excited by hiding in the dark and peering into a window of his own home to watch a pajama party hosted by his prepubescent daughter; and a father who joins his son in bed to teach him how to masturbate.[20]

In short, evangelical sex and marriage experts have concocted their own brand of Christian porn, not least so that we know that they know what they're talking about. That's the implied rationale. The invitations to voyeurism are multiple. Some stories are appalling and meant to repel; others invite direct identification; yet others are clearly boastful. Certainly, the authors' own experience with nonmarital sex and pornography dramatizes the sincerity of their conversion to the righteous path of sacred love within marriage. Yet meanwhile, they—or at least the men—can suggest that the best evangelicals have also been (and presumably still are) studs in bed. At the same time, the surface message of all the autobiographical evangelical writing about sex is precisely the opposite: *Don't try this at home. Don't do what I did.*[21]

ANTIMASTURBATION AND ABSTINENCE guidance is not the only graphically detailed evangelical advice out there. Obsessing over orgasms has also long been an essential ingredient of the evangelical sex advice business. For at least a quarter-century, evangelical sex advice–givers have recognized that every man and woman wants bigger and better orgasms. They know this is as true for their flock as it is for the average forsaken nonbeliever. And so they have turned their attention to techniques for intensifying climax.

God wants His devoted followers to have boundary-dissolving ecstasy each and every time. There is no need to feel unfulfilled and frustrated after sex with a spouse. Evangelicals deserve the very best in sex, and so evangelical experts offer the happy news that holy sex means orgasmic sex. Dozens upon dozens of evangelical publications rehearse the basic facts of life. *Cosmo* meets the Bible.

Evangelicals Linda Dillow and Lorraine Pintus provide one of the most popular guides for Christian women and their orgasmic lives: *Intimate Issues* (published, like the "Every Man" series, by WaterBrook Press, an evangelical Christian publishing house based in Colorado Springs, Colorado, and a division of Random House). Coining the term "soulgasm" as the desired result of sex with your husband—incredible orgasms *plus* intense emotional connection with your husband *plus* God's spiritual presence—Dillow and Pintus describe the experience variously: "Waves of pleasure flow over me; it feels like sliding down a mountain waterfall." Or: "It's like having a million tiny pleasure balloons explode inside of me all at once."[22]

Orgasm equity is key to the Dillow and Pintus vision. They are unapologetic in their insistence that Christian women make their own pleasure a priority. They recommend that women "EXERCISE YOUR LOVE MUSCLE. Your PC muscle (pubococcygeal) is your love muscle." They describe the "SIX SECRETS OF HIGHLY ORGASMIC WIVES," which include not only "grab your Nikes" (because a well-exercised woman is also a pleasure-primed one) but also "educate yourself" about your own body. Above all, they urge women to "let yourself feel":

> As Christians, we often think that focusing on ourselves is wrong, that we should concentrate on giving, not receiving. But in order to move toward physical orgasm, we must give ourselves permission to dwell on our physical responses and emotional feelings. . . . It is not selfish. . . . There is a fascinating paradox as your selfish inward journey to orgasm and intense

personal excitement become a mutual experience and a marvelous turn-on for your mate.[23]

Dillow and Pintus are enormously reassuring in their sensible advice that every woman—like every couple—is unique, and that "there is no 'right way' to make love." So they also stress that while clitoral pleasuring may be the key to orgasm for the majority of women, some women experience their orgasms as centered in the vagina. And they point out that simultaneous orgasm is not a necessary aim; it is perfectly fine for women to come first. Indeed, "some couples find that intercourse is more pleasurable for the women [*sic*] if she has already reached a climax as her genitals are lubricated and engorged."[24]

And they go out of their way as well to answer the query "Is intercourse the only 'proper' way to have sex?" by asserting that, no, "intercourse is not the *only* 'proper' way to have sex," because "God grants us enormous liberty" and "we are free to enjoy sexual variety." They recommend to their female readers the following prayer: *"Lord, keep me growing as a godly and sensuous woman. Keep me from worrying about what is normal and let me dwell on what is a successful sexual encounter for me and my husband."*[25] If all goes well, and all lessons are practiced and learned, Dillow and Pintus assure their female readers that this story of "Bethany" might someday be their own story:

It had never occurred to me that I could come more than once. Then I read that this sometimes happened to women as they grew in giving in to their sexuality and in their trust of their husbands. I think reading about it opened the door—and the next time we were making love I experienced wave upon wave of pleasure. As he entered me, I built up to another orgasm. It wasn't something I tried to make happen, but it was glorious, and my husband felt like "Superman lover."[26]

Testimonials like these are another crucial component of the evangelical sex industry: true tales from real people who find orgasmic bliss through prayer and devotion—and by flexing their love muscles.

WHEN EVANGELICALS TALK ABOUT SEX, they inhabit a world of religious references that make sense to them. A typical recommendation is: "Try this simple act of foreplay: Pray with her."[27] Nor would eyebrows be raised by the answer to the question "*How Do I Shift into Sexual Gear?*: 1. Memorize the first portion of Romans 12:2: Do not be conformed to this world, but be transformed by the renewing of your mind."[28]

Yet, as the experts suggest over and over again, evangelicals struggle with anxiety about what they are permitted to do with one another. As marriage therapists and clergy counselors Louis and Melissa McBurney put it in their essay, "Christian Sex Rules: A Guide to What's Allowed in the Bedroom," they receive "many, many questions from Christian couples who want to know what is and what is not okay to do sexually."[29] Or as Dillow and Pintus note, "Many women we talk with want to be reassured that their sex life is normal."[30] Yet "normal" is not always an easy thing to define, even for the true believer. (And certainly doing so has not gotten any easier in the midst of new pressures and challenges wrought by sexual psychopharmacology and Internet pornography.)

There is no consensus among the faithful as to what constitutes good clean sexual fun. To be told that I Corinthians 7:1–5 reveals that "the Bible clearly promotes the value of regular sexual release" is considered pertinent, if perhaps ambivalently received, information.[31] Being told that the Song of Solomon celebrates oral pleasuring for men and women can be a huge relief for some. A few Christian advice-writers reject the idea that the Song of Solomon offers guidelines for sexual practice, yet many argue otherwise. The LaHayes in their 1976 classic were among the first to suggest that the Song of Solomon, especially verses 2:6 and 8:3, might be translated into tips for genital pleasuring.[32] And Joseph Dillow (Linda's husband) dedicated an entire book to the naughtiness of *Solomon on Sex* in 1982.[33]

In his book, Dillow offers a close reading of Song of Solomon 4:5: "Thy two breasts are like two young roes that are twins, which feed among the lilies," and then riffs on Solomon's interest in "his wife's breasts": "They are very curvaceous like the lily. Their beauty creates within his heart a desire to reach out and fondle them as one would a gazelle feeding by a brook. The notion of frolicksomeness suggests sexual playfulness." And "the female genitals are referred to in 5:1 as a 'garden' and in 4:13 as 'shoots.' In both passages, myrrh and frankincense are described as characteristic scents of her 'garden.'"[34]

Other evangelicals have made similar enthusiastic claims that the Song of Solomon is a detailed account of the sexual foreplay and "total body involvement" enjoyed between King Solomon and his beloved, and that the Song of Solomon describes "passionate lovemaking" and "sexual climax—higher and higher," "ecstasy," "orgasm," and "sexual oneness."[35] It all gets pretty steamy in the retelling. As one writer summarized the accumulated wisdom in 2000, "The Song of Solomon . . . is one of the best textbooks for sexual instruction ever printed."[36]

Another writer assures his male readers: "If you're a husband who wants to be a consummate lover to your wife, learn from Solomon. Once you start understanding the idioms of Solomon's day, you'll see that he knew exactly how to bring his wife to peaks of sexual ecstasy. Do what he did, and your wife will respond as passionately as his." Never mind that a few pages earlier, the same author concedes that "rich and powerful men like King David and King Solomon had not only a multitude of wives but concubines, as well, to sate their need for status and sexual gratification."[37]

Not that Song of Solomon is the final word on sexual dos and don'ts. There are a host of thorny issues that continue to challenge evangelical sex writers as they confront what should be deemed proper or improper behavior in bed. For instance, there is the not-inconsequential matter of oral sex. In this regard, Tim Alan Gardner's *Sacred Sex: A Spiritual Celebration of Oneness in Marriage* stands firmly with the naysayers. Gardner informs the faithful that

> If you receive your sexual information primarily from the magazine rack at the grocery checkout lane, you'll believe things like "every man loves getting oral sex and every woman loves giving it." In reality, however, studies show that this is not true. A majority of women do not like giving or receiving oral sex, and most men don't find it the most enjoyable way to engage sexually. The reason everybody is talking about it is simply because everyone is talking about it.[38]

Evangelicals cannot agree about the righteousness of oral sex. Marriage and sex advice author Karin Brown acknowledges that there is considerable unease among Christians over the activity of oral sex, and she admits that often either the man or the woman does not particularly enjoy it or feels forced into it by their partner. She notes that "so many marriages seem to be plagued with disagreement regarding it."[39] Yet Brown says she favors the activity, although she is careful to advise that it be used solely for foreplay and not as a substitute for intercourse.

There are also sex toys to puzzle over. Take vibrators. This time Karin Brown heads up the opposition: "I personally see no need for them when we have hands, lips and other great body parts to successfully heighten our intimate sexual encounters."[40] But Dillow and Pintus demur. They ask that the faithful apply the following test: "To find out if the use of a vibrator is right or wrong, let's apply the three questions. Is the use of a vibrator prohibited by Scripture? Is a vibrator beneficial to lovemaking? Does the use of a vibrator involve anyone else?" Since scripture does not offer commentary on vibrators—rendering it acceptable from a scriptural perspective—Dillow and Pintus move rapidly to questions two and three. On this basis they conclude: "So if a vibrator enhances a couple's lovemaking and is used exclusively for the couple's private enjoyment, then it is permitted."[41]

This is the commonsensical view adopted by a number of evangelical writers. Examine scripture and if there is nothing to prohibit a specific activity there, then it ought to be permitted. On this score, evangelicals Melissa McBurney and Louis McBurney emerge as virtual sex libertarians. The McBurneys have concluded, with regard to "oral sex, rear-entry vaginal penetration . . . and mutual masturbation," that since "we find no scriptural injunction against any of these," they are all just fine.[42]

Evangelical authors have given thumbs-up to all sorts of activities one might not immediately assume to be appropriate evangelical behavior. Sexy lingerie? This has been interpreted as a definite plus, again with reference to the Song of Solomon.[43] Anal sex? Hard to imagine? On the contrary, while some evangelicals deem anal sex unhealthy, there is the loving couple Reverend Charles Shedd and his wife, Martha, who have testified that their own sexual experiments have included anal sex, and they have publicly pronounced it enjoyable indeed.[44] So too do the Reverends Paul and Lori Byerly of the online site

"The Marriage Bed," which is officially antiporn, feel comfortable recommending both oral and anal sex, as well as a wife masturbating while her husband gets to watch. For the Byerlys, in marriage you can do just about anything. Typical upbeat advice includes enthusiastic endorsement of the "come-hither" move, in which the husband uses his fingers to stimulate his wife's G-spot—"We think the G-spot should be seen as one more way God gave us to share in the pleasure of sex"—as well as the seemingly neutral observation that just because the Bible says homosexual sex (as well as, they note, homosexual kissing) is wrong does not in any way prove that anal sex is wrong. They also note that spanking can be "arousing" and that bondage can be "very arousing."[45]

Recently, evangelicals have also begun increasingly to recommend that couples engage in occasional quickies. As Tim Alan Gardner states in *Sacred Sex*:

> I like to think of healthy marital sexual encounters in three categories. . . . The first grouping is Fast-Food Sex. This primarily includes "quickies" and those spur-of-the-moment rendezvous that take place without a lot of planning. Frequently, only the husband will have an orgasm (though not always). Fast food is fine, on occasion, but too much of it will leave one or both of you lacking passion and feeling taken for granted just as too many triple cheeseburgers will leave you—well, let's just say, not healthy.[46]

Gardner's two other recipes for a healthy marriage are Informal Dining and Five-Star Dining.

Gardner is far from alone. Dillow and Pintus also endorse the quickie, by which "we are talking about the act of sex taking around three to five minutes." The quickie, these women assure their presumably female readers, is absolutely "okay with God."[47]

HOW DO WE EXPLAIN the evangelical advocacy of the quickie? First, there is the worry that with women's growing equality in the world and growing concern with enhancing women's orgasm equity, men don't seem to feel terribly special anymore. Second, there is the much-discussed phenomenon that the supersaturation of the visual landscape with sexualized images—from Internet porn in the home to racy fashions on the street—has been accompanied by a perceived plummet in heterosexual desire. Viewed in this double context, the evangelicals' obsession with male ego-boosting and the novel attacks against masturbation and fantasy make more sense. And this is also the context in which the quickie—fine for the man, less so (usually) for the woman—should be understood.

The extent to which evangelicals embrace their version of the sexual revolution and the feminist movement is striking. As Shannon Ethridge writes: "I'm thrilled that the women's liberation movement brought us freedom to vote, get an education, and find satisfaction in careers."[48] And Stephen Arterburn clearly understands the necessity of husbands serving their wives, especially the many who work outside the home, by cooking, cleaning, doing the dishes, sharing child care responsibilities, and so forth.[49] These are the legacies of women's liberation that the evangelical movement supports 100 percent.

Yet evangelical writers on sex unapologetically contradict themselves. On the one hand, they admonish men that they never have a "biblical right" to demand sexual submission from their wives. They assure wives that they need never engage in any sexual practice they find degrading or unpleasant. In fact, they urgently remind wives that to accept the biblical injunction to wifely "submission" does not mean mindlessly doing whatever their husbands tell them to do.

On the other hand, the authors of the "Every Man" series, for instance, also recommend that wives be sexually available to their husbands at all times. Women should meet their men's needs with tenderness and compassion—and, if need be, with those quickies. Even Shannon Ethridge encourages wives to keep their legs shaved and their vaginas douched at all times.[50] Just in case.

Despite their seeming support for women's equality at home and in the workplace, moreover, evangelical authors spend a great deal of time repeating what they call "a foundational truth: God created men and women to be different."[51]

That women don't want sex as often as men is a regular feature in the archives of Christian sex literature. Dr. Neil T. Anderson, founder and president of Freedom in Christ Ministries, tells us that when he conducted a "For Women Only" seminar in the early 1990s, "to my surprise most of the written questions dealt with sex in marriage. If I could synthesize their questions into one, it would be, 'Do I have to do whatever my husband wants me to do in bed?'"[52] Tim LaHaye is even more blunt: "The sex drive in a man is almost volcanic in its latent ability to erupt at the slightest provocation."[53] James Dobson, president of Focus on the Family, has said: "Many women stand in amazement at how regularly their husbands desire sexual intercourse."[54] More recently, Paul Coughlin, in *No More Christian Nice Guy*, finds it rather irritating that evangelical wives were found—statistically—to be the most sexually satisfied wives in the nation. (He's invoking those early 1990s National Health and Social Life Survey research findings conducted by the University of Chicago team. Never mind that it was only 32 percent of conservative evangelical wives who always had orgasms during sex with their husbands versus a mere 27 percent among mainline Protestant and Catholic American women; no matter which number is considered, the findings were not exactly a ringing endorsement of the state of American heterosexuality. Yet the difference is still cause for right-wing pride.[55]) But Coughlin is focused on something else. He thinks the untold story is that it's evangelical *husbands* who are not so satisfied. Coughlin complains vociferously about wives who give their husbands—who struggled so hard to preserve their own sexual purity in the midst of a sex-obsessed culture—nothing but the sexual equivalent of "frozen dinners" rather than the "fabulous banquets" they need and deserve. Coughlin says that "sex isn't the only reason some guys get married (at least it shouldn't be), but it's a biggie." And he regales readers with sad laments of husbands who suffer from being with wives who offer up "I'm-tired-so-hurry-up sex" or "did-I-detect-life? sex"—or even "new-car sex" or "bigger-home sex"—when *what we really want and need is There's-No-One-Like-You sex.*[56] Coughlin may sound whiny, but he has an audience.[57]

Again emphasizing the idea that women don't want sex as much as men, after reviewing the results of their survey of 1,400 individuals about the "top five love needs," evangelical syndicated radio talk-show hosts Dr. Gary and Barbara Rosberg—authors, individually and together, of at least a dozen books, including *Healing the Hurt in Your Marriage* and *Forty Unforgettable Dates with Your Mate*—make related observations. In their advice book on how best to *Divorce-Proof Your Marriage*, the Rosbergs relate that while for both spouses "unconditional love and acceptance" rank as number one, among husbands "sexual intimacy" is number two but does not even make it onto the wives' top-five list. The Rosbergs elaborate: "Much of a man's masculinity is rooted in his sexuality, a part of his maleness he cannot erase. As most couples discover, men spell intimacy S-E-X." The same cannot be said for the wife: "Wives spell intimacy T-A-L-K. For many women, conversation is the primary way they process thoughts, feelings, ideas, and problems."[58]

The books in the "Every Man" series argue repeatedly that guys use emotions to get sex, while women use sex to get emotions. But the series takes this generic sentiment—so frequently asserted in mainstream culture as well—and amplifies it in wholly new ways. Arterburn's contention is that, put in the most rudimentary terms, if a husband can't do it to his wife every couple of days at least, he *will* stray—at least in his mind, if not with his body.

So what is the self-respecting evangelical wife supposed to do? This is where the quickie comes into play. It is also where some of the more disturbing aspects of evangelical advice come into the picture. For a woman has to be taught to cooperate. She must never ever compare her husband unfavorably to another man. The sin of comparison is as bad as the sin of sexual impurity.[59] She should wear sexy lingerie, if he wants her to do so.[60] But she must also give her husband sex whenever and wherever he wants it. For only in this way will her man be reassured. And a reassured husband is a satisfied husband and a satisfied husband is the key to marital bliss.

A central premise of *Every Man's Battle* is that men must learn to "bounce" their eyes. That is, they should practice and learn to look away immediately when confronted with a sexy image in the same way one would immediately yank a hand back from a hot stove. In this way, a guy can learn to "starve" his brain of all improper fantasies, memories, and images—anything and everything that is sexually stimulating that does not involve his wife. Stoeker and Arterburn recognize that Satan tempts men who will try this—and that the closer a man is to victory, the more Satan will develop ruses and rationalizations. But they express confidence that their step-by-step plan will work. They recommend going "cold turkey." Targeting masturbation alone won't work. The key is to target the eyes and mind. And then, in fact, there will be a huge—as they unabashedly say—"sexual payoff": "With your whole sexual being now focused upon your wife, sex with her will be so transformed that your satisfaction will explode off any known scale."[61]

With reference to the husband who decides finally to give up the visual stimulations that fuel his sexual fantasies, Arterburn and Stoeker directly advise wives: "Once he tells you he's going cold turkey, be like a merciful vial of methadone for him. Increase your availability to him sexually, though this may be difficult for you since your husband might have told you some things that repulse you."[62]

Wives are directly told to have sex with their husbands more often, no matter what it feels like for them. (All in the name of *his* sexual purity.) Having introduced their scientific conclusion that all men need to have their sperm released at least once in any seventy-two-hour cycle, Arterburn and Stoeker approvingly quote the testimony of "Ellen":

> In relation to your own husband, understanding the seventy-two-hour cycle can help you keep him satisfied. Ellen said: "His purity is extremely important to me, so I try to meet his needs so that he goes out each day with his cup full. During the earlier years, with much energy going into childcare and with my monthly cycle, it was a lot more difficult for me to do that. There weren't too many 'ideal times' when everything was just right. But that's life, and I did it anyway."

Voice-over intervenes:

> "So there's a place for the quickie. While a long-term diet of
> drive-by sex is unhealthy, it certainly has a place in defusing the
> power of the seventy-two-hour temptation cycle. Sometimes you
> just don't have the time or energy for the full package, but if
> you care about his purity, you can find just enough energy to get
> him by."[63]

Evangelical women might be unhappy with their men—or with
having sex with their men—but Arterburn and Stoeker argue
that it is all for a good and godly cause. Take the case of "Andrea," again quoted by Arterburn and Stoeker: "Even if I'm
tired or don't feel good, I can appreciate his sexual needs, so I do
my part to satisfy him. I have to admit, though, I've had times
that I felt resentful."[64] Nonetheless, trooper that she is, Andrea
soldiers on.[65]

AFTER A WHILE, IN SHORT, it begins to sound like the real deep-
down taboo—which Arterburn and Stoeker can never openly acknowledge even though it is *the* core basis for their entire
enterprise as well as their success—is that many husbands have
actually lost desire for their wives. Despite evangelicals' constant announcements about revved-up men, it is simply not true
that women want sex less than their husbands.

Further, what the evangelical advisers suggest is that most
men lead lives of quiet desperation. Men far too often feel like
losers and chumps. Evangelical authors repeatedly hammer
home the awfulness of many American marriages, but especially
the misery of masculinity. Men find their lives dull and boring.
In James Dobson's words:

The straight life for a working man . . . is pulling your tired frame out of bed, five days a week, fifty weeks out of the year. It is earning a two-week vacation in August, and choosing a trip that will please the kids. . . . The straight life is coping with head colds and engine tune-ups and crab grass and income-tax forms.[66]

In addition, as another evangelical author notes in passing, "many, many Christian couples are bored silly with their sex lives."[67]

In this insider's view of evangelicalism, men are revealed as worrying that they will be exposed as posers or impostors, fakes or failures. Men fear that their jovial, buddy-buddy interactions with other men are merely a sham to cover up a mutual defensiveness and rivalry. Men wish they had a more gorgeous and thrilling or less critical and demanding wife, but they are afraid they don't deserve one.

The core appeal to men of the new evangelical advice-writing is its seductive promise that they can again *feel like real men*. Conservative evangelicalism holds out the promise of a restored masculinity. It offers men the ideals of self-confidence and strength. It flatters guys with extensive talk about their powerful sex drives. It acknowledges how much men need to have their egos stroked and stoked. And it addresses the supposed "raw power" that comes from holding back on sex.

Evangelicals also taunt men to buck up. They define a "sissy" as someone who cannot eliminate every hint of improper sexual innuendo from his life. As Arterburn and Stoeker insist: "We must choose to be *more* than male. We must choose *manhood*."[68] They mock men who still seek out porn. A porn-achieved intimacy is intimacy attained without risk. And only losers need that kind of cheap reassurance. They promise the faithful guy that he is not a loser because only a loser can't control himself, or has sex with any woman who will sleep with him, or masturbates every time an erotic image assails him.

Some advice-writers seek the transformation of Christian couch potatoes into adventurous, untamed men. In his massively best-selling self-help manifesto *Wild at Heart: Discovering the Secret of a Man's Soul*, John Eldredge of Ransomed Heart Ministries draws on a combination of stories from scripture and new age and men's movement thinking to challenge the stereotypical view that Christian men ought to be dutiful homebodies. Eldredge has a nightmarish vision of modern man as mortgage-burdened and overstressed, paralyzed at the prospect of taking risks in his personal life. Fathers and sons need to escape the world of work and women—not as a means to abandon those responsibilities, but as a means to revitalize their relationship to them.

Eldredge argues that the modern man has been castrated and feminized by the pressures of his middle-class, suburban existence, citing men's movement spokesman Robert Bly's argument in *Iron John* that "some women want a passive man if they want a man at all; the church wants a tamed man—they are called priests; the university wants a domesticated man—they are called tenure-track people; the corporation wants a . . . sanitized, hairless, shallow man." Eldredge's take is that this is *not* what God wants. In his view, the last thirty years in America have resulted in a "gender confusion never experienced at such a wide level in the history of the world." Eldredge is disgusted that "what we hold up as models of Christian maturity" are "Really Nice Guys." He suggests that "this dedication to niceness is the reason there are so many tired and lonely women, so many fatherless children, and so few men around."[69] Christian men especially have become bored—and boring—beyond belief.

Like everyone else in this business, Eldredge engages the confessional mode, admitting his own past failings and struggles. He talks about his own marital crises and the moments when he felt his formerly pretty wife had grown plump and unattractive; he refers to his nagging insecurities about his masculinity. He also includes stories about other boys and men anxious about the size of their penises, the high-maintenance challenge of their girlfriends or wives, and the wounding and emasculation that resulted from their fathers' inability to validate them. This technique invites identification. The book moves on to inspire guys to be "dangerous" men, unconstrained and more fully themselves. Women, he advises, should not be turning their husbands and sons into eunuchs—after all, what every woman really, truly wants is a *wild man*. And when the Bible is correctly understood as reflecting the wishes of "a passionate God," then men will be able to remake themselves in this God's image.[70]

Evangelical writers appear torn between the points they ultimately wish to make. They admit the prevalence of dull men and emotionally and sexually unfulfilling marriages, but also say that God made men to be passionate and wild, thrilling to their spouses, confident in themselves. They want to assure men that they really have powerful sexual motors and raging "mustang minds," and yet they also want men to know that they can win the battle against improper lust.[71] They document widespread agony but promise ecstasy. They pay lip service to gender equality, yet instruct wives to be available as sexual receptacles no matter how badly their husbands are treating them or how ineptly their husbands perform in bed—because this is the only way husbands can learn to cherish them.

These contradictions, far from undermining the power of the advice-writers' messages, are central to evangelicalism's ideological effectiveness. The seeming contradictions are in fact the key to the advice-writers' success, because this is how audiences are stirred up and involved emotionally. Much of the advice literature is reassuring and valuable; without a doubt, for instance, Dillow and Pintus's calm endorsements of regular exercise and self-acceptance can help many women. Similarly, Eldredge's rugged antimaterialism and thoughtful critique of intra-male rivalries could be very beneficial. (At the same time, Dillow, Pintus, and Eldredge have all advanced vicious homophobia.) The good cop–bad cop strategies are also constantly being adapted and updated as the perceived needs for therapeutic self-help escalate under the emotionally bruising impact of daily life in a perpetually insecurity-inducing culture, and even more so as the sexual landscape of America changes. The use of men's movement and new age thinking in Eldredge's *Wild at Heart* is as indicative of the therapeutization of evangelicalism as is the continual absorption of secular sex and marriage self-help innovations in evangelical advice books as well as workshops, conferences, retreats, and associations. But Stephen Arterburn, Fred Stoeker, and Shannon Ethridge have really taken evangelical sex advice in new directions. They rail against porn even as they produce porn. They endorse being Christian as the only good and proper way to be, yet they also document exponential rates of Christian hypocrisy in unprecedented and elaborate detail.

Consider Kevin, who is married with three kids. While working with the youth group at church, he met a beautiful fifteen-year-old girl. "She's a knockout, and looks more like twenty," he said. "Sometimes I'd ask about boys she's known and dated, and we'd joke and laugh a lot. . . . We'd get to talking a little trashy . . . it was exciting. Last week, when my wife and kids were out of town, I gave this girl a ride home. We got to talking dirty again, and somehow I bet her that she wouldn't pull her pants down for me. She did. I lost my senses, and I drove her to a park and we had sex. I'm in real trouble! She told her parents about it, and they may press rape charges!"[72]

Is this story supposed to be somehow representative? After a while, it begins to seem so.

What *is* the appeal of reading a story like this? Beyond the fantasy-stimulating elements, its appeal may also be due to the way it taps into the taboo zone of marital misery. Again, beneath the surface buzz, there appears to be the sobering implication that a whole lot of American marriages have gone sexually dead. The Christian pornographers do not hesitate to describe this ravaged landscape almost as graphically as they describe the fantasies they deem inappropriate. These tales of a haunting marital morass resonate in the Bible Belt, but they are tapping into a deep reservoir of apprehension and disquiet in the secular world as well.

To anyone reading its sex and marriage advice literature, the Religious Right's core message to its followers becomes abundantly clear: *you really can have it all.* You can feel virtuously superior to and voyeuristically outraged by sexual minorities and abortion seekers. And you can know that God forgives all your own prior sins, and that He promises you decades of spectacular sex in marriage.

Delving into the messy vicissitudes of marital heterosexuality, however, was by no means how the Religious Right got its start in the business of sexual politics. Back when most Americans were less easily intimidated about their own sex lives, a mere fifteen years ago, the focus of Religious Right activism lay elsewhere. Reinforcing contempt for homosexuals was how the Religious Right made it big in the first place.

Chapter 3

TRIAL AND ERROR

Mᴜᴄʜ ᴏғ ᴛʜᴇ ꜱᴜᴄᴄᴇꜱꜱ of the marital heterosexual model advanced by the Religious Right rests on the construction of homosexuality as the disgusting opposite of heterosexuality. Heterosexuals might continually be tempted by porn and by infidelity, but they are nothing like homosexuals. And yet, in the profusion of antihomosexual rhetoric generated by the Religious Right in the course of the 1990s, there was a strong pornographic charge as well. The rhetoric served not only to repulse but also to titillate its target audience. There was throughout a voyeuristic fascination with what homosexuals might be doing in bed with each other.

The year 1992 marked the first time the rights of homosexuals became a major theme in a presidential election. Republican president George H. W. Bush took a hard line on the subject to appeal to conservative constituencies in his reelection campaign. The bulk of the fund-raising literature of the right-wing evangelical Christian movement began to focus on the need to demolish gay rights, and the Religious Right mobilized its core supporters by fueling antigay resentment. The mobilization moved swiftly and decisively, and with remarkable coordination. Pat Robertson and Ralph Reed of the Christian Coalition distributed 40 million voter guides (30 million of them in churches) that compared the candidates' positions on abortion, prayer in schools, and homosexual rights. Robertson called the distribution "the most comprehensive effort in the history of the country."[1]

The initiative also reflected a tremendous degree of political calculation. As a strategist for the Bush campaign stated, his campaign's focus on homosexuality was an open attempt to pander to southern evangelical voters. "We need that vote," he said. "You get it on abortion, on prayer in the schools and—I don't want to use the word 'gay'—on other-than-normal life styles."[2]

The literature emphasized that homosexuals were potential sex offenders and child abusers, playing on impulses of fear and loathing. As social historian George Chauncey writes, it was during this moment in U.S. history that "Christian Right organizations distributed thousands of copies of 'The Gay Agenda,' a video that effectively juxtaposed discussions of pedophilia with images of gay teachers and gay parents marching with their children in Gay Pride parades, which made it easy for viewers to imagine they were molesters showing off their prey."[3] A group calling itself the Christian Action Network ran television ads against Democratic presidential candidate Bill Clinton that depicted men in black leather hugging each other at a protest march while a voice-over intoned: "Bill Clinton's vision for a better America includes job quotas for homosexuals." The voice asked: "Is this your vision for a better America?"[4]

Americans were far from unified on the question of whether homosexuality represented a menace to society. Polls revealed contradictory evidence on the growing acceptance of homosexuality in American life. As more Americans knew someone who was openly gay or lesbian, there was a slow, steady climb in the social acceptance of homosexuals. According to a Gallup/*Newsweek* poll conducted that year, 78 percent of Americans favored equal job opportunities for homosexuals, and two-thirds said they approved of the idea of inheritance rights and health insurance for gay partners. Americans were also slightly more than twice as likely in 1992 as in 1977 (29 percent versus 14 percent) to believe that gays should be allowed to adopt.[5] At the same time, fewer than one-third of Americans approved of gay marriage, 53 percent said that they did not consider homosexuality an acceptable lifestyle, and 45 percent said that they considered gay rights "a threat to the American family and its values." Americans were almost evenly divided over whether homosexuals should teach in elementary schools or be members of the clergy.[6]

A *New York Times*/CBS poll that same year reported somewhat lower levels of tolerance for gays and lesbians. It found that only 38 percent of Americans believed homosexuality was an acceptable life choice, and it underscored the existence of a gender gap: "Almost half of American women consider homosexuality an acceptable lifestyle, compared with less than a third of the men." It also found that only about one-third of Americans thought homosexual relations between consenting adults should be legal. (Sodomy was still illegal in twenty-two states. Never mind that in many of those states the sodomy laws covered heterosexual sodomy as well, including oral sex; these were finer points not addressed by the poll.)[7]

Public opinion toward homosexuality was clearly in a process of flux. It was a glass half full or half empty, depending on how you looked at it. Leaders of the Religious Right were about to gamble that they could knock the glass right over.

Their gamble was a response in large part to the fact that 1992 also witnessed the first time articulate and effective gay and lesbian rights groups received heightened national visibility during a presidential election cycle. As Rahm Emanuel, the Democratic presidential campaign's financial director, excitedly admitted, "The gay community is the new Jewish community." Emanuel elaborated: "It's highly politicized, with fundamental health and civil rights concerns. And it contributes money. All that makes for a potent political force, indeed." Estimates in 1992 indicated that while there would be 4 million likely Jewish voters, there might be as many as 9 million gay and lesbian voters.[8]

The Republicans were willing to venture that there was probably another new voter bloc made up of those who could be persuaded that "the new Jewish community" should be defeated. The formal introduction of this perspective came during the Republican National Convention in August 1992 in the form of a speech from Patrick Buchanan. Buchanan specifically underscored that "the homosexual agenda" was among the more distasteful changes a potential Bill Clinton administration planned for the country. Buchanan declared: "It's not the kind of change we can tolerate in a nation that we still call God's country." He also announced that opposition to a gay agenda would be a key plank in the Republican platform. The extremeness of this now-famous "culture war" speech from Buchanan prompted journalist Molly Ivins to comment that it "probably sounded better in the original German."[9]

Buchanan quickly found vocal allies. There were those at the convention who toted signs that read: FAMILY RIGHTS FOREVER/GAY RIGHTS NEVER. However, Buchanan's tough antigay talk marked a sharp new tack in Republican strategy. In 1988 the Republican platform committee had consented to meet with representatives of gay rights groups, but in 1992 such meetings were not permitted. Now the party platform openly stated: "We oppose efforts by the Democratic Party to include sexual preference as a protected minority receiving preferential status under civil rights statutes at the Federal, state and local level."[10]

This new national effort to vilify homosexuals also surfaced in the form of two state-level antigay referenda. An important early state-level mobilization occurred in Oregon when Lon Mabon, head of an organization called the Oregon Citizens Alliance, successfully got a referendum on the ballot that the *New York Times* labeled "the strongest antihomosexual measure ever considered by a state." The referendum, if passed, would have obliged state and local governments and the public schools to set "a standard for Oregon's youth that recognizes homosexuality, pedophilia, sadism and masochism as abnormal, wrong, unnatural and perverse," and it would have permitted discrimination against gays and lesbians in employment and housing.[11] Mabon liked to say: "Homosexuality is not a civil right. It's an aberration."[12] While Colorado's Amendment 2 was less openly nasty in that it did not condemn homosexuality, it did strategically reject antidiscrimination measures. The Colorado concept was to bar the state legislature as well as any Colorado municipality from passing an antidiscrimination law. It was possible that passage of the amendment would cause AIDS patients to lose their health insurance or be evicted from their homes.[13]

American voters proved unreceptive to the most extreme and strident antigay appeals. Mabon's referendum in Oregon was too grotesque for Oregonians, and the Catholic Church joined the majority of state leaders, major newspapers, and Protestant religious organizations in condemning the measure, not least on the grounds that it might encourage hate crimes. Colorado voters, however, did endorse Amendment 2, with the result that antidiscrimination ordinances in Denver, Boulder, and Aspen were repealed, although the amendment was later found to be unconstitutional.

And Democrat Bill Clinton defeated Republican George H. W. Bush.

But the antigay efforts of 1992 were nonetheless historic. As Urvashi Vaid, executive director of the National Gay and Lesbian Task Force, observed at the time:

> It's hateful. The [Republican] party is saying "we don't want you." We're the only ones left to attack. Communism is gone. There's too much support for women's issues. The Los Angeles riots [of April–May 1992] make it impossible to attack blacks, and the party is wooing them anyway. That leaves us as the ones to beat on to divert attention from the economy and other failings.[14]

The Religious Right may have lost the battle for the presidency, but it had no plans to abandon its war on the rights of homosexuals. Having appealed to homophobia on the state and national stages, many within the movement contended that homophobia was still their ticket to success and to the White House—or at least, for the time being, to Congress.[15]

So far as the Religious Right was concerned, 1992 was a watershed because it represented an experiment that failed. The movement's leaders had mobilized around the issue of homosexuality, not necessarily out of conviction, but because they believed that homophobia might be a winning strategy. That homophobia had not worked did not mean that they had chosen the wrong issue, but merely that they had gone about it the wrong way. Next time around, homophobia would simply have to look less like what it really was—that is, hatefulness—and more like what it really wasn't: all-American and healthful common sense. All the strategy required was a makeover.

In the spring of 1994, leading right-wing evangelicals and their allies gathered for a conference that would formally anoint homophobia the new racism that they would use to mobilize their movement. It was a choice that would soon have intense political consequences.

The two-day conference was held on the several-hundred-acre grounds of Glen Eyrie Castle, located on the west side of Colorado Springs. Glen Eyrie is international headquarters for the Navigators, an influential evangelical Christian organization that had purchased the castle for several hundred thousand dollars back in 1953. In the intervening half-century, Glen Eyrie has been host to countless conferences and outreach programs for the evangelical movement, all efforts to further the group's stated mission to help individuals know Christ personally. Only forty people attended the 1994 conference, but they represented the more powerful evangelical lobbying groups in the nation, including Focus on the Family, the National Research Institute, Accuracy in Media, the Family Research Council, the National Legal Foundation, Concerned Women for America, the Christian Coalition, the Traditional Values Coalition, the Eagle Forum, the American Family Association, and the local Colorado for Family Values. No outside media were allowed to attend, though reports on the conference based on eyewitness accounts, tape recordings of the conference, and interviews eventually got out.[16]

Among those in attendance were attorney Robert Skolrood of the National Legal Foundation, a former employee of right-wing evangelical Pat Robertson; Judith Reisman, the anti-Kinsey and antiporn expert long active in the campaign to portray homosexuals as child molesters; Peter LaBarbera, producer of *The Gay Agenda*, the widely distributed video screed against homosexuality; Paul Cameron, a psychologist notorious for his antigay "research findings"; Colonel Ron Ray, an avid opponent of homosexuals in the military; and John Eldredge, onetime member of the Los Angeles drug scene, future author of the bestselling "rugged Christian masculinity" guidebook *Wild at Heart*, but as of 1994 director of seminars and research for James Dobson's powerful, Colorado-based national lobby group, Focus on the Family.[17]

The conference and the tactics discussed there represented in condensed form several key reorientations within the Religious Right in the 1990s. Among these were two nationally coordinated but locally effectual shifts of energy to the grass roots: the first in the realm of politics and the second within the churches. The first was a shift from high-visibility political interventions at the federal level to a wide array of initiatives at the state and local levels, including not just elections and referenda but also the development of legislation and entry into the leadership of Republican Party state committees.[18]

The second involved not only gaining control of major evangelical church organizations, by casting out more liberal and even apolitical evangelicals from leadership positions and replacing them with conservatives, but also creating conservative evangelical groups that would work within the mainstream denominations (like Presbyterians, United Methodists, and Episcopalians) to push a variety of conservative issues and create disputes over sexual politics inside local congregations. Other major goals were to monitor and publicize candidates' voting records, to engage in targeted fund-raising and spending, and to develop disciplined voting blocs.

There was yet another matter of signal significance at Glen Eyrie: the move to "de-religify" the evangelical movement's sexual messages. Situating homophobia as the new central plank of the Religious Right's platform came together with an explicit plan to present the antigay message in *secular* terms in order to reach a wider audience and shape the national conversation. After the defeats of 1992, the Glen Eyrie group wanted to leave nothing to chance.

The unifying aim of the conference was to hammer out a clear set of strategies for combating what it labeled "the militant gay agenda," which was part of a wider move to present gay and lesbian efforts to gain *equal* rights as a problematic and disturbing attempt to achieve *special* rights. The Glen Eyrie project involved such broad and bold initiatives as:

- Creating a nationwide data bank for monitoring and exchanging information on all politicians and activists perceived to be pro-gay
- Pressuring politicians to commit to opposing any gay-friendly legislation
- Discouraging public funding for AIDS-related research and support services (AIDS in this case being perceived as "the result of improper behavior brought on by their [homosexuals'] lifestyle")
- Pressuring evangelical pastors to stop being "wimps" (Robert Skolrood's word) about the homosexuality issue and to make the need to combat homosexuality a central topic within their congregations
- Focusing political campaigns, media blitzes, and fund-raising initiatives specifically on the issue of homosexuality—presented at this meeting (by Eldredge, channeling Dobson) as "one of the key issues of our age," yet an issue

to which the church was only "slowly waking up" and an issue about which "the vast majority of Christians in the country" remained "woefully ignorant"[19]

- Promoting "family values" such that "homosexuality would be regarded as a sad pathology by implication"[20]

Those attending were encouraged to invest in good fax machines (for contacting state and national legislators and sending letters to the editors of newspapers, as well as faxing to churches, which could then "reprint by hundreds"), and they were also educated on the (then-new) technologies of e-mail and Internet forums. They were urged to "know your enemy," "monitor computer bulletin boards," "go on gay and lesbian forums, read their publications" (the Lambda Report was especially recommended), and in general to engage in "intelligence gathering information . . . so we can preempt."[21]

Some attendees persisted in addressing the dangers supposedly inherent in homosexuality in religious terms. Thus, Skolrood spoke of the importance of keeping these "demons from polluting the word of God," invoked "II Corinthians 10:3–5," and asserted that the antigay activists were involved in "a spiritual battle." Colonel Ray contrasted "God's objective order" and "His standard" with "Sodom and Gomorrah."[22]

Other attendees adopted nonreligious fearmongering. Stressing the pernicious influence of homosexuals on teenagers, Judith Reisman (the only Jew in attendance) cautioned that while homosexuals represented only a tiny fraction of the population, their small number belied the dangers they posed to the nation's health precisely "because the recruitment is loud; it is clear; it is everywhere." Because of successful gay recruitment, Reisman estimated, "you'll be seeing [that], I would say, twenty percent or more, probably thirty percent, or even more than that, of the young population will be moving into homosexual activity."[23] John Eldredge, for his part, observed:

> I think the gay agenda, and I would not say this as frankly as I will now in other cultural contexts, I think the gay agenda has all the elements of that which is truly evil. It is deceptive at every turn . . . it is destroying the souls and the lives of those who embrace it, and it has a corrosive effect on the society which endorses it, either explicitly or even implicitly.[24]

"Evil," "deceptive," "corrosive": the fomenters of the new anti-gay agenda worked hard to find language to portray gays and lesbians as a major source of spiritual and social danger for mainstream America.

Eldredge even floated the argument that the American ideals of individualism, personal autonomy, and the pursuit of happiness were problematic. There was, in his view, no such thing as a right to sexual happiness or sexual fulfillment, and he also found it irritating that there were increasing pressures in American culture to show "sensitivity" and "tolerance" and to avoid causing "personal pain."[25]

Still, the politics of homophobia presented a special challenge. It was a delicate matter, especially since Americans were divided on the issue. John Eldredge urged his colleagues to brainstorm fresh ways to "tell America why heterosexuality is best for individuals and society." The peddling of hatred could be a considerable turnoff, Eldredge counseled, and he cautioned the conference to develop a strategy that did not simply demonize homosexuals: "To the extent we can control our public image, we must never appear to be bigoted or mean-spirited. . . . We must never appear to be attempting to rob anyone of their rights, of their constitutional rights."[26] To this end, Eldredge proposed that they learn how better to *package* their message—and thereby preempt any potential reaction to the notions they were promoting as something cruel or hurtful toward a minority, or as more generally privacy-invading or overly religious. That their message was all those things was irrelevant; it was necessary that it not *appear* to be those things.

Strikingly, already at this Glen Eyrie meeting the idea that homosexuality could be cured was put forward as one potentially useful line of argument. One participant recommended to the others to "take [the] high ground on compassion, feature the ex-gay movement," because "born gay is a lie, [a] foundational myth for the gay culture." The task was to "blow away this oppressed minority myth." In response to the worry about what to "do with politicians who have gays in their families," the suggestion was that "you can love someone and still disagree with his problem (compare to alcoholism)." The idea should be to "get back to common sense things," for instance: "How can you be born gay if what you do causes disease?"[27]

In addition, Eldredge warned his listeners to avoid strenuously all "overt appeals to biblical morality in the public square" and never to rely on such assertions as "homosexuality is an abomination to God." Moreover, he said, "most people react negatively if they perceive an effort such as ours as robbing their freedom of choice, telling them what to do." Thus, he stressed further that it was important for the antigay agenda not to be presented as a "takeover" from outside, or in any way a "top-down" endeavor. In every local instance, the best scenario would be one in which the "eight-hundred-pound gorilla" (Eldredge's own term) of the national organization Focus on the Family would be kept out of view, and the resistance to homosexual rights would be presented as emerging from "a genuine grass-roots uprising."[28]

Less than two years after the Glen Eyrie meeting, another gathering of representatives of Religious Right organizations—including the Christian Coalition, the American Family Association, and Focus on the Family—was held in Memphis, Tennessee, to create an antihomosexual networking organization called the National Pro-Family Forum. The group's master plan was to develop a national strategy to advance what would come to be called the Defense of Marriage Act, or DOMA. The first event sponsored by the National Pro-Family Forum transpired during the Iowa presidential caucuses in February 1996. Republican presidential candidates were invited to appear in a church in Des Moines; while a pool of reporters watched, they each signed a pledge declaring their opposition to gay marriage. Cincinnati-based activist Phil Burress was ecstatic. "No one was paying attention to the issue of same-sex marriages up to that point," he said. "And then all of a sudden bam! This was an issue that was being debated nationwide!"[29] Burress had every reason to be pleased.

DOMA sailed through Congress, pushed by Republican Representative Bob Barr of Georgia (himself divorced twice and married three times, but no matter), and then signed into law by President Bill Clinton. That same year the voters in nineteen states passed referenda against gay marriage, and thirty-seven states passed their own "defense of marriage" laws, many of them stating that they would not recognize gay marriages approved in any other state.

ADOPTING A NICER AND SOFTER HOMOPHOBIA proved more difficult for some than might have been expected. Not all conservative Christian leaders or their political allies were able to wean themselves of undisguised disdain for homosexuality.

They might mouth the words "love the sinner, hate the sin" while home alone in front of a mirror, but in front of cameras and reporters they backslid into the politically incorrect view that gays were little more than repugnant sodomites.

Donald E. Wildmon, an ordained United Methodist minister, was chairman of the American Family Association, an organization devoted to the view that only healthful representations of traditional "family values" should appear in American entertainment. The AFA's official position is that it has nothing against homosexuals. The organization's website declares:

> The same Holy Bible that calls us to reject sin, calls us to love our neighbor. It is that love that motivates us to expose the misrepresentation of the radical homosexual agenda and stop its spread through our culture. AFA has sponsored several events reaching out to homosexuals and letting them know there is love and healing at the Cross of Christ.[30]

Yet, in a 1994 booklet on *Homosexuality in America*, the AFA claimed that prominent gay rights activists "have voiced support for pedophilia, incest, sadomasochism, and even bestiality."[31] And as part of a fund-raising campaign, Pastor Wildmon declared: "For the sake of our children and society, we must OPPOSE the spread of homosexual activity! Just as we must oppose murder, stealing and adultery! Since homosexuals cannot reproduce, the only way for them to 'breed' is to RECRUIT! And who are their targets for recruitment? Children."[32]

Senator Trent Lott (R-Miss.) knew how tough it could be to drop old ways and get aboard the new love-the-sinner-hate-the-sin train. In 1996 Lott helped defeat a Senate bill that would have banned discrimination against gays and lesbians in the workplace, calling the legislation "part of a larger and more audacious effort to make the public accept behavior that most Americans consider dangerous, unhealthy or just plain wrong." During an interview in 1998, Senator Lott was asked whether he considered homosexuality a sin. "Yes, it is," he replied, adding, "In America right now there's an element that wants to make that alternative lifestyle acceptable." He caught himself, though, and quickly said: "You still love that person and you should not try to mistreat them or treat them as outcasts." But the old homophobic itch wouldn't let up. He kept going: "You should try to show them a way to deal with that." Alluding to his father's alcoholism, Lott pursued the point: "Others have a sex addiction or are kleptomaniacs. There are all kinds of problems and addictions and difficulties and experiences of this kind that are wrong. But you should try to work with that person to learn to control that problem."[33]

Some friends of the Religious Right persisted in articulating their undisguised revulsion. Back in 1991, Robert Wasinger— then a Harvard undergraduate, later to become chief of staff for Senator Sam Brownback (R-Kans.)—had declared homosexuality a problem because it meant sperm would "swim into feces" during anal sex.[34] Family Research Council representative Robert Knight took a similar view: "Just look at the human body! You can't fool nature. The rectum was not made for sexual activity. . . . It is an exit ramp, not an entry ramp."[35]

Others remained glued to outright hatred. The Reverend Lou Sheldon of the Traditional Values Coalition speculated that any moves toward hate crime legislation might be turned against those who deemed homosexuality sinful. Sheldon even reached for a Holocaust analogy to underscore his point: "What Hitler began to build against the Jews is now being built against people of faith who believe the Scriptures are valid for today and their injunctions against certain sexual behaviors is [*sic*] correct."[36] Likewise, Pat Robertson, former presidential candidate and influential talk-show host, said on *The 700 Club*: "Many of those people involved in Adolph Hitler were Satanists. Many of them were homosexuals. The two things seem to go together." Robertson once cautioned that homosexuals "want to come into churches and disrupt church services and throw blood all around and try to give people AIDS and spit in the face of ministers." And in 1998 Robertson warned that "terrorist bombs, earthquakes, tornadoes and possibly a meteor" might hit Orlando, Florida, because the city council had given permission for rainbow flags to be flown "in God's face" as part of a Gay Days celebration.[37]

By far the most consistently extreme of the hate campaigners has been Baptist pastor Fred Phelps of Kansas. Phelps has devoted his life to disrupting the funerals of men who died of complications from HIV/AIDS. He and his followers attend these funerals with signs that read: AIDS CURES FAGS, GOD HATES FAGS, and WHEN FAGGOTS DIE, GOD LAUGHS.[38] Phelps rose—or descended—to national prominence when he interrupted the funeral of Matthew Shepard, a victim of antigay violence, with a placard that read MATT IN HELL.[39] As late as 2006, Phelps could still be seen on national television.

Overall, such overt ugliness diminished within the ranks of the Religious Right during the late 1990s. As the antigay agenda gathered momentum, so did its stated intention to preempt any interpretation that it fomented hate or disinformation about homosexuals. In 1998 the National Pro-Family Forum launched an unexpected new strategy: a media blitz called "Truth in Love." It featured "ex-gays" who had "walked out of homosexuality into sexual celibacy or even marriage." The effort was cosponsored by the Christian Coalition and an organization called Americans for Truth About Homosexuality. It promoted an early gay-to-straight "conversion" organization called Love in Action (even though one former member sarcastically said the organization should have been called Lots of Action). Subsequently, another "conversion" organization was created, Love Won Out, which organized monthly workshops sponsored by Focus on the Family for individuals "struggling with same-sex desires," along with their family members.[40]

The Religious Right now insisted that "morality is not bigotry," and that it was above all motivated by "love for the homosexual community" and a commitment to *"redemption,* not rancor."[41] Since the mid-1990s, there have been a slew of books on the "truth" of homosexuality, including *The Truth About Homosexuality, Homosexuality and the Politics of Truth, The Truth About Same-Sex Marriage,* and *Homosexuality: Good and Right in the Eyes of God? The Wedding of Truth to Compassion and Reason to Revelation.* The recommendation to heal (rather than hurt) and offer freedom (rather than restriction) is evident in such recent titles as *Can Homosexuality Be Healed?, Strength in Weakness: Overcoming Sexual and Relational Brokenness, Restoring Sexual Identity,* and *A Parent's Guide to Preventing Homosexuality.* Also enduringly popular has been the classic conversion text, *Coming Out of Homosexuality: New Freedom for Men and Women.* All of these texts depend on the idea that homosexuality is curable. This became the new main rallying cry of Christian homophobia.

The work of James Dobson has been essential. Dobson's writings and radio pronouncements on Christian child development have influenced millions of Americans. His Christian parenting guide, *Dare to Discipline,* has sold three and a half million copies. About Dobson, journalist Chris Hedges writes:

> He is heard on *Focus on the Family,* a program broadcast on more than 3,000 radio stations; runs a grassroots organization with

chapters in 36 states; and runs his operation out of an 81-acre campus in Colorado Springs, Colorado, a campus that has its own zip code. He employs 1,300 people, sends out four million pieces of mail each month, and is heard in 116 countries. His estimated listening audience is more than 200 million worldwide, and in the United States he appears on 80 television stations each day.[42]

Voted one of the most powerful evangelicals in America by *TIME* magazine, Dobson has made and broken a few political careers in his day; he certainly gives himself credit for George W. Bush's reelection in 2004.[43]

James Dobson does not like homosexuality, but Dobson also believes homosexual is not something anyone is born to be. An adolescent boy may come to suffer from "a condition we might call 'prehomosexuality,'" when the parents or pastor turn a blind eye to the boy's abnormal behavior. Potential symptoms listed by Dobson include taking pleasure in looking at oneself in the mirror wearing skimpy underwear, feeling aroused while jumping up and down under the shower, trying on fingernail polish, or attempting to suck one's own penis. Speaking of one unfortunate youth who was suffering from such a "prehomosexual" condition, Dobson writes: "Unless he and his entire family are guided by someone who knows how to assist, the probabilities are very great that he will go on to experience a homosexual lifestyle."[44]

Dobson argues that such boys must be turned into real boys who like to mix explosive chemicals or get their heads bashed during a tackle football game. Boys who think or feel otherwise are not real boys, and these fake boys have been damaged in some respects, probably as the result of early sexual abuse.[45]

Dobson's views fit squarely into the main currents of a broad-based evangelical and secular movement that has sought to redefine homosexuality as largely a result of childhood sexual abuse or that sees same-sex attractions as resulting from something some participants in this movement call "gender identity disorders."[46] Andrew Comiskey, ex-gay founder of Desert Stream Ministries together with his wife, an abuse survivor, not only observes that "same-sex yearnings in a man signal his disidentification with his own masculinity" but also ranges freely across the topics of abuse and homosexuality in a way that suggests they are somehow interchangeable.[47]

Homosexuals are now identified by right-wing evangelicals as victims to be pitied rather than perpetrators to be feared. Child abuse is no longer what they do; it's what they've been subjected to. And above all, they are really insecure heterosexual wannabes.

"Sexual abuse is common in the backgrounds of women and men struggling with homosexual attractions," write Bob Davies and Lori Rentzel. "Some women enter lesbianism after years of sexual abuse or other trauma at the hands of fathers or other older males." Davies too is an ex-gay man and executive director of the Seattle branch of the leading ex-gay organization, Exodus International. Rentzel is a former counselor with Love in Action. Davies writes elaborately of a major turning point in his own conversion from homosexuality to heterosexuality after he heard a lecture at the 1982 Exodus International conference in Denver, long before conversion therapies hit the national news.

"You are heterosexual in Christ," the speaker said and I (Bob) shifted uncomfortably in my seat. "No matter how deep your homosexual feelings are, deeper still lies your heterosexuality, buried under a thousand fears."

Am I really heterosexual? I wondered in the following weeks. How could I honestly claim to have a heterosexual identity? I did not feel heterosexual. I was not sexually attracted to women. I still had homosexual feelings for other men.

Over time Davies came to understand the true meaning of what God sought from him. "As I look into God's Word, I realize that all the basics I need to know about who I am are right before me":

In making us after his image, God has invested us with immeasurable value. On a good day I may see myself as Bob Davies—a nice, competent, heterosexual man. On a bad day I see Bob Davies as frustrated, struggling, someone who will never measure up. But when God looks at me, he sees Bob Davies—made in his own image, planned from all eternity, a marvel![48]

Reports from Love in Action and similar ex-gay ministries routinely claim that reparative therapy or conversion therapy can have a success rate of anywhere from 25 to 50 percent, although no long-term follow-up studies of individuals who have successfully "converted" to heterosexuality have been done.

Nonetheless, the reparative treatment of homosexuality is meant to assist individuals in achieving "gender wholeness." It seeks to fix "sexual brokenness" and heal "gender woundedness." Reparative therapists claim that 80 percent of lesbians are victims of rape, while gay men who seek counseling from reparative therapists are frequently informed that their homosexuality might well be the result of a forgotten or repressed incident of sexual molestation.[49]

How exactly does reparative therapy work? A state-licensed reparative counselor in New Jersey remarked in 2007: "The therapy I do really just uses standard, normal therapeutic principles."[50] But it is seldom quite so simple. And it certainly uses anything but "standard, normal therapeutic principles." Furthermore, as one reporter discovered in 2005 when he was preparing an article on the ex-gay movement, if you seek counseling for gay desires, you may well be told (as he was) that a cure will take no less than two years of weekly hour-long sessions at $140 an hour.[51] That comes to more than $14,000.

There are also reparative therapy residential programs, which are sometimes called a kind of new age boot camp. Here there are many rules, including:

- Residents cannot wear jewelry or clothing from brands like Calvin Klein or Abercrombie and Fitch.
- They cannot keep diaries.
- They cannot watch "secular" movies or listen to "secular" music.
- They must wear pajamas to bed every night.
- All belongings are subject to inspection and search every day.
- All sexual fantasies must be reported immediately to a member of the staff.[52]

Much of this might have remained under the radar of American life if it had not been for the wholehearted endorsement of reparative therapies by James Dobson and his Focus on the Family organization. An example is the case of John Paulk. A former male prostitute and drag queen (named Candi), Paulk found Jesus in the 1980s. Subsequently, through Exodus International, Paulk met an ex-lesbian with whom he fell in love. They married in 1992, had a son, and in 1998 found themselves on the cover of *Newsweek* preaching that homosexuality could be cured.[53]

Focus on the Family hired John Paulk to serve as the organization's homosexuality and gender specialist in its public policy division. Dobson softened his hostile rhetoric toward homosexuality after Paulk joined his team. As scholar Tanya Erzen has noted, the influence of Paulk and a handful of other ex-gay leaders of the Religious Right has been significant; after the mid-1990s, the evangelical movement began "utilizing their stories of sexual conversion to move from a politics of condemnation of homosexuality to one of compassion."[54]

Then, in 2001, John Paulk was sighted at a gay bar in Washington, D.C., or so it was reported. Paulk initially denied the charge. However, when confronted with photographs of himself fleeing the scene, Paulk confessed, but claimed he had not known it was a gay bar. He had only needed to find a toilet.[55] Later, after Paulk was confronted again, he sheepishly confessed that he had of course known he had entered a gay bar, but he had gone to the gay bar only to check it out. He swore he had not set foot in a gay bar in fifteen years. He had merely been curious. Paulk subsequently added that it was really not his fault. Gay activists wanted to see him humiliated in public. And, Paulk said, Satan had made him go to that bar that night.[56]

James Dobson kept John Paulk on the payroll at Focus on the Family.[57] In fact, Exodus International's Bob Davies said Paulk was now even better suited to his role as an ex-gay advocate for the Religious Right. "God has done a major overhaul in John's life," observed Davies after Paulk was reinstated on the Exodus board after a momentary hiatus. "He is in a better place spiritually than ever before. We are confident that his ministry will be even more powerful than anything God accomplished through him in the past."[58] All was forgiven.

Certainly, the ex-gay movement has had its occasional embarrassment or setback. There have been the announcements that several Exodus ministries had to close when their directors announced they were in fact homosexuals—and that it was good to be gay. An often-mentioned scandal involves the cofounders of Exodus International, two men who renounced the organization after they fell in love with one another. "Exodus is homophobia with a happy face," the now openly gay couple stated.[59] There has also been the controversy surrounding Dr. Joseph Nicolosi—PhD in psychology, president of the National Association for Research and Therapy of Homosexuality (NARTH), as well as author of several books on how to prevent (and/or recover from) homosexuality, and a key player in the recuperative therapy industry—for conducting conversion therapy on boys as young as three years old.[60] But proponents of reparative therapy have made inroads throughout the United States since the origins of the movement in the late 1970s. In 2007 Exodus International had more than one hundred chapters nationwide.[61]

ON THE LOCAL LEVEL as well as the national, the evangelical-inspired debate about homosexuality scored its successes. In 1992 the demand to replace comprehensive sex education with abstinence-only curricula was a new gambit, one that caught school boards and sex education specialists off guard. The previous strategy had been to chip away at the contents of the comprehensive programs. References to homosexuality were a key part of what conservative parents objected to in the comprehensive curricula. In Plymouth, Connecticut, they demanded that references to "abnormal" sexual activity (homosexuality and masturbation) be removed. In a case in Newport-Mesa, California, they demanded that materials that "validated homosexuality" be suppressed.[62] In dozens of local communities in which nationally organized lobby groups like the American Family Association, Concerned Women for America, Focus on the Family, and the Eagle Forum helped mobilize hundreds of conservative parents to jam school board meetings and demand abstinence-only education, the adoption of the new abstinence-only curricula was sometimes perceived by administrators as a way to defuse the conflicts over homosexuality in their programs.

Now the emphasis of Religious Right homophobia has changed. The antidiscrimination campaigns of gay and lesbian activists have been successful. More heterosexual Americans know out gays and lesbians and are comfortable with them. Even though a majority of Americans still oppose gay marriage, more Americans at least find civil unions acceptable.

Yet the tide has not turned completely. At the grassroots level and in state legislatures, the micro-wars continue. There are hundreds of skirmishes in local communities over sexual orientation in school curricula. Materials that promote tolerance toward LGBTQ (lesbian, gay, bisexual, transgender, and queer) individuals and treat homosexuality as an acceptable life choice meet with calls for these materials to be removed or to be balanced with materials that represent the ex-gay and reparative perspectives. Numerous gay-straight alliances that have sprung up in high schools around the country in reaction to homophobic bullying have been accused by conservative parents and administrators of promoting homosexuality. In Virginia in January 2005, a state legislator introduced a bill clearly aimed at gay-straight alliances that would bar clubs or other groups "focused on supporting, assisting or justifying any lifestyle involving sexual behavior" from Virginia public schools. Arkansas followed Texas's lead in seeking to ban any mention of LGBTQ families in textbooks. And in Alabama a state representative proposed a bill that would prohibit the use of public funds for "the purchase of textbooks or library materials that recognize or promote homosexuality as an acceptable lifestyle."[63]

In 2005 a group calling itself PFOX (Parents and Friends of Ex-Gays and Gays—a counterpunch to PFLAG, Parents and Friends of Lesbians and Gays) sued the Board of Education in Montgomery County, Maryland, a suburb of Washington, D.C. According to PFOX, to engage in consensual gay sex is not a freely chosen activity, but rather something dangerous that can raise rates of AIDS, cause psychological difficulties and violent behavior, promote drug use, and lead to something called "gay bowel syndrome." PFOX complained that a proposed sex education curriculum treated homosexuality as "natural and benign." PFOX insisted that "other views" like its own be included; it claimed that the curriculum amounted to "viewpoint discrimination." PFOX voiced particular concern that students who did not agree with the curriculum would be labeled homophobic. It also—and here was the new twist—expressed distress that information about the existence of ex-gays had been suppressed.[64] In short, PFOX used traditional liberal values of freedom of expression, tolerance, and diversity to its own advantage.[65]

PFOX won its suit. In the flush of victory, the PFOX president announced that "we are going to march across the country and we are going to help parents organize in every county." And: "We want parents to check out the curriculum in every place where sex ed is being taught, and if they are advocating homosexuality without any other diverse views being offered to the children, we will help them with a legal defense."[66]

Two years after its initial victory, PFOX attacked a new curriculum proffered by the Montgomery County Board of Education. It once more complained that "absolutely nothing is allowed to be said that is negative about homosexuality," and it demanded that the curriculum include the advice that homosexuals can change and that anal intercourse is more dangerous than the vaginal variety. A PFOX press release lamented that the curriculum would "demand universal affirmation by students of the gay lifestyle, even if it is contrary to their religious beliefs," and that the new curriculum would introduce anal sex "as just another option."[67] PFOX neglected to acknowledge that many homosexuals never engage in anal intercourse, preferring other activities, while many heterosexuals do engage in it. What is noteworthy is the mixing and matching of older tactics (like stirring up alarmism over anal sex) with newer tactics (like complaining that the "religious beliefs" of children of sexually conservative parents would be challenged).

In addition to shaping debates about sex education, the heightened Religious Right emphasis on sexual orientation's changeability has had further consequences. A recent study by the National Gay and Lesbian Task Force has noted that the latest targets for conversion therapies are teenagers. Parents often coerce their adolescent children into conversion programs despite the evidence that these programs can foster tendencies toward depression and suicide.[68] (The American Psychological Association's position has also been that reparative therapy proves not only useless but potentially harmful to an individual's emotional well-being. Ditto for the American Psychiatric Association.) Among the more than one and a half million young people who run away or are homeless every year, more than half a million are LGBTQ youth.[69]

These days the hot topic in the world of antigay America is adoption. Homophobic ideas have been recast in the secular language of psychological health and well-being. Gary Bauer's American Values organization has contended that "research demonstrates that same-sex parents subject their children to disproportionate risks including gender confusion, and increased risk of promiscuity, teen pregnancy, substance abuse, school dropout, depression, suicide, and other emotional difficulties."[70] Tony Perkins, president of the Family Research Council, has similarly insisted on "the devastating effects of domestic violence, increased substance abuse, mental health problems, sexual identity confusion, depression, and suicide associated with the homosexual lifestyle" and has argued that even if a child raised by lesbian or gay parents manages to be "fortunate enough to escape those realities," he or she "still faces a distinct disadvantage throughout childhood—the irreplaceable influence of the missing biological parent."[71] Instead of the pity- rather than hate-based argument that abuse causes homosexuality, Perkins—in the wake of the 2006 scandal over Florida Republican Representative Mark Foley's overtures to teen male aides on Capitol Hill—reverted to the false old adage, as he told Chris Matthews on the TV talk show *Hardball*, that "there's clear research that shows that homosexual men are more likely to abuse children than straight men."[72]

Not least in reaction to the Religious Right's fixation on the purported ability to cure homosexuality, many gay and lesbian rights organizations have focused on whether or not sexual orientation is biologically determined. We learn from studies that the proportionate length of index finger to ring finger can indicate homosexuality. (The proportionate finger length of some lesbians is said to resemble that of heterosexual men.) The "gay" brain is said to be notably different, especially the "suprachiasmatic nucleus," or the isthmus in the corpus collosum. We hear about a search for "the gay gene," about endocrine balances in the womb, and about differentials between gay and straight in terms of pheromones and senses of smell.[73] And we hear many unnecessarily defensive assertions that homosexuality is innate.

What we have not heard much about is the possibility that a person's sexual identity might have multiple sources—that it might be partially biological, but that it might also be historically and culturally mediated. Nor do we hear that people's sexual longings may well change over time. No one has suggested that conversion therapy occasionally works because some people have bisexual tendencies to begin with. Nor does anyone talk about something even more subtle and complex: the idea that many people have a rich stew of homo- and heterosexual desires within themselves—in their sexual fantasies, their sexual experiences, and their emotional connections and longings.

What if homosexuality *were* 100 percent biological? Leave it to the "kinder" antigay movement to be one step ahead. As antigay evangelical Erwin Lutzer has noted: "We are responsible for our behavior *even if it is genetically motivated.* Surely homosexuals don't want to say that their genes have rendered them helpless robots."[74] The American Family Association has argued that even "if we discovered that being a serial killer or a sociopath was genetic, though we might not blame the serial killer or sociopath for being so, we certainly would not allow him to act upon his serial killing or sociopathic disposition."[75] In 2007, Reverend R. Albert Mohler, president of the Southern Baptist Theological Seminary in Louisville, Kentucky, contended that homosexuality might well be rooted in "some level of biological causation," only to argue that if a prenatal treatment to undo gay orientation were ever developed, using such treatment would be *biblically* justified.[76]

At the same time, the thought of homosexual sex does not evoke the fear and disgust it once did. Paul Volle, chairman of the Christian Coalition of Maine, may have been pleased to announce in a 1998 antigay pamphlet that homosexuals were weird: "What do 'homosexuals' do? They typically engage in oral or anal sodomy, or mutual masturbation."[77] A decade later, these activities are acceptable to all but the most hung-up heterosexuals. Gay sex has simply lost its power to repulse.

By 2007, anal sex and other kinds of anal-area stimulation were no longer gross, no longer taboo, but rather interpreted as perfectly friendly. *Cosmopolitan* announced: "These days, interest in backdoor booty is growing." The magazine had its own theories about why this might be so:

> Due to the prevalence of online pornography and the breaking down of sexual taboos, anal sex is no longer considered something only gay guys do. In fact, according to data released in a recent sex survey by the National Center for Health Statistics, one in every three women admitted to having had anal sex by the age of 24.[78]

And *Glamour* soon adopted its own position statement: "You're not freakish for wanting anal sex."[79] This sort of brazen discussion in venues that cater to heterosexual women would have been unimaginable not so many years ago. In the 1990s, anal sex still equaled gay sex, and gay equaled icky or unnatural. It was not something healthy heterosexuals were supposed to consider a viable or normal option. That couples did consider it, and that they did do it, was beside the point. Just don't discuss it. So what has been happening here?

As sex-advice columnist Dan Savage observed a decade ago: "What's generally considered 'kinky' changes over time."[80] Cultural observers Barbara Ehrenreich, Elizabeth Hess, and Gloria Jacobs noted more than two decades ago that the line between what's straight and what's gay was melting and dissolving, and that we were witnessing nothing more nor less than "the homosexualization of heterosexual sex."[81]

Sexual orientation still signals whom we choose to love or desire, but it no longer defines what we like to do when we do make love. This signals a profound shift in American sexual values over the last two decades. Heterosexuals have energetically adopted what used to be considered homosexual practices to enhance and expand their own sex lives.

However, heterosexuals have not returned the favor. Reluctant to give homosexuals full respect and complete civil equality, the privileged majority has allowed a vocal and aggressive right-wing minority to muddle what might otherwise have been a vital national debate about the complexities of sex and about human beings' rights both to public recognition and to privacy, to information about pleasure and safety, and to self-determination.

For fifteen years, homophobia was a major factor in American electoral politics. Fomenting hostility to homosexuals was an extraordinarily successful tactic pursued by the evangelical Right, a crucial supplement to anti-abortion activism, and an essential replacement for that old mainstay of conservative mobilization: overt racism against African Americans. Homophobia made the Religious Right a political force to be reckoned with. As one reporter observed about South Carolina in 1998, "The state Republican party is certain enough of its constituents' views on homosexuality that it does not even poll on the issue." A Republican Party spokesperson explained to him: "It would be like asking everybody if they're for free ice cream."[82]

Some gambits worked right away but then ran into difficulties. Others were floated and failed. Still others were developed and succeeded. If in prior decades economically vulnerable white Americans were prevented from making common cause with African Americans over issues of social and economic justice, not least because they were paid (in W. E. B. Du Bois's words) in "the wages of whiteness," many downsized, health care–lacking, economically vulnerable Americans of all colors in the 1990s could be said to have been paid in "the wages of straightness."

Over and over, through trial and error, conservative Christian activists developed new arguments and tactics for mobilizing against homosexual rights. It worked remarkably well over the course of the 1990s and only began to unravel by the turn of the millennium. The anti–gay marriage referenda in eleven states coinciding with President George W. Bush's reelection in 2004 may have been the last great triumph of this particular strategy. In the first years of the twenty-first century, the Religious Right, while maintaining a homophobic platform, has been more concerned with wallowing in the miseries of heterosexuality and advancing the cause of sexual abstinence at home and, more recently, also abroad. Yet the antigay campaigns of the 1990s were hugely successful for the Religious Right and were essential to making it a major player on the American political scene.

While the American public has become far more tolerant, the damage from the evangelical movement's assault has been done. In the meantime, moreover, the secularizing and psychologizing strategies developed for the refinement of homophobia have more recently also been adapted wholesale for a much larger new focus of mass hysteria: adolescent sexuality.

Chapter 4

SAVED FROM SEX

IN THE WAKE OF GEORGE W. BUSH'S accession to the presidency in 2001, federal funding for abstinence programs rose exponentially. According to a 2006 report in the *Wall Street Journal*, $111 million was spent between 1998 and 2000, and $779 million was spent since 2001.[1] This spending has profoundly re-shaped program content. In 2003 the government spent $120 million for abstinence-only-until-marriage programs, with $37.5 million more in state matching funds; at that point, a poll showed, 30 percent of public high school instructors were teaching abstinence only.[2] In 2006 the government spent $200 million to advance the cause of premarital abstinence domestically, and abstinence-until-marriage was being taught in 50 percent of public high schools and the majority of private schools. Numerous church-affiliated organizations have received federal money to promote abstinence; indeed, abstinence projects can be a major cash source for the religious organizations that sponsor them.[3] By 2006, more than $1 billion had been spent on abstinence promotion.[4]

Over the years the advice directed to adolescents and young adults about abstinence has gotten ever more explicit, and ever more restrictive. In the 1980s and early 1990s, it was routine for evangelical Christians to create their own compromises for preserving technical virginity while nonetheless having great premarital pleasures. Passionate French kissing, heavy petting, mutual masturbation, and oral sex were generally understood to be fine in the eyes of God and the community alike.[5]

By the beginning of the new century, however, the abstinence advocacy websites and how-not-to advice books had become far more precise and specific. Oral sex was no longer okay. Mutual genital fondling was also now off-limits. Doug Herman, a popular abstinence-until-marriage speaker at public high schools across the United States, put it like this: "If the sun don't touch it, nobody else better either."[6] The Silver Ring Thing, an abstinence organization with a global reach (along with a major merchandising outfit), declared: "Your private areas are not to be used or touched by a member of the opposite sex. . . . No oral, anal, no fondling."[7] In 2002 right-wing pundit Oliver North lent his weight to the cause when he reserved special venom for those advocates of comprehensive sex education who were promoting "far-out theories" in their stress on "the pleasures of sex" and "mutual masturbation."[8]

Even French kissing was now said to induce an urge to go all the way. So it was not quite okay anymore either. Focus on the Family founder James Dobson instructed fathers to tell their sons "not to take anything that doesn't belong to them—especially the moral purity of a woman. Also, tell your boys that sex is progressive in nature. Kissing and fondling will lead inevitably to greater familiarity. . . . Tell them not to start the engine if they don't intend to let it run."[9]

Some of the reasoning behind this new antisexual revolution is justified by citations of religious doctrine. According to abstinence proponents, the Bible condemns premarital sex. Abstinence programmers quote 1 Thessalonians 4:3–4: "It is God's will that you should be sanctified: that you should avoid sexual immorality; that each of you should learn to control his own body in a way that is holy and honorable."[10] There is also a prevalent view in religious abstinence circles that God chooses our future mate and it is foolish and unwise to mess around before marriage looking for the possibility of lifetime companionship. As the female Christian rock group BarlowGirl explains:

We believe that God has one perfect man already chosen for us; therefore we have no need to worry ourselves in searching for him. When the time is right we know God will bring us together. In the meantime we are not hiding in a closet avoiding all males. We are still living our lives, just without the pressure of having to have a boyfriend.[11]

Abstinent singles are now advised to pray on behalf of their future mates long before they ever know who those people will be. As Christian sex experts Linda Dillow and Lorraine Pintus urge young women: "On Monday pray for God to teach him how to love. On Tuesday, pray for joy to characterize his life. Continue on through the other fruits of peace, patience, kindness, goodness, faithfulness, gentleness, and self-control."[12]

A great deal of the abstinence argument, however, is a mix of assertive invocations of God's will and threats that sexual desire within marriage will die unless premarital abstinence is observed. Dillow and Pintus assure their readers through a multitude of examples and stories that only those women who have been premaritally abstinent will be truly, deeply, and consistently desired by their husbands in the long years after marriage.[13] Another Christian sex advice–writer phrases the point this way: "Don't ruin what's waiting for you by acting prematurely and turning what is supposed to be so good and holy into something sinful and shameful."[14] In a 2007 rally in New Jersey, an organizer for True Love Waits, a Southern Baptist group self-designated "the largest group of celibates in America," led the crowd in chanting, "Sex is great! Sex is great!" before continuing with the message to wait until marriage, while another spokesperson for the group boasted to the crowd that she was confident the sex she would have on her wedding night would be amazing.[15] The website www.Love Matters.com announces that "Sex is Awesome! . . . But sex before marriage has emotional consequences that can bring life-long pain."[16] And there is this more gruesome formulation from former missionary Heather Jamison: "Sins such as coveting grieve our Father, but physical immorality mocks Him. Jesus bought my body with a price—His death on the cross. When I wrongfully gave my body [before marriage] to Brian, I gave something that was not mine." Citing the biblical idea that our bodies are temples of the Holy Spirit, Jamison adds: "Sins against the body are different from other sins—they are committed against God's very temple, and they are committed against our very selves. They are acts of degradation and desecration against our own bodies."[17]

Jamison asserts that those who have engaged in premarital sex are highly likely to have "awful" sex after marriage—possibly even for *up to a decade*. By contrast, couples who dutifully abstain beforehand "report a deep level of intimacy in combination with great sex."[18] Along related lines, as one woman quoted by Dillow and Pintus puts it, "I wish, so wish that on my honeymoon night I could have given my husband this beautiful body without fingerprints all over it." So this line of argument is not simply about the ideal of purity for its own sake. Among the smorgasbord of reasons abstinence advocates offer to amplify the point that premarital encounters wreck postmarital lives is the argument that whenever a woman has sex with her husband, if she has had any former lovers—even people with whom she only engaged in such activities as "intense kissing, arousals, and petting"—the former lovers will "intrude" in fantasy, and thus make sexual satisfaction with a spouse that much more difficult to achieve.[19]

And then there is abstinence advocate Lisa Bevere, who advises young girls what she herself learned from her private chats with the Holy Spirit: "He said to me, '. . . Tell them they can go as far with their boyfriends as they are comfortable doing in front of their fathers.'"[20]

ABSTINENCE ADVOCATES go out of their way to say that it is hard to refrain from sex. They work to give the whole enterprise of abstinence an allure of deep significance and heroic struggle. It is a strategy that has proven remarkably effective: millions of young Americans have taken abstinence pledges in the last decade and a half (whether or not they've kept them), and tens of millions have absorbed arguments about the evils of premarital sex. But the aim of the movement is far broader than that.

Abstinence is the new rallying cry of the self-styled sexually sophisticated American. No sex is good sex. Marriage is the dividing line. Before marriage, sex will be very bad. After marriage, sex will be very good. An abstinence vow connects you to the promised land of bliss—have no sex before marriage and you *will* have outstanding sex after marriage.

This movement aims to make fresh and new in human beings all that which has been worn or tainted and used. It also makes clear that all of us who are unmarried are really still virgins, even those of us who are not virgins. As an abstinence advocate tells a crowd of young people at an Indiana rock concert organized by True Love Waits: "It's never too late to be a virgin. No matter what you've done, you can have a secondary virginity, it's there for you to reclaim."[21]

Nor is secondary virginity recommended solely by evangelicals. Secular abstinence proponents make similar points. An official Florida Department of Health website tells us:

> It's never too late to make healthy choices. You can still decide to stop sexual activity now even if you have already had sex, or if you have engaged in other forms of sexual arousal or gratification. Many people realize they weren't ready for sex and choose secondary virginity. Take back control. Secondary virginity means that you care enough about yourself and your future to save sex for the right person and the right time—marriage. Deciding to start over is the hardest part. Your decision to choose abstinence shows to others that you value yourself.[22]

The abstinence movement preaches that love means being able to say you're sorry for your mistakes—sorry for engaging in sex before marriage—and then being forgiven by God, by your church, by your friends, and by your future spouse. Love means making a vow to God and to yourself to respect yourself and love yourself and hold yourself back from making those mistakes again. Never again will you have sex before your wedding night. Never again will you permit yourself to be manipulated by your own base desires or the unscrupulous desires of others. But if you do, all can be forgiven.

As the influential South Dakota abstinence cheerleader Leslee Unruh (a prime mover behind the 2006 law criminalizing all abortions in that state, a law subsequently overturned by voter referendum) has said about the many young women who have sex and then return to her for counseling: "I don't care if she starts over seven times, or twenty times. I'm going to believe in her each time she comes back."[23]

There are plenty of reasons why young people can find these messages appealing. Perhaps they don't want to be pressured, or they're not interested yet—or not anymore. They may not be ready for the potential emotional intensities of a relationship that includes sex—or, on the flip side, they may wish for romance but are finding only offers of intercourse. The individual's right to say no—anytime, anywhere (a right for which the feminist movement fought long and hard from the 1970s through to the 1990s)—and the moral imperative of consent in sexual relations has been respun into a one-size-fits-all program that says everyone should say no before marriage. It has left no room for people, especially girls, to negotiate practices, to say, "No, not that, but yes, this," making female sexual agency once again seem dirty and suspect.

The abstinence movement also succeeds because it is a self-help and self-improvement movement that holds out the promise of perfection. The movement doesn't care that it's completely contradictory. While it declares that even mutual genital fondling and tongue-kissing are unremittingly evil and sure to lead to disease, depression, and death, it keeps its potential market base as large as possible by making sure that you recognize that there are no real consequences for messing up. The only thing you have to do is join the chorus of voices making sure everyone else feels ashamed about the sex they may be having.

Then again, making other people feel crappy and confused about sex is not exactly a trivial or trifling thing.

There is a suggestive testimonial included in an abstinence primer about a young girl named "Alicia," whose romance with "Rick" involved happy kissing and fondling, but then went all the way to intercourse.

> Then one night we had sex. It was worse than I could even imagine. I felt dirty and very separated from God. I hated myself for doing something I've grown up believing was so wrong. I had the guiltiest feeling I ever had.
>
> Rick walked me to my car and asked me what was wrong. I burst into tears. I told him I hated it. I never wanted to do it again. Then Rick told me that he loved me, and the weirdest thing was that I couldn't tell him I loved him back. I had no feelings for him anymore. We sat in front of his house for a long time. We both cried. We knew what we did together was wrong.[24]

One reaction to this experience might have been: sex takes practice. If it wasn't pleasurable, maybe the couple needed to slow things down the next time. Or try different ways of touching. Or maybe Rick is just a jerk, even though the story does not give that impression. Or maybe he was the one who was anxious about performance and needed more sensitivity from her. The possibilities for understanding what to make of this first encounter are almost infinite.

But that's certainly not the intended message here. Rather, Alicia dutifully renounces not only coitus but everything else as well:

> Now I know that "too far" doesn't mean only intercourse, but also the stages leading up to it. Too far is when you crave the

physical more than the spiritual. Too far is when sexual thoughts take over your relationship. Too far is when you don't want to stop. . . . For me, kissing should be the limit. I've decided not to go any further than this until I'm married. With God's help, I can be pure from this day on.[25]

Abstinence testimonials insist that all pleasure derived from sexual contact is horribly awful and deserving of remorseful feelings. Here's one young man's story in all its perplexing glory:

I messed up big time my junior year of high school. I started having regular sex with my girlfriend. I was a Christian, therefore the momentary pleasure was there, but the relationship was a miserable one. I am still scared from the instances that took place. . . . I will never completely forget what happened during my junior year in high school. But I worship an awesome and forgiving God. I know I shall reap what I sow, and that is the most important thing to know. I can't tell you how ashamed I am, all because of a few months of pleasure. The biggest statement I would like to make is the fact that I would give anything to take it back and to have my virginity still to this day.[26]

Somehow here it is the Christian faith that ("therefore") is the cause of the pleasure, and somehow God is forgiving, and yet this boy will nonetheless "reap" what he sows. Logic is not the point; the reader is meant to take away the sense of intense emotion and the combination of authoritative real experience of sex coupled with assurances that sex is awful.

It is precisely *the frequent imperfection of actual experiences of sex* that the abstinence recommenders use in order to push for secondary virginity. As one pro–secondary virginity organization phrased it in 2007: "If you slipped but now realize that you don't want to go down that road, again, at this point in your life then hello . . . abstinence is for you! It may even be a bit easier for you to abstain because you already know that the talk is so much more than the act."[27] Here the clear implication is that actual sexual contact with another body turned out to be far less pleasurable than the individual had hoped—or had been taught by a hypersexualized culture to expect.

What also emerges in this discussion is an urgent and powerful longing for sex to be good, to be *special*—and to make its participants feel special themselves. Here's one final testimonial:

> I started having sex at 14, it was normal in my class, but I got pregnant and had Mickey. Then I decided to take back my virginity. My boyfriend said if I wasn't doing it with him I must be doing it with someone else, so we split up. It was only ten months until our wedding but he wouldn't wait. Even though I'm a mum I feel like I'm a virgin, I never think about sex. I'm going to wait until I get married. I want sex to be special next time.[28]

It's this waiting, abstinence advocates insist, that is always worth it.

The arguments are not just religious. Even secondary virginity, we are told, is a matter of physiology. Sex before marriage alters the body in destructive ways. As abstinence enthusiast Unruh has said, couples who do not engage in premarital intercourse will be able to count on simultaneous orgasms after marriage: "The hormonal symphony between the two, you can have it right away." And for those who don't wait until marriage? They can expect an entirely different outcome, says Unruh. "The secretions from one person are different from the next person," she says, and when people have sex before marriage, they inevitably "mess up their bodily processes." As for those who have had sex before marriage but have chosen to reclaim their secondary virginity, Unruh holds out hope. They too will enjoy superb marital sex because over time secondary virgins can restore their bodily processes and regain their hormonal equilibrium.[29]

Meanwhile, in the abstinence literature, sexual violence and abuse are never handled as themes separate from the constant injunction to premarital chastity. The potential dangers of violence and abuse, including incest, appear in the texts only as yet another excellent reason to avoid premarital sexual contact. Initially, it can seem difficult to determine what purpose these often grotesque and terrifying stories of violence and abuse—tales that range from date rape to sexual torture of children—could possibly have within the abstinence advice literature, especially because the stories are frequently so disturbing and outrageous. They are simply too awful to be titillating. But the message they convey is unmistakable: consent is not a moral value worthy of discussion, much less a value worthy of defense.

It is, in the end, not inadvertent coincidence but rather quite deliberate that, in *Gift-Wrapped by God*, Dillow and Pintus include a lesbian love story along with a story of Satanic child abuse in their catalog of nonmarital horrors. No matter, apparently, that Bible study leader "Darcy" was utterly devoted to the (also Bible-studying) woman with whom she had the four-year love affair, while the evil done to "Natalie" was "not far removed from the horrors of the many Nazi concentration camps of Adolf Hitler's regime. Natalie's Auschwitz was within her soul." The ending of both stories is pretty much the same. Both women get rescued by God. Darcy prostrates herself before her minister, cuts off all contact with her female lover, and finds her reward with the love of a "godly man."

> The Lord continues to fill me up with HIMSELF! And now He
> has blessed me with Paul. How grateful I am that the walls be-
> tween my sexuality and my spirituality have crumbled. I am a
> whole woman, and I am excited to become Paul's wife. God is
> gracious. I have no words to thank him.

Natalie, for her part, eventually falls in love with "Joe," himself
"severely sexually abused as a child"—which had caused him to
make all those "unhealthy choices of sexual relationships with
both men and women."[30] Dillow and Pintus, in short, are happy
to play on homophobia—even as they also adopt the most up-
to-date homophobic theories that see sexual abuse as a cause of
homosexual desire rather than its outcome.

IN ADVICE BOOKS and on the Internet, in Christian schools and
in mainstream public high school sex education curricula, in
public presentations by religious and secular abstinence gurus,
and in teenagers' peer-driven abstinence organizations, the
message about premarital sex is that it is not just immoral but
also demeaning.

Already in the 1960s and 1970s, there were conservative parent protests against overly explicit sex education in public
schools. Once Ronald Reagan became president in 1981, right-
wing activists succeeded in passing the Adolescent Family Life
Act. This act made possible federal funding of programs across
the country that encouraged adolescent sexual abstinence and,
although largely forgotten now, also helped pregnant teens develop parenting skills. Still, the abstinence campaign did not really gain popular or political traction until more recently.

The mid-1980s were not an accidental birth date for this politically effective movement. Those years coincided with in-

creased public awareness that HIV/AIDS was not a "gay disease" and could afflict the heterosexual population. Public health policy and medical experts, government officials, and reproductive and sex rights activists began to demand widespread and aggressive condom campaigns on television, on billboards, and in schools. They insisted that the condom not be seen as an awkward inhibition of pleasure or a sign of distrust, but rather as an erotic sex toy or a sign of respect, even love. However, some conservative activists and experts began to argue that there was no such thing as safe sex and that Americans should "just say no."

An early champion of the right-wing position was former pastor Ken Abraham, a prolific inspirational writer and frequent collaborator with high-profile figures. In 1985 Abraham published *Don't Bite the Apple Till You Check for Worms*, a how-not-to guide for the young and curious that included tips on "Becoming Maximum Marriage Material." Abraham cleverly noted that the letters VD could mean "Very Dangerous." His message? "Premarital Sex: Hot It's Not."[31]

But a book does not make a movement. To really mobilize people around an issue, it helps to create situations where they make public commitments to their cause. In this case, it also helped to recast the abstinent as neither repressed nor marginal or devoid of passion. Instead, they were cast as trendsetters and—as *Newsweek* announced in a cover story in 1994—as the new "cool."[32] No sex until marriage? How hip is that?[33]

It might have appeared a stretch of anyone's imagination that the mantra "no sex until marriage" could be a hit with American teens. As one—apparently naive—British journalist put it, teen sex is, after all, "the only perpetually renewable resource known to mankind."[34] Yet those who proffered the successful branding of the abstinent teen as a new wave in style and fashion took the long view.

The abstinence pledge burst onto the scene in the early 1990s, the brainchild of the Christian Sex Education Project (founded in 1987). Together with True Love Waits, the Christian Sex Education Project hyped the abstinence pledge with commitment cards. Here the young person signed a statement that read:

> Believing that true love waits, I make a commitment to God, myself, my family, my friends, my future mate, and my future children to a lifetime of purity including sexual abstinence from this day until the day I enter a biblical marriage relationship.[35]

Soon there were T-shirts and buttons that declaimed: PET YOUR DOG, NOT YOUR DATE. But these were still treated as curiosities for general public amusement; also, the majority of Americans assumed that teens would seek sex. Abstinence still had an air of defensiveness about it.

Since 2000, the situation has changed considerably. Prominent athletes and beauty queens (including A. C. Green, Lakita Garth, and Erika Harold) have joined the abstinence cause.[36] There is an entire subset of the Christian rock youth culture scene devoted to representing abstinence as the choice for the countercultural anti-authoritarian.[37] And the flood of merchandise available to meet the new market niche allows young people to strut around with stuff that makes clear they are not strutting their stuff. At Unruh's Abstinence Clearinghouse Online Store, based in Sioux Falls, one can purchase the popular I'M WORTH WAITING FOR (removable) tattoo. One can buy "Suckers," cherry-flavored lollipops with a heart in them: "A fun way to get the message to teens: Don't Be a Sucker! Save Sex for Marriage." And there is stop sign–emblazoned "No Trespassing Underwear" (boxers and bikinis), part of a "Keep It Underwear" line of clothing that announces: "Saving sex until marriage is not only safe and smart, it's cool, too! Keep It Underwear aims to approach the serious subject of abstinence in a light-hearted way by letting teens show their statement of choice—even if it's just to themselves!"[38] More recently, there is Yvette Thomas's "WaitWear" line of T-shirts and underwear. Under the slogan "Where Purity, Passion and Power Meet Phashion!" Thomas, a never-married mother of three, a practicing evangelical Christian, and an abstinence advocate, offers such items as a boy's brief in hot pink emblazoned NO VOWS NO SEX, and in red I'M SAVING IT!, along with T-shirts stating TRAFFIC CONTROL—WAIT FOR MARRIAGE, as well as VIRGINITY LANE—EXIT WHEN MARRIED (this last one replete with two arrows positioned over the nipples and pointing downward to the private parts).[39] A Catholic organization offers T-shirts with a more discreet message: ABSTINENCE MAKES THE HEART GROW FONDER.[40]

Humor and gentle admonition are only two strategies in the arsenal of these antisexual revolutionaries. Bids to stimulate condescension, fear, and loathing are also in play.

Girls and women who desire sex before marriage are to be pitied by the righteous. They will be utterly shattered by despair and abjection, forever envious of their more perfect virginal sisters. If they do engage in premarital sex, it is because they have a lousy body concept, or because they believe that they cannot get someone to love them any other way. They will always "feel cheap and dirty . . . like damaged goods."[41] They will always have "that sick, used feeling of having given a precious part of myself—my soul—to so many and for nothing."[42] That is, unless they get back on the road to righteousness and forsake sex immediately and pray to God for healing.

An extraordinary amount of creative energy goes into communicating disdain and contempt, especially for girls who are sexually active before marriage. In the brave new world of the present, desire alone cannot make sex acceptable. Abstinence-advocating organizations and advice-writers veer sharply back and forth between the concession that females' sexual desires can be as strong as males' and an insistence that young women who seek sex outside of marriage are simply doing it because they are pathetically desperate for attention. They demonstrate their lack of self-esteem by desiring sex. Because sex is "worth the wait."

On the most fundamental level, sexual activity, on the one hand, and, on the other, self-respect and success in school and sports and later life are presented as mutually exclusive.

And then there is the ick factor. Take this public school abstinence classroom exercise:

> Boys and girls are invited to chew cheese-flavored snacks and then sip some water, after which they are to spit the resulting "bodily fluids" into a cup. After a game in which the fluids are combined with those of other students, ultimately all cups are poured into a pitcher labeled "multiple partners" sitting adjacent to a pitcher of fresh water labeled "pure fluids." In the final segment, each boy and girl is asked to fill a cup labeled either "future husband" or "future wife" with the contents from one of the pitchers.[43]

The Georgia-based abstinence organization that came up with this exercise has received more than half a million dollars in government funding.

IN 2002, WHEN *Newsweek* reprised its cover story on "The New Virginity: Why More Teens Are Choosing Not to Have Sex," it was apparent what drove the attractive teens profiled to steer clear of their own and other people's erogenous zones. A sixteen-year-old from Colorado who had seen a Christian slide show on abstinence in the eighth grade observed that it was picture after picture of sexually transmitted diseases: "It's just one of the grossest things you've ever seen. I didn't want to touch a girl, like, forever." His seventeen-year-old girlfriend agreed: "If that doesn't scare kids out of sex, nothing will." As *Newsweek* noted, these kids are "sure that whoever they marry will be disease-free."[44]

Fear of disease has been a powerful tool in the efforts to secularize the evangelical abstinence message. School programs as well as a large variety of local federally funded program offerings can avoid being accused of violating the constitutionally guaranteed separation of church and state, and the message can be made palatable to anyone who might feel put off by the Religious Right.

There is in fact a laserlike intensity to the focus on the potential deadliness of sex. Not only do abstinence advocates argue that "there is no condom that can protect you from a broken heart and a shattered dream."[45] They also say that, in the age of HIV, "the only safe sex is no sex," and "the wrong sexual encounter can mean a death sentence."[46] Relying on condoms during intercourse is the equivalent of playing Russian roulette with a revolver.[47] Even if there's just one bullet, the odds are high that you'll soon be dead.

Once upon a time, condom advocates made the point that HIV is a blood disease, not an STD. The real issue, if you wished to stay healthy, was not how many partners you had, but what practices you engaged in and whether there was latex between you and the pathogen. When a sex rights activist in the mid-1980s criticized the calls for monogamy that constituted the conservative response to the HIV/AIDS epidemic, she noted that by the same sloppy logic—the fact that something can be transmitted sexually means it must be an STD—the common cold is also a sexually transmitted disease.[48] Gone are the days when a sex rights advocate could speak in public schools to young people about how to make safe sex hot or speak to them about how to negotiate practices and keep mutual touching both pleasurable and safe. School systems that dare to offer such programming now get hauled into court by irate parents.[49]

Now abstinence advocates use the fear of disease to frighten kids away from sex entirely, rather than encouraging them to learn how best to take precautions. They seldom urge teens to get tested for disease before they make out and fondle one another. And they *never* suggest that teens talk with potential partners about possible practices or educate teens on how to transition into sexual activity knowledgeably and safely once they do start. Such ideas, so the argument runs, would only promote teen sex.

Adolescents who turn to abstinence advocacy websites find many excellent reasons to be afraid. They can find the statement that "65 million Americans are living with an incurable STD" and that "1 out of 4 sexually active teens will get an STD this year." They can read this: "It is estimated that 20 percent of all Americans age 12 and older are infected with genital herpes." Or this: "In one single act of unprotected sex with an infected partner, a teenage woman has a 1 percent risk of acquiring HIV, a 30 percent risk of getting genital herpes, and a 50 percent chance of contracting gonorrhea."[50]

Teens can also go to a website on "Safe Sex and the Facts" and read this horror story:

> At age 16 John had sex with Andrea. Just one time. He enjoyed the experience but felt guilty and decided the risk of sexually transmitted diseases (STDs) and pregnancy were just too great.

He did not have sex again until nine years later when he married Cindy, who was a virgin. Three months after their wedding Cindy began having painful symptoms. Unknowingly, John, who had never had any symptoms of disease, had brought two STDs into his marriage.

There is a lot one can ask about John. For instance, if John had been taught about condoms, might John have used a condom? Could he have gotten himself tested before he had sex with the woman he chose to marry? Did Cindy find her problems treatable? Apparently this does not matter to the story's point either. Instead, the moral is that

> thirty years of the sexual revolution is paying an ugly dividend, and those most at risk are teenagers. This is true partially because teenagers are more sexually active than ever before, but also because teenage girls are more susceptible to STDs than males or adult females. . . . [We need] to discuss the severity of the problem as well as what must be done if we are to save a majority of the next generation from the shame, infertility, and sometimes death, that may result from STDs.

Again, the story line does not end here. The website also includes statistics intended to stand a reader's hair on end: "It is estimated that 1 in 5 Americans between the ages of 15 and 55 are currently infected with one or more viral STDs, and 12 million Americans are newly infected each year. That's nearly 5% of the entire population of the U.S.! Of these new infections, 63% involve people less than 25 years old." And then there's this: "The bottom line is that condoms cannot be trusted."[51]

A major move used by every abstinence advocacy group is to insist that it is offering "the truth," "the facts," "the science," and "the information" that Americans need to keep themselves safe. Abstinence advocates present themselves as the real scientific experts. Whether it is the doctors who have joined together in an organization like Physicians for Life or who advise right-wing lobbyist groups like Concerned Women for America, what counts as science, as well as social scientific "expertise," is more and more in the eye of the beholder. Routinely, abstinence advocates lump together different diseases to make the overall picture more frightening, exaggerate the ease of contracting various diseases and the harms they cause while minimizing the possibilities of treatment and cure, and misrepresent the effectiveness of condoms for preventing transmission of disease.

Moreover, the websites misrepresent their opponents— whether those opponents are liberal or radical activists or whether they are established medical professionals or social science analysts—by either twisting their words to support conservative and pro-abstinence positions or directly accusing these opponents of spreading lies or misleading facts.

It is indicative that one of the earliest abstinence organizations—it has been around since the mid-1980s—calls itself Project Reality. The organization aims no less than to revise what counts as reality—and indeed what counts as truth. When Libby Macke, the director of Project Reality, has gone on the offensive against "abstinence-plus" programs (programs that assert that abstinence is the best strategy but that include information on condoms and contraceptives owing to the perception that some adolescents do engage in sexual encounters), she has sought to have these programs "examined and defunded" on the grounds, among other things, that "many so called 'abstinence-plus' programs actually encourage sexual activity among youth by assignments such as condom relay races, condom shopping trips and fantasizing about sexual activity and condom use." She has also labeled research that illustrates the effectiveness of such programs as itself "erroneous and misleading."[52]

When academic sex researchers release their reports these days, they can pretty much count on having their findings turned into something unrecognizable by the abstinence movement. Take the oft-cited studies based on the research of scholars at Yale (Hannah Brückner) and Columbia (Peter Bearman) that were published in the *American Journal of Sociology* in 2001 and the *Journal of Adolescent Health* in 2005. These studies found that adolescents who took abstinence pledges ended up having sex on average eighteen months later than those who had not taken the pledge. They also found that when these teens did finally have sex, they were one-third *less* likely to use protection, thus making themselves vulnerable both to disease and to unwanted pregnancy.[53] And only 12 percent of the virginity pledgers kept their promise. As sexuality researcher Marty Klein pointed out in analyzing the findings, "That means abstinence fails 88 percent of the time—*six times as often as condoms fail in typical use,* six times as often as the method that abstinence advocates say is unreliable."[54]

In the hands of abstinence organizations, however, this research comes out looking rather different. Gravity Teen, one of the most influential secular abstinence groups, has discussed the Yale-Columbia findings under the headline: "Do Teens Really Stick by Their Abstinence Pledges?" The answer Gravity Teen gives is: "Seems so!" The group sums up the findings this way:

> A major study released in a recent issue of the American Journal of Sociology found that teens who took an abstinence pledge were 34% less likely to engage in premarital sex, and were far older when they did begin to have intercourse. Among black females, for example, the median age of sexual debut for those

who took the virginity pledge was 18.6, compared with 16.3 for those who did not take the pledge.[55]

In a similar vein, Physicians for Life merely rearranges the words of Brückner and Bearman to make them sound like defenders of abstinence programming. Under the heading "True Love Waits Pledges Shown Highly Effective, Other Studies," they write:

> Teenagers who pledge to remain sexually abstinent until marriage are 34 percent less likely to have sex than those who do not take virginity vows, according to a study to be published in the American Journal of Sociology. "Pledging decreases the risk of intercourse substantially and independently," authors Peter S. Bearman and Hannah Brückner wrote.

The Physicians for Life essay also includes this subhead, "Since the beginning of True Love Waits in 1993, we have believed pledges do make a difference," and continues: "Bearman is professor of sociology and director of the Institute for Social and Economic Theory and Research at Columbia University, and Brückner is assistant professor of sociology at Yale University."[56] It is easy to conclude that the words in this subhead were written by Bearman and Brückner, but the person quoted is Chris Turner, a media relations manager for True Love Waits.

Along related lines, the Abstinence Clearinghouse has refuted a 2006 study published in the *Journal of Public Health* and entitled "'Virginity Pledges' by Adolescents May Bias Their Reports of Premarital Sex—Most Adolescents Disavowed Their Pledge Within a Year." The research drew on a nationally representative sample of teens who participated in the National Longitudinal Study of Adolescent Health. More than twenty thousand adolescents were interviewed in 1995, and more than fourteen thousand were reinterviewed in 1996. Among the key findings were these:

> More than 1 in 10 students who reported being sexually active in 1995 said that they were virgins in 1996. Students who reported they were sexually active in the second survey were more than three times as likely as their peers to deny they had taken a pledge of virginity. . . . On the other hand, 28 percent of nonvirgins who later took a virginity pledge retracted their sexual histories during the 1996 survey. . . . Sexually active teens who later took virginity pledges were four times as likely to deny previous reports of sexual activity than were those who had not taken virginity pledges.

The analysis by Janet Rosenbaum, a graduate student in health policy and statistics at Harvard University, had two central points:

1. Adolescents' revisions of their sexual histories had everything to do with whether or not they were taking on or rejecting a born-again Christian identity.
2. Self-reports are an unreliable research source.

As Rosenbaum also stated: "Studies of virginity pledges must focus on outcomes where we know we can get good information, such as medical STD tests."[57]

In the current climate of shaming around premarital sex, self-reporting—even on anonymous surveys—is remarkably unreliable. The Abstinence Clearinghouse, however, was quick to rebut: "Since the survey studied in this paper was conducted ten years ago, new and reliable data has been collected. Teens who make a virginity pledge report greater amounts of sexual abstinence and for longer periods of time. Also, teens who did not make a virginity pledge are twice as likely to experience an unmarried teen pregnancy."[58] Exactly what these "new and reliable data" consist of remains unnamed.

Comparable confusion is evident on the many websites that purport to offer "just the facts" about sexually transmitted diseases. Statements found on abstinence advocacy websites refer to "the risk of deadly STD transmission," as if STDs were invariably deadly. They casually mention "the danger of contraceptives," although they never explain what those dangers might be. Do these refer to the potential risk of thrombosis from the birth control pill? Do they refer to the minuscule chance of damage to fertility caused by IUDs? Do they refer to the "danger" that adolescents and young adults might possibly find that sex can be safe—an activity that can be pleasurable and enjoyable and empowering? It's all left intentionally unclear and frightening.

It has thus become more difficult for adolescents to find accurate and sufficiently detailed information to educate themselves and protect themselves from unwanted pregnancy and disease if they do choose to have intimate contacts. (How long do sperm stay alive? Can one acquire HIV through cuts in the hand?) It is likewise increasingly difficult to alert the public through the mass media about the abstinence advocates' rewriting of reality without having one's own arguments ridiculed, dismissed, or selectively distorted.

The resulting sense of helplessness is palpable in comments by scientists, like this one from a specialist on viruses and cancers in reference to the anti-HPV (human papilloma virus) vaccine: "I never thought that now, in the twenty-first century, we could have a debate about what to do with a vaccine that prevents cancer." He added:

Politics plays a role in all these decisions, and so does belief. I have no problems with that. But this is religious zealotry masked as politics, and it runs against everything that I as a scientist believe in, that I have devoted my life to. We are talking about basic public health now. What moral precepts allow us to think that the risk of death is a price worth paying to encourage abstinence as the only approach to sex?[59]

Keep in mind that there are several dozens of strains of HPV; only *two* of those strains can lead to cervical cancer and only another two can cause genital warts (which can be removed). All four of these dangerous strains are now preventable with this new vaccine. However, government-appointed experts as well as abstinence organization leaders have openly argued that the medical community should be hesitant about promoting a vaccine for HPV because it might "encourage promiscuity," or even just encourage monogamous teen sexual activity. A physician who is a member of the federal government's Centers for Disease Control's Immunization Committee and who formerly worked for Focus on the Family has gone even further, suggesting that if a vaccine were ever developed to prevent HIV transmission, perhaps it should not be made immediately available either. "We would have to look at that closely," he has said. "With any vaccine for HIV, disinhibition [that is, lack of fear about having sex] . . . would certainly be a factor, and it is something we would have to pay attention to with a great deal of care."[60]

AND HERE IS WHERE THE FOCUS shifts from physical to mental health, a far fuzzier but no less emotionally effective focus. Important recent examples are the studies that purport to conclude that premarital sexual activity causes chemical changes in the teenage brain and can spur serious depressive tendencies.

Silver Ring Thing has worked to publicize "information" like this: "New studies show that clinical depression in adolescent boys and girls is related to sexual activity and drinking."[61] Both the Abstinence Clearinghouse and the Care Center have stated:

> With every act of sexual activity the persons involved release oxytocin, a hormone in the brain, which creates permanent bonds in the brain, linking the two people together. Because the couple has bonded, there is heartache when a breakup occurs. For teens who have not been educated in their sex education classes about this bonding effect, and to [*sic*] lack the maturity to deal with the sudden loss of intimacy and the very real pain and distress, this can lead to depression and suicide.[62]

The Abstinence Clearinghouse has also provided a sample letter that citizens can use whenever there is a battle in their local school district over whether to provide adolescents with comprehensive sex education. It "can be copied, personalized and sent to your school administrators in support of abstinence education." "Dear Superintendent," the letter begins. "For more than forty years, contraception sex education programs have been teaching children in public classrooms that sexual activity is acceptable behavior for adolescents and that it can be virtually risk-free." This is unacceptable, the letter goes on to warn, not least because "sexually transmitted disease (STD) rates are skyrocketing among our nation's youth" and "half of all sexually active teens will have at least one STD before age 25." Further, the Abstinence Clearinghouse letter contends, "a 2004 Centers for Disease Control (CDC)–funded report showed that for girls, the link between teen sex and depression and suicide was so great that the researchers concluded 'any involvement in teen sex was indicative of the need for mental health screening'"(!) and that "a follow-up report shows that for male and female teens, the depression follows sexual activity, demonstrating a causal relationship." Wrapping up, the letter declares that condoms are not effective against many STDs and that virgins invariably do better in their professional and personal lives (including financially) than nonvirgins.[63]

What would have been deemed hallucinatory notions ten years ago are now treated with gravitas. The Department of Health and Human Services in 2006 issued guidelines for grant applications for sex education programming that stated that curricula *must* include teaching about "the potential psychological side effects (e.g., depression and suicide) associated with adolescent sexual activity" and that "non-marital sex in teen years may reduce the probability of a stable, happy marriage as an adult."[64]

Whatever wall there may have been in past decades between church-based abstinence advocates and state-backed public health policies disappeared during President Bush's second term. Abstinence advocates and their counterparts in government can be one and the same person.

A notable case in point was Dr. Eric Keroack, appointed in 2006 as deputy assistant secretary overseeing family planning and reproductive health matters at the Department of Health and Human Services. Dr. Keroack was concerned about women who have multiple sexual partners because, according to him, "people who have misused their sexual faculty and become bonded to multiple persons will diminish the power of oxytocin to maintain a permanent bond with an individual."[65] Dr. Keroack also contended that "premarital sex is really modern germ warfare."[66] It was not his lack of credentials or common sense that finally forced Dr. Keroack from office in 2007, but rather a financial scandal.[67] In October 2007, Bush's newest nominee for Keroack's post was Susan Orr, formerly of the right-wing Christian lobbying group Family Research Council, who believed that contraceptives were part of a "culture of death."[68]

The Bush administration announced in 2006 that it was formally "clarifying" for the states that they should feel free also to use federal abstinence-promotion monies (that's a pot of $50 million annually) to discourage all nonmarital sex among Americans between the ages of nineteen and twenty-nine. Wade Horn, assistant secretary for children and families at the Department of Health and Human Services—the same man who in 2002 brought us the program to encourage more marriages among the very poor in the United States—claimed the clarification was spurred by recent news that more American women in their twenties were deciding to have babies out of wedlock.[69] The new guidelines explicitly encouraged states to "identify groups" of people who "are most likely to bear children out of wedlock" and then target those groups with "the truth that abstinence is the only 100 percent effective way of avoiding unwanted pregnancies and sexually transmitted diseases." Horn said, "The message is 'It's better to wait until you're married to bear or father children,'" and "'the only 100% effective way of getting there is abstinence.'"

Never mind that a recent study by the Guttmacher Institute—based on interviews with more than thirty-eight thousand people—revealed that 95 percent of Americans, including those born as far back as the 1940s, have had premarital sex. Horn was undeterred. Warding off critics, he assured MSNBC, "The Bush administration does not believe the government should be regulating or stigmatizing the behavior of adults." He just thought it would be good to encourage people to delay sex. "The longer one delays, the fewer lifetime sex partners they have, and the less the risk of contracting sexually transmitted diseases."[70]

ALTHOUGH WADE HORN had only discreetly gestured to the "groups" of people "most likely to bear children out of wedlock," this comment bore traces of a much longer history of assumptions about race and extramarital reproductivity in America. Abstinence education originally had an enormous amount to do with race. From the very beginning, Bill Clinton's welfare reform of 1996 was packaged as a way to push unwed mothers, especially women of color, to find ways to go back to wage-paying work. Throughout the effort to get the welfare reform bill, called the Personal Responsibility and Work Opportunity Reconciliation Act, passed through Congress, the most prevalent images circulated in the mainstream media were of women of color, draining taxpayer money to support their illegitimate babies while refusing to work for pay. Only after the act passed did major newsmagazines report the truth that the majority of women on welfare were white. Ultimately, it was neither a coincidence nor clever deal-making tactics that caused the abstinence education addendum tacked on to the bill to pass without protest.

As Cris Mayo, education policy professor at the University of Illinois, has pointed out in a thoughtful analysis of the welfare reform bill, within a few years after the debacle over African-American surgeon general Joycelyn Elders's recommendation that masturbation was an acceptable topic for high school sex education classes (a public outcry forced her to step down), "abstinence education became a centerpiece in the war against welfare." While the welfare reform bill's abstinence addendum expressly said that federal funds should be given to support abstinence education "with a focus on those groups which are most likely to bear children out of wedlock," Mayo observes that "included in drafts of the act are an array of statistics pointing to the link between single motherhood and poverty, the rising rate of illegitimacy among black Americans, rates of criminal activity among young black men raised by single mothers, and the rate of criminal activity in neighborhoods with a greater incidence of single parent households." In short, Mayo notes, "Rather than focusing concern on the relationship between poverty *per se* and criminal activity, these statements link single motherhood, and also female sexual activity, with criminality and social decay."[71]

After 9/11, race was for a while less frequently discussed in the United States. Hurricane Katrina in 2005 brought images of African American "welfare mothers" back on to American TV screens (and once again subjected them to the condescending scrutiny of middle-class and white Americans), but on the whole our national attention was redirected to the war in Iraq and the wider global war on terror. Muslims at home and abroad were presented as posing a greater danger to our well-being than impoverished African Americans ever could.

Nonetheless, having a historical memory about the long-standing intersections of racial and sexual politics in U.S. culture is indispensable for understanding the roots of the ideological confusion of the present. Among other things, conservative religious leaders now pretend that the Religious Right was born in reaction to the legalization of abortion in *Roe v. Wade* in 1973. In fact, the Religious Right was born in reaction to the

Internal Revenue Service's effort in 1975 to revoke the tax-exempt status of the Christian conservative Bob Jones University, owing to its racially discriminatory policies: the school first denied admission to African Americans and then forbade interracial dating. Moreover, evangelical leaders were initially not at all united in hostility to *Roe v. Wade*.[72] So too abstinence advocates have tried to erase from public memory the abstinence movement's racist roots. Unwed mothers, especially when they were women of color, functioned—like homosexuals—as yet another "other" to the married heterosexual model the Religious Right was determined to promote.

The attack on African American women, whether sincerely felt or simply strategically utilized, was yet another move in the wider effort to make the abstinence movement palatable to the majority of Americans who were initially put off by the sanctimonious busybody and conservative religious approach of the early abstinence advocates. That young women might find the messages of self-respect and goal achievement proffered by the abstinence movement appealing for their own reasons—and perhaps especially appealing in light of the relentless assault on female self-esteem and body image in American culture—does not change the fact that an emphasis on abstinence as the road to achievement erases all the ways in which an informed and empowered female sexual agency can be compatible with achievement of other life goals.

THE CURRENT WAR OVER SEX in this country is not just a culture war. It is an emotional war, one that sets up battle lines *inside* individuals. It is a war that works to put women in their place, as well as to confuse and disorient men. It is a war whose shock troops bank on the inevitable imperfections of sex and the equally inevitable feelings of vulnerability that sex can induce just as it can induce feelings of pleasure.

In the current climate of anxiety about the death of lust and romance, the abstinence movement succeeds not least because it plays on—and foments further—profound fears of not being deeply desired. Indicatively, evangelical sex and marriage advisers Dillow and Pintus are all about eroticizing the crucial wedding night event—replete with black lace or white satin lingerie and tales of the "sweet ache," "mounting passion," and "liquid warmth" suffusing the bride's body as the groom undresses his beautifully pure gift from God and makes sensuous love to her—as the starting point for lifelong mutual bliss.[73]

The most striking aspect of the abstinence movement is how it blames all the emotional ambivalences and complexities of marital (as of any) sex, all the inevitable moments of alienation, longing, confusion, or incomplete satisfaction, on premarital experiences. The idea that premarital intimacies—with other people or with a subsequent spouse—might be a resource that enhances or strengthens individuals, both in their sense of self-ownership and in their capacities for enduring and passionate relationality, is never remotely considered.

It is remarkable how recent the talk about the value of abstinence is; as of the mid- to late-1990s, it was still a notion advanced only by a few. Yet no less remarkable is how pervasively this notion of the value of abstinence has taken hold since the turn of the millennium. This is evident not least in the way critics of the abstinence movement have conceded the terms of debate. Almost all attempts to defend comprehensive sex education, for instance, now begin from the premise that abstinence is surely a worthy ideal, but that it would be good to supplement the advocacy of abstinence with information about condoms and contraceptives.

A similar compromise position has emerged since combating the global HIV/AIDS pandemic became a priority for the U.S. government in 2003. What had been an internal U.S. conversation became an international discussion. But with the U.S. government setting the parameters for that discussion—also by setting the funding guidelines and overseeing the distribution of billions of dollars across more than twenty of the world's poorest nations—nongovernmental organizations (NGOs), health workers, and politicians, both in the countries most affected and in other donor nations, have all been obligated to engage the debate over HIV prevention worldwide on terms initially set by the Religious Right in the United States.

Chapter 5

MISSIONARY POSITIONS

<hr />

WHAT HAD ALREADY BEEN AN INCOHERENT, cruel, and mendacious abstinence program directed primarily at America's teens was now being aggressively exported to adults and adolescents alike in countries dependent on U.S. funding for family planning and public health services. In his State of the Union address in January 2003, President George W. Bush unveiled his plan to make "fighting the international HIV/AIDS pandemic a U.S. priority."[1] Bush described it as "a work of mercy beyond all current international efforts" and argued that the United States "can lead the world in sparing innocent people from a plague of nature"—much as "this nation is leading the world in confronting and defeating the man-made evil of international terrorism." The president thus urged Congress to "commit $15 billion over the next five years, including nearly $10 billion in new money, to turn the tide against AIDS in the most afflicted nations of Africa and the Caribbean." Bush promised that "this comprehensive plan will prevent 7 million new AIDS infections, treat at least 2 million people with life-extending drugs, and provide humane care for millions of people suffering from

AIDS, and for children orphaned by AIDS." "Seldom," he asserted, "has history offered a greater opportunity to do so much for so many."[2]

On May 21, 2003, Congress passed the United States Leadership Against HIV/AIDS, Tuberculosis, and Malaria Act of 2003 (Public Law 108-25). The law established the President's Emergency Plan For AIDS Relief (PEPFAR). It was "the largest commitment ever by a single nation toward an international health initiative." Fifteen of the most afflicted nations were chosen as "focus countries" and designated to receive $9 billion of the $15 billion. With the exception of Guyana, Haiti, and Vietnam, all were in Africa: Botswana, Côte d'Ivoire, Ethiopia, Kenya, Mozambique, Namibia, Nigeria, Rwanda, South Africa, Tanzania, Uganda, and Zambia. Collectively, the fifteen focus countries "represent at least 50 percent of HIV infections worldwide."[3] The remainder was to be donated to bilaterally managed programs in more than one hundred other countries ($5 billion) and to the international Global Fund to Fight AIDS, Tuberculosis, and Malaria ($1 billion).[4] Subsequently, five other "PEPFAR lite" countries would be designated for special attention: Cambodia, India, Malawi, Russia, and Zimbabwe.

From the start, there was controversy over how best to distribute the funds across different categories of need (for example, medical care for those already infected versus prevention). Ultimately, 20 percent was set aside for prevention. Then there was controversy over what kinds of prevention efforts would be funded. Christian conservatives, upset that condom use might be promoted at all, contended that the endorsement of condoms "promotes promiscuity."[5] As a result of this, a number of restrictions on the use of funds designated for prevention were put in place.

The original funding requirements of PEPFAR in 2003 read like this:

- 55 percent of monies for the treatment of individuals with HIV/AIDS (especially with antiretroviral drugs)
- 15 percent for palliative care for individuals with HIV/AIDS
- 10 percent for helping orphans and vulnerable children
- 20 percent for HIV/AIDS prevention (with fully 33 percent of this to be used for "A" programs, that is, abstinence-until-marriage strategies)

There remained some wiggle room for condom distribution in the two-thirds of funding not set aside for abstinence in the category of HIV/AIDS prevention.

Yet the promotion of condoms was restricted in multiple ways and would be further restricted in subsequent years. It was not just that PEPFAR's prevention work was based on an "ABC" approach in which "A" (Abstinence) and "B" (Be faithful) were considered at least as important in reducing the spread of HIV as "C" (Condoms). The Bush administration insisted that condoms were appropriate only when abstinence or fidelity was not a plausible option, that is, among groups they designated as "high-risk"—defined as truck drivers, sex workers, migrant workers, and occasionally substance abusers. This approach failed to consider that the majority of the sexually active population of older adolescents and adults, both outside and inside of marriage, also needed condoms to prevent sexually transmitted infections, not to mention unwanted pregnancies.

In addition, PEPFAR was passed with an amendment written by Representative Chris Smith (R-N.J.) demanding that any foreign-based NGO receiving funds from PEPFAR through the U.S. Agency for International Development (USAID) sign a statement declaring its opposition to sex trafficking and prostitution. Smith took the view, which Congress endorsed by passing the amendment, that voluntary prostitution was a "despicable" practice that involved "the severe degradation and exploitation of women, the literal rape of countless women around the globe," and that those who would defend the legalization of voluntary sex for sale and saw prostitution as "a worker's rights issue" were "doing a grave disservice to women" and "demean[ing] the value of women." There is a world of difference between prostitution and sex trafficking (and making the distinction is important for public health reasons as well as for effectively reducing the incidence of trafficking and slavery), but Smith asserted otherwise.[6] Segueing back and forth between references to those who believed that prostitution was "a legitimate form of employment" and horror stories of women "being raped every day" and eight- and nine-year-old victims of trafficking, Smith asserted that any organization that refused to declare its opposition to prostitution was morally indistinguishable from "a group that is also comprised of the very slavers that have these women and will not let them go." In Smith's view, moreover, "condom distribution in a brothel" could at best be seen "only as a short-term endeavor," for providing a steady supply of condoms—rather than eradicating prostitution—edged awfully close to "standing toe to toe with the oppressor against the oppressed."[7] This amendment had the direct effect of making it more difficult for NGOs to do prevention programs with the very sex workers the Bush administration and Congress had conceded were most at risk.

By fiscal year 2006 (with guidelines announced in late 2005), prevention funding faced even sharper restrictions than before.

The one-fifth of the pie devoted to HIV/AIDS prevention was again split up, with further reduced support for condom distribution. Now only 50 percent of the prevention monies could be used for programming related to sexual transmission; the other half would go to projects for blood supply safety and the prevention of mother-to-child transmission. Of the remaining 50 percent dedicated to sex, fully two-thirds now had to be focused on messages "A" and "B," leaving only 33 percent for condoms.[8] Public health organizations, although allowed to address "high-risk youth" in non-educational settings, were not permitted to promote condoms within high schools.[9]

Also in 2005, Smith's amendment demanding that foreign-based NGOs sign an antiprostitution statement was extended to include American-based NGOs working overseas as well. Previously, the Justice Department had been worried that such a restriction would curtail the constitutionally guaranteed free speech rights of Americans; as of 2005, the Justice Department was no longer worried. Congress also endorsed far stricter guidelines that required USAID to make certain that all organizations comply with the requirement to oppose prostitution before those organizations could receive funding.[10] In their eagerness to enforce these restrictions, Congress and USAID saw to it that programs in both Asia and Central America that had been doing successful prevention outreach with sex workers had their funding cut.

As the abstinence-and-fidelity program went global, it was not merely about an export of "values." The effect was much more concrete. The move to denigrate as well as to restrict condom availability, both by earmarking funds and by restricting which groups could receive condoms, had been put into action in some of the African countries most devastated by poverty and the pandemic, including countries in which, in some regions, the adult HIV infection rate had been estimated as being as high as 25 percent. (It is noteworthy that HIV appeared in Africa just at the moment—the mid-1980s—when heavy foreign debt burdens and economic crises forced massive cuts in already underprepared national health care systems.[11]) These are also frequently countries in which women and girls—often both socially and economically disempowered—are the ones most vulnerable to HIV infection. This remains true even in peacetime. In some nations, war and genocidal violence accompanied by mass rapes have wrought incalculable additional harm.[12]

Even as the United Nations in November 2007 revised downwards the estimates of new infections (mostly based on new data from India), at least two and a half million people were newly infected with HIV in 2006.[13] More than half of the new infections occurred in sub-Saharan Africa, and among those with the highest rates of new infection were girls in their late teens and married women in their twenties and thirties.[14]

What should have been a comprehensive war on HIV instead turned into a war on condoms. Since 2003, the unprecedented "work of mercy" that is PEPFAR has both provided phenomenally impressive levels of care for millions of individuals already infected with HIV and contributed to the systematic undermining of global prevention efforts. Owing to incessant attacks from right-wing evangelicals, condoms have now become associated with increased risk and recklessness. Rather than seeing condom distribution as an important aid to women in their struggle for both reproductive and sexual self-determination, the guidelines in PEPFAR have treated condoms as though they were themselves an obstacle to advancing the causes of women worldwide. Already in 2003 the United States donated only 300 million condoms internationally, compared to the approximately 800 million it had donated annually toward the end of the first President Bush's term a decade earlier.[15] And in the meantime, PEP-FAR has funded overtly homophobic organizations, while deliberately downplaying the prevention and treatment needs of same-sex practicing individuals in African nations.[16]

What PEPFAR's prevention division has done, in effect, is to finance some kinds of sex and defund other kinds. It has also made many kinds of sex more dangerous. The results have been deeply disturbing.

The even more limiting guidelines announced in late 2005 continued to restrict condom provisions to "high-risk groups," and there remained great confusion within PEPFAR focus countries about whether they were permitted to advocate for and distribute condoms to the general population, including youth and married people, even as some public health officials and activists argued that in a pandemic where up to 25 percent of entire national populations might be infected, *everyone* was a member of a "high-risk group."[17] Countries that could not demonstrate that two-thirds of their prevention monies were going to be used solely for abstinence and fidelity messaging would not receive U.S. funding of any sort.

PEPFAR maintained that funding would not be dispensed to any nation that distributed information about condoms until an also mandatory statement about the "failure rates" of condoms was "coupled with information about abstinence as the only 100 percent effective method of eliminating risk of HIV infection."[18] Defenders of this approach contended that condoms were unreliable protection against disease not least because people could not be counted upon to use them consistently or correctly. They clearly saw denigrating condom effectiveness as the best response to this problem, in lieu of promotion of correct and consistent use. As one senior NGO official remarked: "No public health intervention is 100% effective," and to lead with failure rates is "so contrary to public health that it will sabotage any condom promotion."[19] Or, as AIDS Foundation East-West fund-raiser David Veazey remarked: "It would be the same as a seat-belt commercial saying, 'Buckle Up! But there is a 10 percent chance that the seat belt won't save you in an accident.' Not only would people continue to drive—because they have to—but they probably wouldn't see the point in wearing a seat belt either."[20]

When these funding guidelines were made public, twenty-two member states of the European Union reacted in alarm, releasing a statement on the occasion of World AIDS Day. They declared themselves "profoundly concerned about the resurgence of partial or incomplete messages on HIV prevention which are not grounded in evidence and have limited effectiveness." They urged leaders of African nations to continue to promote condoms as the first line of defense against the pandemic. And British secretary of state for international development Hilary Benn advocated condoms in no uncertain terms: "I don't think people should die because they have sex."[21] The U.S. government was undeterred.

As a result of the new PEPFAR guidelines, eleven focus nations immediately requested exemptions from the two-thirds requirement. These waivers were granted, albeit only for one fiscal year. Nations were allowed to reduce "AB" to 33 percent from the formal requirement of 66 percent. Nine additional nations were obligated to expand their abstinence and fidelity programs as a percentage of their prevention funding in order to compensate for reductions elsewhere.[22]

In 2006 a Government Accountability Office (formerly known as the General Accounting Office, or GAO) study disclosed that seventeen nations in Africa were finding that the 66 percent requirement presented "challenges to their ability to respond to local prevention needs." In one country, the budget for outreach work with groups such as sex workers, sexually active youth, and sero-discordant couples (couples in which one partner was HIV-positive and the other was HIV-negative) had been cut from $8 million to $4 million to meet the "AB" earmark.[23] Additionally, the GAO found that in nine focus nations, officials said, "the abstinence mandate forced reductions in programs to inhibit mother-to-child transmission of the virus."[24] The GAO report also indicated that several focus nations remained unclear about "ABC" guidelines when it came to which condom-promoting activities were allowed by PEPFAR.[25]

Studies in three of the PEPFAR focus nations—Botswana, Nigeria, and Kenya—revealed utter confusion among citizens who had been exposed to "ABC" messaging; significant percentages of those questioned held incorrect or negative views of condoms and/or were inconsistent in condom usage.[26] A further 2006 study in South Africa, home to approximately 40 percent of all people currently living with HIV globally, and the southern African region more broadly found that "low condom use among people with multiple concurrent sexual partners," along with "gender inequality" and "high levels of gender and sexual violence," were "to blame for the rapid spread of the disease."[27] Already in 2004, a study of South African sex workers servicing miners found that women were unable to demand condom use. The study further found that boys ridiculed one another for both abstinence and condom use, and men often rejected condoms out of a combination of "fatalism and machismo."[28] And in 2005 the country constantly held up as the exemplary model for the benefits of the "ABC" approach—Uganda—was facing an unprecedented condom shortage. In place of the old billboards advertising condoms (once a common sight, but taken down in December 2004), there were now billboards showing a beautiful young woman's face and declaring, "She's keeping herself for marriage . . . What about you?"[29] Millions of condoms were moldering in warehouses (the government had declared them to be of poor quality), and the Ugandan government, under the influence of the American government, refused to produce or import more. According to one news report, the situation became so acute that "some men have begun using garbage bags as condom substitutes to prevent HIV infection."[30]

THE UGANDAN STORY gets mentioned every time advocates of an abstinence-until-marriage program make their case on how best to combat the spread of new HIV infections in the developing world. The Family Research Council writes: "Several reports show that the decline in AIDS prevalence in Uganda was due to monogamy and abstinence and not to condoms."[31] Or as John S. Gardner, former deputy assistant to President Bush and (from 2001 to 2005) general counsel of the U.S. Agency for International Development (USAID), wrote in an essay called "Condomania: The ABCs of African AIDS Prevention Need the A and B," it is precisely the prioritizing of abstinence and faithfulness over condoms "that has been so successful in reducing Uganda's AIDS epidemic." Public health advocates in Africa who stubbornly complain about the U.S. government's insistence on abstinence and fidelity, in Gardner's view, simply display "a shocking attitude toward Africans [that] contradicts the plain evidence from Uganda."[32]

It was the extraordinary success in reducing infection rates in Uganda in the 1990s that encouraged U.S. government leaders in their efforts to make abstinence and fidelity cornerstones of PEPFAR's prevention programming. During the 1990s, the Ugandan government of Yoweri Museveni had promoted an "ABC" approach to HIV prevention as well as campaigns with slogans like "love carefully" and "zero grazing," which, while not insisting on monogamy, encouraged reduction especially in the number of casual sex partners. In addition, collective organizing of support networks at the grass roots helped empower women and men to speak more openly with each other about sexual practices and safety.[33] Yet conservative pundits and lobbyists in the United States insisted repeatedly that the Ugandan success story proved that condoms were not the answer to HIV in Africa; they saw Uganda as exhibit A for the important lesson that people should have less pre- and extramarital sex.

As both houses of Congress got set to debate the Bush plan to combat AIDS in 2003, a Harvard University medical anthropologist, Edward C. Green, was invited to appear on Capitol Hill on March 20 to testify before the House Subcommittee on Health. "In view of all the sad news we hear about AIDS, especially in Africa," Green began, "it is my pleasure to share some good news." Green pointed to his first chart: it illustrated a dramatic decline in HIV infection rates in Uganda in the prior dozen years, from 21 percent to 6 percent. Green elaborated that the overall decline in infection rates had little to do with what public health experts might have anticipated, namely, expanded condom use. The use of condoms had risen in Uganda, he conceded, but almost exclusively among "those who need them most, namely those relatively few who are still having multiple partners." For the vast majority of Ugandans, he contended, rates of condom use had not changed significantly at all. Furthermore, "it may be noted that condom user rates in Uganda are not higher than those of other countries" that had witnessed no comparable drop in new HIV/AIDS infections. "Where Uganda stands out is in its relatively low levels of multi-partner sex," Green testified.[34]

Green is the author of *Rethinking AIDS Prevention*. In a chapter pointedly entitled "Questioning Condoms," Green reflects on the politically sensitive question: "Are condoms the answer to African AIDS?" Green emphasizes the distressingly high failure rates of condoms in Africa, due to factors that include incorrect usage and poor quality, and concludes that condoms are definitely not the answer to African AIDS.[35] (It is perhaps not entirely irrelevant that—although as recently as 2002 Green told a reporter, "I'm a flaming liberal, don't go to church, never voted for a Republican in my life"—Green's position at Harvard is partially funded by USAID as well as a Christian organization.[36])

On May 19, 2003, Edward Green returned to Washington to testify before the Senate Subcommittee on Africa. Speaking again on how Uganda had managed to reduce its HIV infection rates so significantly, Green said: "The take-home message for the U.S. Senate is that, while condoms were part of the education for youth, the emphasis was on persuading children to postpone sexual activity until they were older, until they were married." Green reiterated that the available evidence from Uganda demonstrated that "reduction in the number of sexual partners was probably the single most important behavior change that resulted in prevalence decline. Abstinence was probably the second most important change."[37]

A few weeks after the passage of the President's Emergency Plan For AIDS Relief in June 2003, President Bush embraced the president of Uganda, Yoweri Museveni, and praised his work in AIDS prevention. Religious conservatives rushed to concur. The Ugandan plan to combat AIDS "doesn't use the distribution of condoms as the first line of defense," effused Family Research Council director Ken Connors.[38]

Nor did Edward Green's efforts on behalf of the president's plan go unrewarded. He has served since 2003 as a member of the President's Advisory Council on HIV/AIDS (PACHA). In 2004 Green was appointed as a specialist consultant to a five-year project, funded by PEPFAR, on AIDS prevention in Uganda, Rwanda, and Ethiopia.

There are multiple possible reasons for Uganda's decline in HIV prevalence rates in the course of the 1990s. The evidence is messy in many ways. Uganda experienced the onset of the HIV/AIDS epidemic earlier than nations in southern Africa, and it is actually possible that high mortality rates may partially explain the reduction in prevalence rates. Some scholars have suggested that sex may not have been the only source of early infections, but that reused needles for medical injections or cutting practices used for healing purposes may have contributed to the early spread of infections. Early vigorous government leadership and the involvement of religious organizations in decreasing the stigma associated with infections were crucial as well. Once the connection with sex was evident (initially Ugandans referred to the wasting disease that was affecting so many people as "Slim"), the incidence of casual sex may indeed have declined, and there are regions of the country in which condoms were never readily available, and thus the decline in infections is likely to reflect a restriction in the number of partners. At the same time, measuring prevalence has remained difficult, with some estimates based on screening pregnant women and extrapolating from them to the general population, and others based on random samples of the adult population.[39]

Nonetheless, taking all the evidence together, while some of the available data suggest that reductions in the number of casual partners contributed to falling HIV rates in the early 1990s in Uganda, continued partner reduction has not been a plausible explanation for falling rates in subsequent years, since the numbers of multiple partners once again increased. As public health researcher Helen Epstein observed in 2005: "Condom use increased at the same time, and this must be why HIV infection rates have remained low." Moreover, with regard to the issue of abstinence messaging, Epstein noted:

> Between 1988 and 2001, the average age at which young Ugandan women started sexual activity rose by less than a year, even though the national HIV rate fell by some 70 percent. Most Ugandan girls begin having sex at around age seventeen, a year or so younger than in Zimbabwe, where HIV rates are about five times higher. More than half of all Ugandan women have been pregnant by age nineteen. HIV rates in pregnant teenage Ugandan girls fell rapidly during the first half of the 1990s, but during this time, the rate and ages at which these girls became pregnant—a marker of their sexual activity— barely changed at all.[40]

The NGO Population Action International has phrased the point even more forcefully: "Contrary to some media reports, Uganda is not an example of an 'abstinence-only' prevention program. Rather, the decline of HIV/AIDS prevalence rates in Uganda offers testimony to the triumph of the multi-pronged ABC approach." While the abstinence component succeeded in delaying (albeit by less than a year) the average age of first intercourse in Uganda, the statistics also "indicate that higher proportions of young people became sexually active." At the same time, between 1995 and 2000,

> the percentage of Ugandans using condoms during sex with non-marital, non-cohabiting partners rose significantly, from 20 percent to 38 percent of women and from 36 percent to 59 percent of men. The percentage of young people (aged 15–24) in

Uganda using condoms during premarital sex also increased impressively between 1995 and 2000, from 26 percent to 50 percent of women and 44 percent to 58 percent of men.[41]

Careful research on the rural Rakai District of Uganda conducted by scholars from Uganda as well as Columbia and Johns Hopkins—based on an annual survey of ten thousand people between 1994 and 2002 and published in 2005—also suggested that age at sexual debut declined in both sexes, while there was a rise in young adults participating in nonmarital sex and having multiple partners; they too concluded that a rise in condom use (from 19 percent to 38 percent among males age fifteen to sixteen, for instance) must have been the cause of stable rates of HIV incidence.[42] As the *New York Times* summarized the findings, the study "found no evidence that abstinence and monogamy explained the overall decline in HIV prevalence," and—as lead author Dr. Maria J. Wawer commented—"condoms are essential" to reduce the number of new HIV infections. Another scholar from Johns Hopkins quoted by the *Times* observed that the study's findings underscored once more that "condoms are the main preventive tool against HIV," adding: "Condoms have to be everywhere alcohol and sex are sold."[43]

By 2005, however, condoms were suddenly no longer widely available at free clinics. Condoms imported from Germany and China were labeled unusable and not distributed. Meanwhile, the government of Uganda ceased to distribute domestically produced condoms. All foreign-made condoms, including those manufactured in the United States, were now subject to government inspection, owing to alleged concerns about defective brands. The country, by some estimates, required 80 million free condoms in a year—but it only managed to make 8 million available. Meanwhile, the price of condoms tripled.[44]

Yet at just this moment, the Ugandan government announced that it had no plans to address the condom shortage. As the minister of state for primary health care said, the condom shortage in Uganda *was* the plan: "The ministry is going to be less involved in condom importation but more involved in awareness campaigns; abstinence and behavior change."[45] Meanwhile, the news got even worse: condoms not only became less easily available but also less socially acceptable.[46]

In late 2006, the UN's "AIDS Epidemic Update" noted that Uganda's fabled era of a decrease in its HIV pandemic was officially over. New HIV/AIDS infections were again rising, while "knowledge and practice regarding condom use has become erratic with only half of Ugandans reporting using a condom the last time they had sex."[47] The restrictions of condoms to "high-risk groups" also proved most unhelpful. Of those Ugandans newly infected in 2005, 40 percent were married.[48] As a researcher for the Center for Public Integrity tersely observed: "In Uganda, which successfully promoted a comprehensive program before PEPFAR, the incidence of the virus has nearly doubled since shifting its focus to comply with PEPFAR's A and B guidelines."[49] Yifat Susskind of the women's rights organization Madre summarized: "It took only two years for HIV rates to double after U.S. missionaries-turned-policymakers effectively shifted the emphasis of the country's AIDS prevention programs from condom use to abstinence."[50]

Crucial players in justifying the new disinterest in condom distribution were Janet Museveni, first lady of Uganda, as well as the U.S.-based evangelicals and Republican lawmakers she often consulted on such matters. Mrs. Museveni flew to Washington in the midst of congressional debates about HIV/AIDS funding and asserted that abstinence programming had been the key to Uganda's successful reduction in HIV infection rates in the 1990s. She was active as well in developing abstinence programming within Uganda. Mrs. Museveni believed that safe-sex initiatives, such as those that involved the distribution of condoms, were irresponsible and immoral. In her view, "There is no safe sex outside of faithfulness in marriage."[51] She also accused condom advocates of racism. As she put it, "They think Africans cannot control their sex drives."[52]

Mrs. Museveni urged her country to undertake a "virgin census . . . to find out the percentage of the youth who never had sex [and] those who have reverted to secondary abstinence," and she sponsored a march of seventy thousand virgins through the capital city of Kampala.[53] She formed the National Youth Forum, an organization that receives U.S. funding to promote its abstinence-only message and has close ties to the Children's AIDS Fund, a Virginia-based organization that also receives U.S. funds to promote its abstinence-only program. Mrs. Museveni also lobbied the minister of education to let True Love Waits pamphlets be distributed in Ugandan schools. As Sharon Pumpelly of True Love Waits would later recall, Janet Museveni "became extremely instrumental in opening doors. Schools would close down for four hours at a time to allow us to bring True Love Waits in to teach the students."[54] Pumpelly said as well that the single most important lesson she learned from her many years promoting True Love Waits in Africa is this: "I really believe we're missing an incredible witness of who Christ is and His power by not telling young people worldwide that with God's help they really cannot have sex until they're married and receive all that God has for them."[55] (Meanwhile, True Love Waits is hardly the only American evangelical organization active in Uganda. There is also Franklin Graham's Samaritan's Purse—recipient of a multimillion-dollar U.S. government contract for HIV prevention—which combines abstinence messaging with evangelizing. As one of its organizers told Helen Epstein, when asked about the role of faith, "It's HUGE. . . . Abstinence is near impossible without the helping hand of the Lord.")[56]

The irony is that the country that in 2003 had served as the touchstone for pressuring the U.S. Congress to permit the ear-marking of prevention monies for abstinence messaging had by 2005 become an exemplar for what was wrong with PEPFAR's priorities. As the *New York Times* noted, while Washington was "moving away from condom advocacy in all its overseas AIDS programs," Uganda "is the only place [where] this policy has been so fully embraced by the government."[57] As Melinda Gates of the Gates Foundation has said: "In some countries with wide-spread AIDS epidemics, leaders have declared the distribution of condoms immoral, ineffective or both." Gates adds:

> Some have argued that condoms do not protect against HIV, but in fact help spread it. This is a serious obstacle to ending AIDS. In the fight against AIDS, condoms save lives. If you oppose the distribution of condoms, something is more important to you than saving lives.[58]

CRITICISMS OF PEPFAR's "AB" programs have been intense and have come from diverse quarters. The British medical journal *The Lancet* published a full-page editorial naming PEPFAR's ap-proach "ill-informed and ideologically driven." *The Lancet* called for "a complete reversal of policy," concluding, "Many more lives will be saved if condom use is heavily promoted alongside mes-sages to abstain and be faithful."[59] Paul Zeitz, director of the Global AIDS Alliance, called PEPFAR's abstinence policy "basi-cally unworkable."[60] The Health Gap Global Access Project issued this statement: "The AB-only message suggests that HIV-negative people can prevent infection by moral fortitude, and by detecting and avoiding 'carriers.' Current U.S. AB-only prevention policy—despite spending hundreds of millions of dollars—is adding bodies to the viral death march."[61] Richard Holbrooke, former ambassador to the United Nations and now head of the Global Business Coalition on HIV/AIDS, asserted in late 2006 that PEPFAR's treatment program was not going to be sustainable if prevention could not succeed: "If the number of people who need antiretrovirals increases every year, it becomes a bottomless pit. . . . We have to turn the corner, the actual number of people with the disease needs to go down."[62] Ambassador Stephen Lewis, the UN special envoy for HIV/AIDS in Africa, delivered an anguished keynote address in 2006 at the closing session of the sixteenth International AIDS Conference in Toronto. Abstinence-only programs will never work, Lewis said, because "ideological rigidity almost never works when applied to the human condition."[63] The year before, Lewis had noted that "there is no question that the condom crisis in Uganda is being driven and exacerbated by PEPFAR and by the extreme policies that the administration in the United States is now pursuing."[64]

Public health experts have also observed that "abstinence-only initiatives do not address the social and political realities of many women in the world, for whom abstinence is simply not an option—such as women who are vulnerable to male violence if they refuse to have sex, or women who have to resort to sex work for their livelihood."[65] The *Boston Globe* wrote that abstinence-only programs "are of little help to some of those most vulnerable to infection, including impoverished young women under pressure to have sex for economic or cultural reasons."[66] The British *Guardian* commented that "many women are not in a position to abstain from sex" and that even wives were not safe within marriage because "many are infected by their husbands."[67]

Close to 40 million people have died from HIV/AIDS, and another estimated 33.2 million currently live with HIV/AIDS.[68] Meanwhile, the world suffers from a condom shortage just as "a billion young people worldwide are about to enter their reproductive years; they form the largest reproductive generation in human history."[69] An international panel of public health experts in Beijing in 2006 stated:

> Condom distribution is known to prevent HIV transmission. It is inexpensive and should be a vital part of all prevention programs. But . . . the Bush administration insists that condoms be provided only for "high risk" sexual encounters and rarely for adolescents. Furthermore, government-sponsored literature perpetuates a myth of condom failure that undermines the repeated evidence of international and domestic studies. We urge free distribution of condoms worldwide.[70]

And in 2007 the call from the World Health Organization (WHO) and the United Nation's UNAIDS program to undertake a massive campaign in southern Africa to encourage male circumcision because it has been shown to reduce the spread of HIV was linked to announcements that circumcision should not be seen as a substitute for condomized sex.[71] Other possibilities—such as a microbicide used vaginally by women to prevent HIV transmission or a preventive HIV vaccine— remain a decade away from success. This means that condoms (and not just male condoms but also female condoms, which prove even more effective than male condoms) remain "the only technology currently available for protection against sexually transmitted HIV."[72]

Yet neither the mounting infection toll nor the flood of expert opposition has made a dent in the Religious Right's stance on the use of condoms to prevent the transmission of HIV/AIDS, even as leading evangelical ministers have increasingly addressed the worldwide AIDS pandemic as a worthy cause.

A PRIME EXAMPLE of the complicated nature of the evangelical war on AIDS can be seen in the advocacy work of Rick Warren, pastor of Saddleback Church in Lake Forest, California, one of the largest evangelical churches in the United States, and organizer of the Global Summit on AIDS and the Church. Warren has said that he seeks allies across the political spectrum to end the global AIDS pandemic. "I'm a pastor, not a politician," Warren says. "People always say, 'Rick, are you right wing or left wing?' I say 'I'm for the whole bird.'"[73] In this way, Warren has been able to win the admiration—or at least the cooperation—of a diverse coalition of influential individuals and organizations.

Bill Gates has worked with Warren, agreeing to appear via video at Saddleback Church's World AIDS Day event. The rock star Bono knows Warren and has also appeared at a World AIDS Day event; Bono additionally arranged for Warren to serve as the official pastor at a Live 8 concert held in Philadelphia in 2006. Media magnate Rupert Murdoch calls Warren his good friend and pastor; Murdoch has donated generously to assist Warren in his fight against AIDS. (Warren's book *The Purpose Driven Life*, with more than 26 million copies sold, is one of the best-selling nonfiction books in American history and is published by Murdoch.) Considered "a straight-down-the-middle evangelical," Warren represents a charismatic new breed of evangelical leader, one with genuine crossover appeal; he's a regular fellow who favors Hawaiian print shirts, gives bear hugs, and loves classic rock. At an anniversary celebration for Saddleback Church, he pulled out an electric guitar and opened with a rendition of Jimi Hendrix's "Purple Haze."[74]

At the same time, Warren strongly opposes abortion rights, thinks homosexuality is a sin (Warren has been willing to meet with gay leaders, but he has also compared homosexuality to bestiality), and believes that all Jews will end up in hell after the apocalypse.[75] Warren also assisted Mel Gibson with publicity for *The Passion of the Christ*. Despite his desire to be seen as non-ideological, Warren sent letters to 150,000 pastors in 2004 urging them to encourage their parishioners to vote for George W. Bush.

Warren has generated a tremendous amount of capital and human resources for his campaign to combat HIV/AIDS on a global scale. He and his wife, Kay, have vowed to give away 90 percent of the profits Warren makes from *The Purpose Driven Life*, several millions of dollars. Since 2002, when Warren first acknowledged that the issue of a global HIV/AIDS pandemic was something he should address, he has thrown himself into the cause. Warren readily admits that, before 2002, "HIV/AIDS was not on my agenda; it was not even a blip on my radar." But all that changed after Kay Warren brought the tragedy of global AIDS to her husband's attention. "Over the years I've learned that when God speaks to my wife I'd better listen!" Warren wrote.[76] Warren chose Rwanda to be his first "purpose driven nation" and has grown quite close to Rwandan president Paul Kagame, whose private helicopter Warren borrows when he visits his Rwandan church projects.[77]

Several thousand Saddleback missionaries have traveled to Rwanda and elsewhere in the developing world to advance Warren's PEACE Plan (Partner with or Plan churches; Equip servant leaders; Assist the poor; Care for the sick; and Educate the next generation). Warren's ambitious goal is to defeat "the five global, evil giants of our day": spiritual emptiness, egocentric leadership, extreme poverty, pandemic diseases, and illiteracy and lack of education. The plan's website explains: "Simply put, the PEACE Plan is about ordinary people, empowered by God, making a difference together wherever they are."[78]

Warren has developed two further strategies relevant to his fight against HIV/AIDS. First, there is CHURCH—Caring and Comfort; Help with counseling and testing; Unleashing a force of volunteers; Reducing stigma; Championing healthy behavior; and Help through medications and nutrition.[79] Second, there is STOP—Save sex for marriage; Teach men to respect women and children; Offer treatment through churches; and Pledge yourself to one partner for life. As Warren has said about HIV/AIDS, it is not good enough merely to slow the pandemic using secular methods like condom distribution or recommendations for partner reduction—AIDS must be stopped. And to stop AIDS, there is only one proven method that works. "If you want to stop it," Warren says, "now you have to bring in the church."[80]

On condom distribution, Warren tends to hedge. "My personal position is I will use whatever works," he has said. "And with people who don't want to use condoms, if there's certain people who have religious beliefs on that, well then I will work with them in other ways. Those who will use them, and I'll encourage them in that, too."[81]

At the sixteenth International AIDS Conference in Toronto in 2006, Warren was again asked his views. His reply was summarized: "He's not against condoms—that is, being distributed by others. . . . But he doesn't do so, nor do the 7,000 Christian activists that Saddleback has already dispatched on missions around the globe."[82]

Pastor.com, the immensely popular website Warren has established, features the *Ministry ToolBox,* a free weekly newsletter "to help those in ministry grow healthier churches." Here we find an interview with an International Mission Board missionary based in Swaziland, Mary Wood, who teaches African children an "ABC" program at odds with the more standard version: "Abstain, Be faithful to your marriage partner, and follow Christ." Asked why she leaves condoms out of her "ABC" plan, Wood tells people that condoms fail because the HIV virus passes through small holes in them. "If I wanted to be rich," Wood tells middle-schoolers in Swaziland, "I would have stayed in America and invested in a condom company. But I care for you and don't want you to get sick. That's why I'm here to talk to you about HIV and answer any of your questions."[83]

The International Mission Board is a missionary organization sponsored by the Southern Baptist Convention, the same church that sponsors True Love Waits. IMB missionaries appear to support the use of condoms for married couples where one partner is HIV-positive, but they believe the only true solution to the HIV/AIDS pandemic is abstinence programs.

That abstinence programs start from problematic premises and that condoms do not have holes in them that permit the HIV virus to pass through appears beside the point. Those committed to "AB" strategies have seen little reason to revise or rethink their perspectives.

If there turns out to be a problem with "AB" strategies, they contend, it will not be because abstinence-until-marriage programs cannot work. It will be because "AB" programs were not given a proper chance to prove their effectiveness. What is needed is *more* abstinence-until-marriage planning. This is the same argument that was being made in 2007 by advocates of abstinence education for American teens in the face of mounting evidence that abstinence programs either did not make any difference at all or were in fact accompanied by raised rates of STIs (sexually transmitted infections), HIV infections, and unwanted pregnancies.[84]

Even before AIDS rates began to rise again in Uganda, Edward C. Green made a dire prediction: "We're going to reach a point where infection rates will start going up again and then experts will say ABC never worked, that there was probably something wrong with the data all along."[85] This theme was picked up by *National Review* editor Kathryn Jean Lopez, who, while mocking Bill Gates because he was still "airlifting condoms into Africa," noted that the real dilemma was that folks were unwilling to give abstinence programs the chance they deserved:

> Unfortunately, the ABC approach may not spread and flourish, even in Uganda. Because of "conventional wisdom of the world," major donors to Africa do not favor the A and the B of it. According to [Edward C.] Green, "If you look at the current national Strategic Framework for HIV/AIDS, which is a blueprint for all the activities supported in Uganda to combat AIDS, you will see that there are virtually no A or B elements there. The document is all about condoms, STDs, future vaccines, future microbicides and testing."

As Lopez saw it, the mistake remained that too many public health officials had just not caught on to the fact that "throwing condoms at the problem has simply not worked in Africa."[86]

In 2007, when Bush asked Congress to commit another $15 billion to combat the HIV/AIDS pandemic for the next five years, the Family Research Council, worried that Democrats might succeed in revoking the Bush administration's earmark for abstinence programming, once more argued that the promotion of condoms was both financially irresponsible and potentially lethal. The FRC's vice president for government affairs,

Tom McClusky, said, "By taking out the abstinence provisions, the Democrats are giving a death sentence to a number of Africans."[87]

Republican presidential contender and evangelical Christian Mike Huckabee had this to say in September 2007 in response to a CNN query about whether he supported U.S. funding of organizations that distributed condoms in Africa:

> I've been a little reluctant to think that condoms alone are the most effective way. . . . It certainly is more effective than not having them. But I think helping people understand that condoms do have a failure rate, and they are not totally 100 percent successful. And it gives some people a false sense of security thinking that they can still live dangerously and recklessly and that that's going to be a fail safe protection when it obviously is not.[88]

But the 2008 Republican nominee, Senator John McCain (R-Ariz.), reflected even less comfort with the subject. Asked by a reporter whether condoms help to stop the spread of HIV, McCain said, "You've stumped me. . . . I'm not informed enough on it." Pressed to clarify whether he agreed with President Bush's prioritizing of abstinence over contraception, and whether he also opposed comprehensive sex education, McCain turned to one of his aides: "Brian, would you find out what my position is on contraception—I'm sure I'm opposed to government spending on it, I'm sure I support the president's policies on it. . . . I've never gotten into these issues before."[89]

IN AUGUST 2005, DKT International, a U.S.-based nongovernmental and not-for-profit organization that had already supplied hundreds of millions of condoms in more than two dozen developing nations, sued the United States Agency for International Development and its administrator, Andrew S. Natsios. DKT International stated that a $60,000 USAID subgrant it had been awarded by USAID for work in Vietnam had been unfairly withdrawn. The declared basis for rescinding the grant had been DKT's refusal to meet federal eligibility restrictions that USAID funds may never be "used to provide assistance to any group or organization that does not have a policy explicitly opposing prostitution and sex trafficking."[90] DKT had refused to certify such a policy, arguing that the free speech rights of DKT's American employees would be violated if it did. DKT also challenged the premise that the U.S. government had a right to declare otherwise eligible organizations ineligible for federal funding if "they do not expressly adopt the government's policy on prostitution." It was unconstitutional, DKT contended, for the government to make "an organization's eligibility for USAID funding [conditional] upon that organization declaring its adherence to a particular government policy."[91] DKT also noted that this USAID eligibility restriction "will likely result in stigmatizing and alienating many of the people vulnerable to HIV/AIDS—the sex workers—and may result in limiting access to the group DKT is trying to reach in its fieldwork in Vietnam."[92]

Vietnam was in the midst of a severe AIDS crisis with an unusual epidemiological profile. More than one hundred thousand persons in Vietnam were infected with HIV; of this number, nearly twenty thousand had developed AIDS. More than eleven thousand had died. The highest prevalence rate was among intravenous drug users (34 percent of them were infected; they constituted 70 percent of all infections); the second-highest rate was among female sex workers (6.5 percent), a significant percentage of whom also used IV drugs. "Injection drug use is the engine driving HIV/AIDS" in the country, and the Vietnamese government had been strongly supportive of needle exchange programs.[93] DKT was also assisting with providing safe needles.[94]

Vietnam has an estimated forty thousand prostitutes. According to a 2002 study, 39 percent of truck drivers in the port city of Can Tho and 20 percent of migrant workers in another city had slept with a prostitute in the past year.[95] (Note that all of these people met the PEPFAR criteria for inclusion in the category of "high-risk groups.") And as late as June 2005, USAID had given express permission to the NGO Family Health International to fund a condom-lubricant project sponsored by DKT, a project expressly geared toward encouraging sex workers and their clients to engage in safe-sex practices. (The lubricant packets were marketed by DKT as sensation enhancement, but just as important was that lubricants reduced the chance of condom rupture.) USAID funding appeared to be moving ahead until a DKT representative, after signing an agreement with USAID, voided his signature when he realized that USAID was expecting him to certify that DKT explicitly opposed prostitution. When DKT's request for a waiver was denied, the federal funding was rescinded.[96]

Two weeks after DKT filed its lawsuit, a second nongovernmental and not-for-profit organization, Population Services International (PSI), found its funding cut by USAID. Like DKT, PSI was a huge purveyor of condoms in the developing world; PSI operated in over sixty countries and was the second-largest organization in the world involved in international family planning after Planned Parenthood. The problem, at least according to Senator Tom Coburn (R-Okla.), was that PSI sponsored a program that educated prostitutes in Central America about condom use. PSI hired former prostitutes in several Central American countries to speak to current prostitutes, many of whom were illiterate. Together they played a card game called Lotería (lottery), which resembled bingo and featured a board with images that the women matched with pictographs held up by the educator. Those who matched all their images received small prizes. The real objective of the game was to explain to prostitutes how to prevent HIV/AIDS and how to use condoms properly. For example, if a pictograph of a palm tree was chosen, the educator might discuss how condoms prevented AIDS like a palm tree prevents sunburn. As a regional director for PSI explained: "We can't just stand up in a bar and say 'AIDS will kill you.' With an interactive game, we can hold their attentions, sometimes for as long as an hour." But an indignant Senator Coburn wrote to President Bush, "PSI has applied for tens of millions more to continue the project. There is something seriously askew at USAID when the agency's response to a dehumanizing and abusive practice that exploits women and young girls is parties and games."[97] Not long after the president received Coburn's letter, PSI learned that its funding for Lotería had been slashed.

Lotería is an example of "social marketing," a concept developed for the field of family planning by Philip D. Harvey, the man who founded both DKT and PSI.[98] Harvey thinks of himself as a "sort of Robin Hood" of public health; a former Peace Corps worker in India, he runs the largest vibrator and porn mail-order business in the world, Adam and Eve, based in North Carolina.[99] For decades, Harvey has put a substantial portion of the profits he makes enhancing Americans' sex lives into subsidizing contraceptives and condoms in the developing world.

Social marketing promotes public health not only through clinics and government agencies but also through the market, especially at the lowest levels, from street vendors to traditional medicine men to taxi drivers and bars and karaoke halls. Entire swaths of the population are more reachable this way than through more official channels. Whatever products are marketed are also subsidized, so that even the poorest customers can afford them. Social marketing also seeks to make products desirable. With contraceptives, it seeks to put the pleasure back in protection.

Thus, social marketers have introduced colored condoms and ribbed condoms and flavored condoms. And they have included packets of lubricant with condoms. Social marketers like to make condoms seem sexy and exciting, arguing that sexy condoms are condoms people will seek out and want to use. Condoms sold as fun and pleasurable have proven far more effective than condoms sold simply as health-promoting. Studies also indicate that people are far more likely to practice safe sex when they have to pay a token fee for a condom than when it is handed to them for free.[100] (This turns out to be true for items like malaria nets as well.) Social marketing deploys strategies of the marketplace to promote safe sex. And it has worked.

Until DKT refused to state an opposition to prostitution and lost its USAID funding, Vietnam had been among DKT's most successful projects. DKT worked through social marketing that delivered subsidized condoms and oral contraceptives to the general population and through targeted interventions directed to the most vulnerable and high-risk populations. DKT marketed two brands of condoms as well as an oral contraceptive, available through nine thousand pharmacies and two thousand additional outlets in the nation. Four out of five households in Vietnam have a television, and so DKT also used television in addition to press and radio advertising to promote condom and contraceptive use. These techniques all yielded impressive results. Between 1993 and 2006, DKT provided more than 513 million condoms and 26 million cycles of contraceptive pills in Vietnam.[101]

During the period when USAID funded DKT, the availability of condoms stabilized and condom sales steadily climbed. In the years after 1998, DKT implemented the "100% Condom Access" project, especially critical in reaching IV drug users as well as sex workers and their clients.[102]

DKT's "100% Condom Access" project had been operating under the auspices of Family Health International (FHI), which was directly sponsored by USAID. USAID had given permission for DKT to receive subgrants from FHI to participate in a project called IMPACT (Implementing AIDS Prevention and Care Project). This project had implemented AIDS prevention in six of the highest-risk of Vietnam's sixty-four provinces. Its objective was to reach prostitutes and their clients more effectively by using a combination of peer educators and media blitzes, including entertainment events and contests with HIV/AIDS prevention messages and nontraditional outlets for condom distribution.[103]

After DKT lost its USAID funding, DKT-sponsored condom shipments from the United States to Vietnam were suspended, and DKT had to seek out alternative sources of condoms. As for USAID, it announced that it now had a new partner organization in Vietnam, one willing to endorse the federal agency's antiprostitution guidelines.

In February 2007, Judge Raymond Randolph of the U.S. Court of Appeals for the District of Columbia ruled that USAID policy did not violate DKT's First Amendment right to free speech. In 2006, in an earlier ruling, a U.S. District Court judge had sided with DKT, noting that just because an organization or an individual receives federal money or benefits does not mean that the individual thereby forfeits his or her rights to free speech. (That goes for veterans, children in public schools, public radio stations, and everyone else as well.)[104] But when USAID appealed that decision, Judge Randolph reasoned that no NGO had an obligation to apply for or receive government funding. If an NGO wished to receive government funding, then, as Judge Randolph phrased it, that NGO "must communicate the message the government chooses to fund."[105]

In January 2006, Randall L. Tobias replaced Andrew S. Natsios as the administrator in charge of USAID. Natsios had won few friends in the public health arena when he incautiously remarked in an interview that antiretroviral drugs represented a waste of money in Africa because these drugs had to be administered on a regular daily schedule and Africans "don't know what Western time is."[106] (Mr. Natsios was reassigned as U.S. special envoy to Sudan.) For public health officials and advocates, however, Randall Tobias was not an improvement. When Tobias served as U.S. global AIDS coordinator for the Bush administration, he had repeatedly argued that condoms did not prove effective as a means for preventing the spread of HIV/AIDS.[107] Tobias also expressed a strong commitment to "partnering with communities [around the world] to find solutions to such issues as sexual coercion and exploitation of women and girls, as well as fighting sex trafficking and prostitution, while still serving victims of these activities."[108]

But Tobias was not long in his new position. In the spring of 2007, Tobias, who is married, abruptly resigned as USAID administrator after he publicly acknowledged that he had several times employed a Washington escort service "to have gals come over to the condo to give me a massage." Tobias also admitted a preference for massages "with Central Americans," though he insisted there had been "no sex."[109] When asked for comment, State Department spokesman Sean McCormack kept a straight face. "The lives saved and made better around the globe by Randy's work at the State Department constitute a rich legacy on which he can look back with justifiable pride," McCormack said.[110]

THE RELIGIOUS RIGHT is not simply a religious movement or a political movement; it has also, and above all, been a sexual movement. Nowhere has this been more evident than in the way the U.S. government's involvement in the project of HIV/AIDS prevention globally was invested with a sexually conservative agenda from the very beginning. While the outpouring of funds and energy for treatment and care is impressive and continues to be urgently needed, the good that is being done is continually undercut by an obsessive insistence on casting aspersions on the effectiveness of condoms, restricting the distribution of condoms, and, more generally, telling people in other parts of the world how to organize their sexual lives. Right-wing evangelicals have been so successful in muddling the conversation and confusing categories of analysis that their critics have frequently been quite intimidated.

At present it is unclear which way American policy overseas will go. An extensive 2007 study by the Alan Guttmacher Institute, based on evaluation of surveys among twenty thousand African adolescents, found that fewer than half of the adolescents surveyed in four African nations (Uganda, Malawi, Ghana, and Burkina Faso) were able to correctly identify ways of preventing HIV infection, and their knowledge of pregnancy prevention strategies was even lower.[111] In view of these kinds of findings, international pressure on the United States to change its public health focus to incorporate more accurate information and better access to condoms and contraceptives is likely to grow. If more Democrats and Republicans alike can come to understand the effects of PEPFAR's prevention policy priorities as brutal and crushing—especially given the economic conditions in the hardest-hit nations—there is a chance that future harms can be diminished. Or perhaps all that is needed is something more mundane: to realize how embarrassing it is to be so wildly out of step with international public health consensus. Or even something more cynical: to confront the fact that, as President Bush's global AIDS coordinator, Mark Dybul (an appallingly vigorous defender of the abstinence emphasis in PEPFAR), put it in late 2007, "We can't treat our way out of this epidemic." As National Public Radio's Susan Dentzer summarized Dybul's growing awareness, in view of the 8 million people around the world "already in need of anti-retroviral treatment, the world may prove unwilling to foot the bill to put all who need them on the drugs. That's a key reason why preventing even more cases is so critical."[112]

Senators and representatives in the U.S. Congress have been proposing bills that, if passed, would reverse the worst damages done by the Christian Right's anticondom crusade. Among the most important is Representative Barbara Lee's (D-Calif.) bipartisan-sponsored PATHWAY initiative of March 2007, HR 1713—the other sponsor is Representative Chris Shays (R-Conn.)—which, if passed, would remove the 33 percent earmark for abstinence funding in President Bush's PEPFAR program and also force PEPFAR to specify more clearly how it will work to reduce the particular vulnerabilities of girls and women to HIV infection in the most impoverished nations.[113] There is also some hope of further bipartisan support for removing the 33 percent abstinence funding earmark; former Senator Bill Frist (R-Tenn.), who is very active in a variety of bipartisan "health diplomacy" projects, in December 2007 stated publicly that he thought the abstinence earmark was wrong.[114]

Most recently, when the late Representative Tom Lantos (D-Calif.) wrote the draft for the reauthorization of PEPFAR in early 2008, he removed the abstinence earmark and also the requirement that recipients of PEPFAR funds sign the antiprostitution pledge. Representative Chris Smith of New Jersey, as well as the conservative evangelical groups Family Research Council and Focus on the Family, have fought back and lobbied for the restoration of the abstinence earmark, as well as for excising any mention of gay men in the bill.[115] The future is open, but the terms of conversation remain restricted.

There are other ways to organize sexual politics. Europeans, for instance, start from the premise that individual sexual self-determination is the most precious moral value requiring energetic defense. And there are signs as well that Americans are beginning to lose patience with the narrow sexual agenda of the Religious Right.

Chapter 6

IN PURSUIT OF HAPPINESS

THE RELIGIOUS RIGHT is a capacious tent in which many agendas and approaches have found a home. There are conservative evangelicals who promise worldly prosperity and success (if only you trust enough in God's plans).[1] There are others who gird themselves for Armageddon.[2] There are the vehement defenders of "Merry Christmas" and school prayer and the enemies of evolution and intellectualism and "liberal elitism."[3] There are highly intellectual (and themselves elite) members of the Religious Right.[4] There are those who see the culture clash with neofundamentalist Islam as the current big threat, and those who work to justify the ongoing war in Iraq as a properly Christian cause.[5] There are those who raise money for and organize tourism in Israel not least in the expectation that at the End of Days a majority of Jews will convert to Christ.[6] But right-wing evangelicalism achieved power in American politics primarily through its sex activism. And in fifteen years of steady effort, it managed to undo the most important achievements of the sexual revolution of the 1960s and 1970s.

This was accomplished, however paradoxically, through a selective appropriation and adaptation of key aspects of that old sexual revolution. A core component has been speaking in graphic detail both about sexual discontent and dysfunction and about the possibilities for ecstatically orgasmic and emotionally fulfilling bliss. Without the promise of pleasure, the Religious Right would not have found nearly as many adherents as it has; repression alone is not sufficiently appealing.

Evangelical sexual conservatives took up some of the main concerns of the feminist women's movement of the 1970s and 1980s. An interest in intensifying women's sexual pleasure has been a central focus of evangelical sex advice from the start. Many women's frustration at male fascination with pornography and emotional nonpresence during sex—another feminist theme—and the need to help men get comfortable with physical and emotional mutuality have also been taken up.[7] So too have the classic women's movement themes of concern about domestic violence, child sexual abuse, and sexual exploitation of women been addressed. More recently, evangelicals have moved to adapt both feminist and mainstream advice about body image, in addition to generating a vast Christian dieting and addiction recovery industry.[8] There is also an anti-authoritarian evangelical youth counterculture.[9]

In its activism around issues of sexuality, the Religious Right has found ways as well to incorporate the insights of the new age men's movement into its own program to transform an insecure, Internet-ogling bumbler into a virile he-man who is competent at both male-male friendship and rivalry and hot heterosexual romance.[10] The movement has been wildly successful in part because of its extraordinary ability to present its own program as therapeutic. None of this, however, should distract from the fact that right-wing evangelicals have also been sadistic and punitive, eager to play to the most base human desires to feel superior to others who fail to live up to the expected norms.

While the roots of the Religious Right lie in antiblack racism (a history that has now been largely overcome but still goes woefully underacknowledged), it got its start in American national politics by organizing against abortion and homosexuality.[11] In the wake of the legalization of abortion in *Roe v. Wade* in 1973, and in response to the growing public visibility of gays and lesbians in the 1970s and 1980s and their demands for an end to discrimination, evangelical conservatives could count on these two issues, along with more general calls for restrictions on sex education and the restoration of "traditional family values," as their major fund-raising and mobilizing tools.[12] All through the 1990s, playing to homophobic reflexes was one of the Christian Right's most popular tactics. But nothing has been more successful in the early twenty-first century than its ability to hijack the national conversation about heterosexuality.

Initially, telling the heterosexual majority what to do was not even on the agenda. In the first half of the 1990s, the antiabortion cause had been running into some difficulties. Americans had grown wary. They were beginning to harbor doubts about some of the movement's more extreme tactics—like shooting doctors.[13] Polls revealed that Americans of both genders remained able—by a slim but stubborn majority—to identify emotionally with the situation of women who sought to end their unwanted pregnancies. At the time, consensual heterosexual sex still seemed to most Americans like a pretty basic all-American right, and the assault on abortion felt like it could grow into an assault on whatever else anyone might want to do with their lives and bodies as well.

Since the turn of the millennium, right-wing evangelicals have become emboldened in new ways. A big boost came through the election in 2000 of George W. Bush, the first conservative evangelical Republican president.[14] Putting individuals sympathetic to the Religious Right agenda into key positions in the federal government and pouring federal funds into projects developed by Christian conservatives inevitably transformed the power dynamics.[15] Yet just as important were the advent of Viagra and the explosive growth of Internet porn—and the ensuing anxiety about the relationships between desire, performance, satisfaction, and intimacy.[16]

In all of its culture war campaigns, the Religious Right was most effective where it was able to formulate its arguments in secular terms. Christian conservatives certainly used pseudo-scientific arguments about physical health in their battles for sexual conservatism.[17] But nothing has been as useful as the adaptation of the language of psychological health, particularly the endlessly inventive invocation of the ideal of self-esteem.

None of us can block out entirely the many injunctions to accept ourselves but also improve ourselves, no matter how contradictory these goals are. The incessant talk about sex and self-esteem hooks into much wider therapeutic aspects of our culture: like a pendulum that constantly swings from telling us to make peace with ourselves and our situations as they are, in all their imperfect ordinariness, to telling us that we really must do battle with ourselves and our situations, that self-improvement is essential, and that greater happiness is always just around the corner. The Religious Right has managed to redirect much of the national conversation about sex—with lasting consequences that go way beyond biannual national election rituals—not least because it merged so thoroughly with the popular culture it claims to combat and despise.

Moreover, the refurbished focus on psychological damage in sexually conservative arguments manages to lend to the current state of the conversation a sense that it is both pro-woman and pro-equality—even when it is neither.

The abstinence campaigns are the most obvious example of the psychologizing strategy. Whether religious or secular in orientation, websites and books that plead for premarital chastity invariably contend that delaying the onset of sexual intercourse is a sign of heightened self-respect. Over and over, young people are told that self-restraint is self-empowerment. Scholastic or athletic achievement is presented as mutually exclusive with sexual activity; the prospects for a strong and happy future marriage are said to be in inverse relationship to premarital experience. Secular conservatives also use the language of self-esteem to make their case for a return to restraint.

The success of the Religious Right is most evident in the way many self-defined sexual liberals now rush to concede that a delay in sexual debut is desirable and that keeping the number of sexual partners in a lifetime to a minimum is an important sign of psychological health and self-valuing. Experience is no longer seen as a resource. Even those who advocate for comprehensive sex education feel the need to insist that "abstinence is a laudable goal" (Deborah Arindell of the American Social Health Association, an STD awareness group, in 2006), or that all they are asking for is "abstinence-plus" education (as in Representatives Barbara Lee and Christopher Shays and Senator Frank Lautenberg's bipartisan Responsible Education About Life [REAL] Act, introduced in March 2007), or that abstinence is what they have been advocating all along but, alas, one must be realistic and include information about condoms and contraceptives (as in the arguments of the coordinator of sex education in the Baltimore school system interviewed on NPR in October 2007).[18]

Even more momentous is the way the language of psychology has infused the discussion of abortion. Although the anti-abortion movement had seemed stalled in the 1990s, it has returned in new forms and found new adherents across party lines. It has also succeeded in putting in place numerous restrictions at the state level to limit women's, especially young women's, access to abortion. One-third of all women between the ages of fifteen and forty-five now live in counties in which abortions are not available; one-quarter of women must travel fifty miles to obtain an abortion, and in some parts of the United States the trip is hundreds of miles. Yet one in every two pregnancies in the United States is unplanned, and one in three American women will have an abortion in her lifetime; a significant percentage of these are women over age twenty-five who are already mothers.[19] In few areas of sexual politics is there so wide a gap between the lived experience of ordinary people and what can be discussed in the public domain.

In 2007, in *Gonzales v. Carhart*, the Supreme Court upheld the Partial Birth Abortion Act, passed by the U.S. Congress in 2003. This act criminalized certain methods of abortion that are used in fewer than 1 percent of all abortions performed (0.17 percent, for instance, in the year 2000)—and then only in order to preserve the health of the woman.[20] But doctors now have good reason to fear that all second-trimester abortions could be interpreted as criminal.[21] The language of the majority opinion authored by Justice Anthony Kennedy has even more significant implications for that vast majority of abortions that take place in the first trimester. The decision is likely to serve as the basis for state legislators' efforts to introduce information into mandatory pre-abortion counseling sessions about the potential psychological damage having an abortion could supposedly do to a woman.[22] The decision marks a key moment in the efforts of the Religious Right to portray restrictions on abortion not as limiting women's fundamental right to control their reproductive capacities but rather as somehow beneficial to women. As Wanda Franz, president of the National Right to Life Committee, likes to say: "We think of ourselves as very pro-woman. We believe that when you help the woman, you help the baby."[23]

Gonzales v. Carhart is the first Supreme Court ruling to reverse the decriminalization of abortion guaranteed since *Roe v. Wade*. As Representative Jerrold Nadler of New York observed in the wake of the decision:

> The Supreme Court has declared open season on women's lives and on the right of women to control their own bodies, their health and their destinies. Overturning a decision only a few years old, the Court has, for the first time since *Roe v. Wade*, allowed an abortion procedure to be criminalized. What has changed since the Court last considered nearly identical legislation? The facts haven't changed. The widely held opinion in the medical profession that this ban would endanger women hasn't changed. The Constitution hasn't changed. Only one thing has changed: Justice O'Connor retired and President Bush and a Republican Senate replaced her with a reliably anti-choice vote on the Supreme Court. It is clear today that the far-right's campaign to pack the Supreme Court has succeeded and that women and their families will be the losers.[24]

Justice Kennedy had himself in the past been a supporter of women's right to choose. In this new decision, however, his word choices were especially telling:

> Respect for human life finds an ultimate expression in the bond of love the mother has for her child. The Act recognizes this

reality as well. Whether to have an abortion requires a difficult and painful moral decision. . . . While we find no reliable data to measure the phenomenon, it seems unexceptionable to conclude some women come to regret their choice to abort the infant life they once created and sustained. . . . Severe depression and loss of esteem can follow.[25]

Despite the admission that there were "no reliable data," and despite the concession that negative emotional consequences for the woman were not inevitable but rather "can" follow, the ideas of diminished female self-esteem and the prospect of post-abortion depression have, in this precedent-setting case, been elevated into judicial concepts.

Justice Kennedy's words were largely based on a friend-of-the-court brief filed by the Justice Foundation, a conservative nonprofit litigation firm. The Justice Foundation brief included statements from 180 women who declared that their abortions had caused them feelings of despair and lasting regret. A typical statement was from Tina Brock of Nicholson, Georgia:

Little did I know when I made that choice to abort my baby 21 years ago that it would affect the rest of my life. Supposing to be [sic] a legal, simple procedure, my abortion sent me down a long road of severe depression. People need to know abortion hurts women![26]

For several years, abortion opponents have been floating this idea that abortion is psychologically damaging. The office of Representative Henry Waxman (D-Calif.) conducted a survey of "crisis pregnancy centers" in which callers posing as seventeen-year-old pregnant girls encountered a range of fraudulent information, including the false advice that abortion raises the risk of breast cancer, negatively affects future fertility, and causes severe psychological distress. Waxman's report noted that "significant psychological stress after an abortion is no more common than after birth." But at one center a caller was told that in the year after an abortion the suicide rate "goes up by seven times," while another center informed a caller that post-abortion stress was "much like" that seen in Vietnam veterans and "is something that anyone who's had an abortion is sure to suffer from."[27]

Anti-abortion activism has profoundly reshaped the national conversation and also deeply affected supporters of legal abortion. Despite the gap between lived reality and rhetoric, and while a (slim) majority of Americans still support the retention of *Roe v. Wade*, a majority also within that pro-choice group now call for more restrictions on access to abortion, especially for teens. For many, abortion is only understandable in dire circumstances; to more and more people, the mere desire to terminate an unwanted pregnancy does not sound like an acceptable reason to seek an abortion.[28]

Anti-abortion activists worked long and hard to present abortion, not as a last-resort method of fertility control when other forms of contraception have failed or have not been used, but rather as a horrific form of murder. It has become clear in the last several years that the aim is not just to stop abortion. If that were the aim, then anti-abortion activists would do much better if they vigorously promoted contraceptives, handed out sex toys, and recommended a variety of imaginative noncoital "outercourse" practices that produce glorious sensations but do not result in pregnancies. Instead, the aim is to infuse with shame all sexual expression and experience outside of heterosexual marriage. Neither of these campaigns would be nearly as effective if they were presented solely in religious terms.

THE DISCUSSIONS OVER SEX in Europe start from entirely different premises. No politician or public health official in Europe would ever seriously debate whether condoms are an effective means to prevent the spread of HIV/AIDS infection. German billboards frankly proclaim, THE ONLY PEOPLE WHO ARE PERVERTED ARE THE ONES WHO DON'T USE CONDOMS.[29] Nor is there a public outcry in European countries over the suitability of public HIV/AIDS awareness campaigns for safe sex that mix humor and explicitness or that take nonmarital heterosexual or homosexual activity as a given. A billboard in German train stations shows a brightly colored, bouncing condom that asks: HAVING AN AFFAIR? TAKE ME WITH YOU![30] An Italian billboard features a working-class senior citizen who uses condoms and has had 8,127 ASCERTAINED ENCOUNTERS and not one STD.[31] The French may be slightly more discreet, opting for the slogan: PARIS PROTECTS LOVE. But posters at bus stops across Paris consist of photos of traffic signals where the green lights are condoms.[32] In 2005 center-right (and Catholic) French president Jacques Chirac proposed that a condom vending machine be placed in every French high school.[33]

There was no great public debate when the Netherlands, Germany, and Switzerland legalized prostitution. The aim was to provide prostitutes with access to police protection and to reduce their vulnerability to pimps and sex traffickers; in addition, the understanding was that consensual adult behavior should in any event not fall under the purview of the law. Austria and, more recently, Hungary and Slovenia have decriminalized prostitution for similar reasons.[34]

Nor was there extensive controversy when, in recent years, first-trimester abortions were decriminalized in Portugal and made more widely available in France and Switzerland.[35] Throughout western Europe, and despite the Catholic Church's opposition, access to abortion is taken by popular majorities as a non-negotiable aspect of half the human race's right to manage its reproductive potential when contraceptives fail. When, in 2007, the Archbishop of Canterbury expressed concern that abortions in England were too easily available, his critics responded that the prevalence of abortions was a signal that British women were taking motherhood more seriously than in the past and were more carefully choosing when to have their children.[36] Meanwhile, abortion rates among teens in particular are notably lower in European countries than they are in the United States. This is coupled with higher rates of contraceptive use.[37]

The European Union recognizes same-sex unions across national boundaries and has made official rejection of homophobia a key marker of the suitability of candidates for European Union offices and of nations for European Union accession.[38] The mayors of both Paris and Berlin are openly gay, but their gayness is unremarkable and politically irrelevant.[39] Spain has recently joined Belgium and the Netherlands in legalizing not just same-sex unions but same-sex marriage.[40] The Italian government recently ran an anti-homophobia billboard campaign.[41] And perhaps most importantly, the European Court of Human Rights takes as foundational the view that guaranteeing a citizen's ability freely to determine his or her own intimate relations is an intrinsic component of a democratic society.[42] A scholar summarizes the court's stance this way: "Both the right to desired sexuality and the right to freedom from undesired sexuality must be safeguarded. Only then is human dignity in regard to sexuality fully and completely respected."[43] Sexual violence, coercion, abuse, exploitation, and harassment are not illegal because they are immoral, but because they are violations of another human being's rights to sexual self-determination.[44]

Adolescent sex education campaigns take both one-night stands and deeply romantic love affairs as perfectly reasonable activities for youth, and adolescents from the age of sixteen on are assumed to have the right to sexual expression free from adult interference. The aim of sex education is to facilitate negotiation skills over practices and to emphasize the importance of consent. "Only when both want it" is a key slogan.[45]

Europeans typically view teen sexual exploration and experimentation as a natural and healthful stage of human development.[46] French, German, and Italian popular magazines directed at teenagers routinely offer explicit discussions of the pleasures of petting and caressing as well as reports on what intercourse feels like the first time.[47] Government-sponsored ad campaigns go out of their way to promote condom use for adolescents.[48] Teens can get free condoms, medical care, and advice at youth clinics, all without parental consent.[49] In Europe, youths' rights to confidentiality are considered as important as those of adults.

Europe and the United States still have comparable rates of teen sexual activity, but it is the American teenage girl who currently has a higher likelihood of pregnancy. Although teen birthrates have finally dropped somewhat in the last several years, they have declined much less steeply since the 1970s in the United States than they did in western Europe.[50] The U.S. teen pregnancy rate (84 out of every 1,000 girls) is more than three times higher than Sweden (25), Denmark (23), and Finland (21), and more than four times higher than Germany (16) or the Netherlands (12).[51]

American teens not only have more abortions than European teens. American teenagers also have a higher rate of sexually transmitted diseases than their European counterparts. The rate of HIV infection among American teenagers is higher than it is among European teens: "Approximately 50 young people a day, an average of two young people every hour, are infected with HIV in the United States."[52] The United States continues to have the highest level of teen pregnancies in the industrialized world, and of the 19 million cases of STIs annually in the United States, almost half afflict young people between the ages of fifteen and twenty-four.

As *New York Times* columnist Nicholas Kristof has written:

> While teenagers in the U.S. have about as much sexual activity as teenagers in Canada or Europe, American girls are four times as likely as German girls to become pregnant, almost five times as likely as French girls to have a baby, and more than seven times as likely as Dutch girls to have an abortion. Young Americans are five times as likely to have HIV as young Germans, and teenagers' gonorrhea rate is 70 times higher in the U.S. than in the Netherlands or France.[53]

The prevailing American view that premarital sex and "risk" are intrinsically linked is inaccurate. As one Swiss-authored essay in the *Journal of Adolescent Health* reported in 2006: "In many European countries—Switzerland in particular—sexual intercourse, at least from the age of 15 or 16 years, is considered acceptable and even part of normative adolescent behavior." Switzerland has one of the lowest rates globally of abortion and teen pregnancy.[54] Like most other European nations, Switzerland offers comprehensive sex education, unimpeded access to contraceptives, and confidential health care. As another Swiss commentator put it, "The main difference is that in the States sexual activity is considered a risk. Here we consider it a pleasure."[55] The Canadian government, like most European governments, takes the view that sexual intercourse is typical for teens and officially informs parents not to be alarmed but rather to talk frankly with youth about consent, contraceptives, and disease prevention as well as body image and emotions.[56]

It would be fair to conclude that European teenagers are more comfortable with sex and their own sexuality than their American counterparts. They are not educated to experience the guilt, shame, anxiety, and taboo-breaking melodrama that Americans—teens and adults—tend to bring to their sexual encounters. The United States also has the highest rate of sexual coercion in the industrialized world.[57]

Survey after survey shows that despite early serial experimentation, love and faithfulness in Europe definitely remain "in." A recent study shows that U.S. teenagers on average actually have more partners than either European or Canadian teenagers.[58] Europeans have exhibited no decline in their ability to handle romance or maintain enduring passion and love with one other special person. At the same time, they do openly accept that long-time partnership is not an ideal for everyone; there is also widespread recognition that, over the course of a lifetime, individuals might seek to move between monogamy and nonmonogamy.[59]

European sexual cultures are far from perfect. The rise of Islam within Europe has particularly challenged Europeans to defend their own more liberal sexual values without reaching for racism in response, and in this they have frequently failed; from Britain to France to Sweden, the Netherlands, Germany, and Austria, hostility to Islam has been expressed specifically in arguments over issues relating to sexuality.[60] In the Netherlands and in several of the German states, it has been the conservative and Christian Democratic politicians who have proposed that foreign nationals from predominantly Muslim countries who apply for Dutch or German citizenship should not only be required to demonstrate their knowledge of Dutch or German history and laws but also affirm their comfort with both homosexuality and female sexual independence.[61]

Still, the conversations in Europe begin from the conviction that autonomy and self-determination in sexual expression and in the formation and maintenance of intimate relationships are themselves key measures of a good and just society, no matter if the subject is adolescent sexuality or marriage, same-sex unions or reproductive choice, prostitution or disease prevention. Europeans also believe that the personal is private, and sex-related matters simply do not determine elections as they have done in the United States in recent years.

THERE ARE SIGNS NOW that grassroots resistance to the Religious Right's sexual program has been mounting across the United States—and that the resistance is getting more confident as well as creative. In cities and towns across the nation, there have been growing numbers of parents fighting back against the abstinence education movement and demanding comprehensive education. At Shamrock Middle School in DeKalb County, Georgia, parent protest succeeded in getting the abstinence curriculum "Choosing the Best" (which receives millions in federal funds and relies on fear- and shame-based messages as well as conveying, as one critic put it, "misinformation, and biased views of marriage and sexual orientation") shelved. Parents argued that the curriculum was bringing religion into the schools and demanded that administrators explain why the curriculum "was accepted without first reviewing its scientific accuracy." In a high school in Sarasota, Florida, after conservatives tried to ban Planned Parenthood from the schools on the grounds that its programs included information on condoms and contraceptives, the school decided to run dual sections of its life management skills class to satisfy both sets of parents, one based on abstinence and one on comprehensive sex education. In Lansing, New York, parents complained that a "pregnancy center" program allowed into the public schools had a "moralizing tone" and used dirty sneakers "to symbolize lost virginity." The parents also pointed out that "the program's emphasis on marriage made children of non-traditional families uncomfortable." The school board voted to remove the programs.[62]

At the state level, there are also promising attempts by governors and legislatures to preempt the worst effects of the "conscience clause" laws that allowed pharmacists to refuse to fill prescriptions for emergency contraception (or any contraception). As of 2006, California, Illinois, Maine, Massachusetts, and Nevada all required pharmacists to fill all legal prescriptions.[63] In November 2007, a New Jersey law went into effect that prohibits pharmacists from refusing to fill prescriptions "solely on moral, religious or ethical grounds."[64] Comparable bills that require pharmacists to dispense birth control may also be passed in Missouri, West Virginia, and Wisconsin.[65] Related to this trend are the pharmacy board decisions in 2006 in Illinois and Massachusetts that obligated the major pharmacy chain Wal-Mart to provide emergency contraception (EC) in the wake of the FDA's 2006 approval of the over-the-counter marketing of EC to women age eighteen and older.[66]

In 2004 there were only three states (Pennsylvania, California, and Maine) that refused federal funding for sex education in the schools owing to the federal requirement that the schools teach abstinence. By the end of 2007, eleven more states had announced their refusal of federal funds for sex education. One of these was New York, which in 2006 had received more abstinence funding from the federal government than any other state besides Texas and Florida. Governor after governor, invoking the federal government's own commissioned 2007 study finding that abstinence programming had essentially the same outcomes as comprehensive programming in terms of both sexual debut and rates of unwanted pregnancy and disease, made the simple argument that abstinence education was not working. Some governors asserted that they would offer comprehensive education because that was what was best for the youth in their state. As a spokesperson for the Sexuality Information and Education Council of the United States said, "This wave of states rejecting the money is a bellwether. . . . It's a canary in the coal mine of what's to come." And as another comprehensive sex ed advocate observed: "I think this could be the straw that breaks the camel's back in terms of continued funding of these programs. . . . How can they ignore so many states slapping a return-to-sender label on this funding?"[67]

The success of the American Civil Liberties Union and a broad array of gay and lesbian rights organizations in making the case for same-sex partners to marry is also encouraging. Although civil unions remain an inadequate substitute for the right to marry, it is excellent news that the intensity of the debate about same-sex marriage and the quality of the arguments put forward in its defense have made the American public more comfortable with the compromise solution of civil unions and thereby have made politicians more comfortable endorsing this solution as well. Already in 2004 a majority of Americans approved of civil unions; the numbers have risen since then.[68] Although an unconscionable amount of pain is still being inflicted at the local level in seemingly never-ending controversies over whether and how homosexuality may be discussed in sex education classrooms, all polls suggest that the balance of opinion is tipping against homophobia, not just toward tolerance but even toward an openly affirmative comfort with diversity of sexual orientation.

The most promising shift across the United States may be the younger generation's growing comfort with contraceptive use. Although the United States still has the highest teen pregnancy rate in the developed world, the rate has recently gone down. A mere 14 percent of the decline in the teen pregnancy rate can be attributed to increased abstinence among teens, and that increased abstinence is largely to be found in the fifteen- to seventeen-year-old category; fully 86 percent of the decline is due to increased use of contraception, especially among the seventeen- to nineteen-year-old set.[69] Even though a distressingly high proportion (32 percent) of American teens have absorbed the false information put out by sexual conservatives that condoms do not protect against HIV, condom use among sexually active adolescents has gone up.[70] In 2005, 63 percent of sexually active high school youth reported using a condom during their most recent sex, an impressive increase over the 46 percent who reported doing so in 1991.[71] Nonetheless, there are still 20 percent of sexually experienced female teens in the United States who use no method of pregnancy prevention at all, compared to 33 percent who use the birth control pill; these are shocking statistics when compared with female teens in France (59 percent on the pill versus 12 percent using no method at all) and Germany (73 percent on the pill versus 1 percent using no protection).[72]

Two recent events, the removal of subsidies for contraceptive pills at college campus health care centers (which also brought to light the news that 39 percent of college women rely on oral contraceptives) and the unplanned pregnancy of Britney Spears's sixteen-year-old sister, have brought the voices of articulate young college and high school women onto the pages of major news outlets, unabashedly expressing their commitment to contraceptive use. They have also created a larger space for both peer and familial conversations about the issue.[73] As of 2007, the mainstream media still quote abstinence advocates in counterpoint to advocates of comprehensive education, but the two sides are no longer treated as equally valid. The main effect of the reporting has increasingly been to expose the enormity of the gulf between how Americans actually live their daily lives and the intimidating histrionics of the Religious Right.

Despite these signs of progress, much remains to be recovered in the wake of our new sexual revolution. At present, Americans still experience a hypersexualization of our culture paradoxically coexisting with decreasing comfort with our own bodies and relationships. As former president of Planned Parenthood Faye Wattleton once observed with regard to this American cultural schizophrenia around sex:

> We're basically an illiterate society sexually. We're not well educated. We're not much better educated than our parents, and even though sex is merchandised and exploited, there is very little sexuality education available in American schools. It is almost as though we had to repay our guilt for exploiting sex so explicitly in our society by preserving a shroud of ignorance.[74]

Above all, Religious Right rhetoric and activism have devastated the foundational moral concepts of self-determination and consent. These should be the cornerstones of all ethical and legal reflection with respect to sexuality. Not sexual orientation, not marital status, not the number of partners, not the practices one prefers to engage in: none of these should be the basis for debates over sexual morality and sex-related law. Among the many precious values that have been lost in the new sexual revolution—including an appreciation for human diversity; a determination to protect the rights of minorities; an understanding of pleasure and happiness as in themselves moral goods; a respect for the privacy of others; and a sense of curiosity rather than threat in the face of the intricacies of sex and love—the greatest loss comes from the confusion over self-determination and consent. These values are eroded every time someone treats prostitution and sexual slavery as indistinguishable, treats homosexuality and child abuse as morally comparable, lumps together promiscuity with sexual coercion, or refuses to include discussion of how to ask for and recognize consent and how to negotiate practices in sex education and anti-date-rape programming.

What remains missing from the general mix is a defense of sexual rights that does not privilege those who match the norm over those who do not, that does not lie about the complexities of human desire, that does not need to pretend that sex is perfect every time (if only you follow the rules and/or buy this product), and that does not root sexual rights only in the negative imperative to reject sexual victimization but also affirms humans' rights to sexual expression, sexual pleasure, and the freely chosen formation of intimate relationships. What's missing is the basic idea that sexual rights are human rights—for adolescents, for sexual minorities, and for individuals both within and outside the institution of marriage.

ACKNOWLEDGMENTS

THIS BOOK IS THE PRODUCT of collective effort. I am immensely grateful for the collaborative brainstorming energies directed my way. Will Lippincott, agent extraordinaire, and Lara Heimert, spectacular editor, were there from the start, offering their energy and thoughtful critical acuity every moment I needed them. They were pushing me always to think harder about what has been going on in this country over the last decade and a half, and about how to explain that especially to people who know they have been feeling uncomfortable yet can't quite find the right words to express the sense that something is wrong—but also how to make clear that, as one of my (as it happens conservative Republican and Catholic) midwestern students put it, "things do not need to be the way they are."

One of my most important albeit diffuse debts is to the remarkable number of strangers who, in taxis or trains or planes, at street corners or in building corridors, in weight rooms or grocery stores, at banks or in doctor's offices, having randomly, politely, learned what I was working on, felt moved to share with me intense episodes from their lives as well as their thoughts and feelings (including anger, confusion, and frustration) about God, about romance and sex, and about parenting and politics. I feel honored, humbled, thankful, for the trust that was placed in me.

I would like to thank as well my colleagues for making me feel so welcome in New York, especially Beth Baron, John Patrick Diggins, Joshua Freeman, Mary Gibson, David Nasaw, Marta Petrusewicz, and Helena Rosenblatt. Most of all, I thank William Kelly for being the phenomenal person that he is and for doing so much to make work one of my favorite places to be.

Other individuals have also stepped in, some early on, some at the last minute. I want to express my appreciation especially to Elizabeth Stein for her superior textual reorganization skills and to Marc Epprecht, James Putzel, Tim Allen, Justin Parkhurst, and Mardge Cohen for sharing their expertise on Africa. Andre Levie and Mel White helped me find key sources. Jessica Hammerman, Antonia Levy, Karin Schützeichel, Ben Tyner, and Francesca Vassalle provided indispensable research assistance and insight.

Friendship truly is its own kind of amazing grace, and it was friends who kept my sanity and optimism in good repair. The Bilsky-Rollins, Hart-Soga, and Kucich-Sadoff households provided nurturing extensions of home as well as general hilarity and perspective. Michael Geyer, Anson Rabinbach, and Omer Bartov, mentors in the history of religion, European history, and Holocaust studies, were not at all convinced that it was a good idea for me to take time off from the study of twentieth-century Germany to write about America at the turn of the millennium; their ongoing support is appreciated all the more. David Halperin, Danny Goldhagen, Till van Rahden, Jim Henle, Madeleine Amberger, and Paul Betts helped me make good decisions at critical junctures. Joan Wallach Scott, Brendan Hart, and John Barnhill generously worked through a late draft of the manuscript, offered numerous essential suggestions, and did their level best to try to save me from myself.

A handful of cherished individuals have anchored me on the other side of the Atlantic, given me shelter, and shown me good times in Berlin, Bern, Hamburg, Paris, and Zurich. Pascal Strupler and Cornelia Theler patiently explained the intricacies of European politics to me. Caroline Arni, Jan Feddersen, Gunter Schmidt, and Todd Shepard are part of this book in more ways than they can know. All read early versions of chapters and gave me helpful criticisms and good counsel. But more than that, their brilliance and passion infuse how I look at the world. My life would be much impoverished without them.

Kristin Herzog has throughout been an incredible source of inspiration and support—often precisely when she was most skeptical. No one has done more to model for me what it means to live a life of faith.

Finally, those who have done the heaviest lifting are also those whose existence makes me feel the most blessed. To Michael, Lucy, Brendan, Anne, and Kevin: thank you from the bottom of my heart for proving that love is indeed what makes a family. Above all, Michael Staub's wisdom and strength have made everything possible. I cannot thank him enough.

NOTES

Chapter 1: Anxiety Nation

1. Candies shoes has run an ad campaign replete with this tagline and T-shirts. See "Sex Sells: Marketing and 'Age Compression,'" CBCNews, January 9, 2005, available at: www.cbc.ca/consumers/market/files/money/sexy/marketing.html.

2. Dani Veracity, "The Great Direct-to-Consumer Prescription Drug Advertising Con: How Patients and Doctors Alike Are Easily Influenced to Demand Dangerous Drugs," NaturalNews.com, July 31, 2005, available at: www.newstarget.com/010315.html.

3. Bruce Handy, "The Viagra Craze," *Time*, May 4, 1998, p. 50. Serious research and anecdotal accounts alike offer conflicting evidence on whether Viagra intensifies orgasms: some men using Viagra can maintain erections and ejaculate but don't have much of an orgasm, while others actually have prolonged and painful erections that can themselves provoke impotence. Strikingly, even in Pfizer's earliest research trials, while Viagra helped anywhere from 60 to 80 percent of trial subjects, the placebo "helped" 24 percent.

4. American Urological Association Executive Committee, "AUA Policy Statement, January 1990," *AUA Today* (May 1993): 8.

5. Meika Loe, *The Rise of Viagra: How the Little Blue Pill Changed Sex in America* (New York: New York University Press, 2004), p. 32; Leonore Tiefer, "The Viagra Phenomenon," *Sexualities* 9, no. 3 (2006): 285–86.

6. Handy, "The Viagra Craze."

7. David Schnarch, *Resurrecting Sex: Solving Sexual Problems and Revolutionizing Your Relationship* (New York: HarperCollins, 2002), pp. 184–98.

8. D. Udelson et al., "Engineering Analysis of Penile Hemodynamic and Structural-Dynamic Relationships," *International Journal of Impotence Research* 10 (1998): 89. See also D. Udelson et al., "Axial Penile Buckling Forces vs. Rigiscan TM Radial Rigidity as a Function of Intracavernosal Pressure," *International Journal of Impotence Research* 11 (2000): 327; I. Goldstein et al., "Axial Penile Rigidity as Primary Efficacy Outcome During Multi-institutional In-office Dose Titration Clinical Trials with Alprostadil Alfadex in Patients with Erectile Dysfunction," *International Journal of Impotence Research* 12 (2000): 205.

9. Jack Hitt, "The Second Sexual Revolution," *New York Times Magazine*, February 20, 2000, p. 36.

10. Joe Kita, "The Sex Crusaders," *Men's Health*, November 2001, p. 102; Dr. Hilda Hutcherson, quoted in Noelle Howey and Gayle Forman, "Can Your Doctor Improve Your Sex Life?" *Glamour*, July 2004, p. 95; Gail Saltz, "The Sex Files," *O*, November 2006, p. 235.

11. Zachary Veilleux, "Synchronized Schwinging," *Men's Health*, December 2001, pp. 98, 100.

12. Dr. Ridwan Shabsigh, quoted in Erica Jong, "Women Demand Pleasure, So Men Invent Stiff Pill," *New York Observer*, May 4, 1998.

13. Douglas Martin, "Thanks a Bunch, Viagra; The Pill That Revived Sex, or At Least Talking About It," *New York Times*, May 3, 1998.

14. N. R. Kleinfeld, "In the Vortex of 'Viagra Madness': Long Days for Urologist as Men Clamor for Prescriptions," *New York Times*, May 6, 1998.

15. Ibid.

16. Loe, *The Rise of Viagra*, p. 14; Adam Harcourt-Webster, "Viagra: The Hard Sell," BBC News, February 5, 2005, available at: news.bbc.co.uk/1/hi/business/4222045.stm.

17. Viagra ad, *Men's Health*, December 2001, p. 99.

18. Martin, "Thanks a Bunch, Viagra."

19. Hitt, "The Second Sexual Revolution," p. 62.

20. Sanjay Gupta, "Move Over, Viagra," *Time*, September 1, 2003.

21. Richard A. Friedman, "A Quest for Better Sex Meets 'Not Now, Dear,'" *New York Times*, August 22, 2006.

22. Jon Nordheimer, "Some Couples May Find Viagra a Home Wrecker," *New York Times*, May 10, 1998.

23. Leonore Tiefer, "The Medicalization of Women's Sexuality," *American Journal of Nursing* 100, no. 12 (December 2000): 11.

24. Loe, *The Rise of Viagra*, pp. 154–57.

25. Cerniplex ad, MedSpan Laboratories, available at: www. evitamins.com/product.asp?pid=5939; Jennifer Berman et al., "Female Sexual Dysfunction: Incidence, Pathophysiology, Evaluation, and Treatment Options," *Urology* 54 (1999): 385–91; Jennifer Berman and Laura Berman, *For Women Only: A Revolutionary Guide to Overcoming Sexual Dysfunction and Reclaiming Your Sex Life* (New York: Henry Holt, 2005), p. 70.

26. UroMetrics promotional material, distributed in 2000, reproduced in Loe, *The Rise of Viagra*, p. 142.

27. Edward O. Laumann, Anthony Paik, and Raymond C. Rosen, "Sexual Dysfunction in the United States: Prevalence and Predictors," *Journal of the American Medical Association* 281, no. 6 (February 10, 1999): 544.

28. Michael Seeber and Carin Gorrell, "The Science of Orgasm," *Psychology Today*, November–December 2001, p. 50; Moira Brennan, "The Opposite of Sex," *Ms.*, August–September 1999, available at: www. msmagazine.com/aug99/sex-oppositeofsex.asp. As of September 2002, there were 178 cites of these numbers in the medical and psychological literature; see John Bancroft et al., "Distress About Sex: A National Survey of Women in Heterosexual Relationships," *Archives of Sexual Behavior* 32, no. 3 (June 2003): 194.

29. John Leland, "The Science of Women and Sex," *Newsweek*, May 29, 2000. In an otherwise critical analysis of the *Newsweek* item, the *Village Voice* still insisted that "the truth is that 40 percent of American women experience some form of sexual dysfunction." Tristan Taormino, "The Female Hard-On," *Village Voice*, June 13, 2000. Also, see the 43 percent cited in the *New York Times Magazine* (Hitt, "The Second Sexual Revolution," p. 37) and quoted online: "While many women are sexually satisfied, up to 43 percent of women suffer difficulty reaching female orgasm" (www.achieving-female-orgasm.com).

30. Kita, "The Sex Crusaders," p. 99.

31. Mary Duenwald, "Effort to Make Sex Drug for Women Challenges Experts," *New York Times*, March 25, 2003.

32. Ruth G. Davis, "Is a Sexless Marriage in Your Future?" *Cosmopolitan*, December 2003, p. 144.

33. Schnarch, *Resurrecting Sex*; Michele Weiner-Davis, *The Sex-Starved Marriage: A Couple's Guide to Boosting Their Marriage Libido* (New York:

Simon & Schuster, 2003); Barry W. McCarthy and Emily J. McCarthy, *Rekindling Desire: A Step-by-Step Program to Help Low-Sex and No-Sex Marriages* (New York: Brunner-Routledge, 2003); Kathleen Cervenka, *In the Mood, Again* (Oakland, Calif.: New Harbinger, 2003).

34. Scott Omelianuk, "Not Tonight, Honey . . . Meet DINS, the Exhausting New Syndrome That's Making Couples—and, in Particular, Men—Too Tired to Have Sex," *Details*, June–July 2003, p. 115.

35. Ralph Gardner, "Generation Sexless," *New York*, January 13, 2003; Sean Elder, "Why My Wife Won't Sleep with Me," *New York*, April 15, 2004. See also Caitlin Flanagan, "The Wifely Duty," *Atlantic Monthly*, January–February 2003.

36. McCarthy and McCarthy, *Rekindling Desire*, p. 4. The McCarthys later assert that "40 to 60 million Americans" are in low-sex or no-sex marriages; ibid., p. 208.

37. Friedman, "A Quest for Better Sex Meets 'Not Now, Dear.'"

38. Dr. Phil McGraw, quoted in Sean Elder, "The Lock Box," in *The Bastard on the Couch: Twenty-seven Men Try Really Hard to Explain Their Feelings About Love, Loss, Fatherhood, and Freedom,* ed. Daniel Jones (New York: HarperCollins, 2004), p. 112.

39. Stephanie A. Sanders, John Bancroft, Cynthia A. Graham, and Jennifer Bass, "A Prospective Study of the Effects of Oral Contraception on Sexuality and Well-being and Their Relationship to Discontinuation," *Contraception* 64 (2001): 51–58; Hollis Kline, "Is the Pill Damaging Your Sex Life?" *Psychology Today*, November–December 2001; Howey and Forman, "Can Your Doctor Improve Your Sex Life?" p. 91; Alison Motluk, "Does the Pill Kill Your Sex Drive?" *O*, January 2006, p. 79.

40. See, for example, Camille Noe Pagán, "Not Tonight, Honey," *Women's Health*, November–December 2005, pp. 92–93; Neil Chethik, "Housework: The Link to Sex," in *VoiceMale: What Husbands Really Think About Their Marriages, Their Wives, Sex, Housework, and Commitment* (New York: Simon & Schuster, 2006), pp. 115–27.

41. Duenwald, "Effort to Make Sex Drug."

42. Cited in Omelianuk, "Not Tonight, Honey . . . ," p. 115.

43. Nicole Beland, "When His Sex Drive Takes a Nosedive," *Cosmopolitan*, February 2003, p. 124.

44. Lucy O'Brien, "Sense of a Woman," *Details*, March 1996, p. 84.

45. Omelianuk, "Not Tonight, Honey . . . ," p. 115.

46. Joan Sewell, *I'd Rather Eat Chocolate: Learning to Love My Low Libido* (New York: Broadway, 2007). See also the responses in Dan Savage, "Savage Love," AV Club, March 21, 2007, available at: www.avclub.com/content/savage/mar-21–2007.

47. Martin Enserink, "Let's Talk About Sex—and Drugs," *Science*, June 10, 2005, p. 1578.

48. See "A Cream That Makes Sex Better?" *Glamour*, July 2004, p. 95; Katherine Hobson, "A Drug for Arousal: It's Not Just Men Who Want Some Help with Sexual Performance," *U.S. News and World Report*, January 24, 2005; Tara Parker-Pope, "Health Matters: For Women's Sexual Problems, Drug Treatments Get New Attention," *Wall Street Journal*, August 21, 2006.

49. Heather Hartley, "The 'Pinking' of Viagra Culture: Drug Industry Efforts to Create and Repackage Sex Drugs for Women," *Sexualities* 9, no. 3 (2006): 363–78.

50. See the comments of Laura Berman and Hilda Hutcherson, quoted in Howey and Forman, "Can Your Doctor Improve Your Sex Life?" p. 92; see also Enserink, "Let's Talk," p. 1578.

51. Already in 2000 Goldstein introduced his own wife at a forum on "Desire, Arousal, and Testosterone" so that she could testify to the blessings of male hormones on her own body. Addressing the audience, Sue Goldstein spoke glowingly of her experiences with the natural steroid hormone dehydroepiandrosterone (DHEA): "It's really an amazing product—DHEA. I have been taking it for two months and it has taken away my night sweats and I feel twenty again. I am fifty and there are no side effects. This is the future of the field"; Sue Goldstein, quoted in Loe, *The Rise of Viagra*, p. 150.

52. Gail Saltz, "Bring Back That Lovin' Feeling," *Good Housekeeping*, March 2006, pp. 124–26.

53. Kara Jesella, "O, Yes!" *Health*, November 2006, p. 117.

54. See "Introducing Intrinsa," About Intrinsa, available at: www.aboutintrinsa.com.

55. Cerniplex ad, MedSpan Laboratories (see note 25).

56. Betsy Querna, "Low Libido," *U.S. News and World Report*, July 6, 2005.

57. Lauren Wiener, "How's Your Sex Life?" *Shape*, January 2007, p. 32.

58. Jenna McCarthy, "Sixteen Secrets to Exciting Sex," *Self*, May 2005, p. 225.

59. Laura Berman, quoted in Ellise Pierce, "Twenty-four Things Love and Sex Experts Are Dying to Tell You," *Redbook*, June 2006, p. 102.

60. Shana Aborn, "Love the One You're With," *Family Circle*, June 2006, p. 91.

61. On the importance of challenging the perceived dichotomy between what's real and what's invented, see Ian Hacking, *Mad Travelers: Reflections on the Reality of Transient Mental Illness* (Charlottesville: University of Virginia Press, 1998), pp. 1–6; Emily Martin, *Bipolar Expeditions: Mania and Depression in American Culture* (Princeton, N.J.: Princeton University Press, 2007); Jonathan Metzl, *Prozac on the Couch: Prescribing Gender in the Era of Wonder Drugs* (Durham, N.C.: Duke University Press, 2003).

62. "How Normal Is Your Orgasm?" *Glamour*, July 2006, p. 101.

63. Jesella, "O, Yes!" pp. 116, 118, 172.

64. David Amsden, "Not Tonight, Honey. I'm Logging On," *New York*, October 20, 2003.

65. Adrian Turpin, "Not Tonight, Darling, I'm Online," *Financial Times*, April 1, 2006.

66. Dr. Judith Reisman, testimony before a hearing of the Senate Subcommittee on Science, Technology, and Space, November 18, 2004, available at: www.drjudithreisman.com/archives.testimony.doc.

67. Dr. Jeffrey Satinover, quoted in Ryan Singel, "Internet Porn: Worse Than Crack?" *Wired News*, November 19, 2004, available at: www.wired.com/news/technology/1,65772–0.html; and in Jan LaRue, "Senate Subcommittee Hears Experts on Pornography Toxicity," December 2, 2004, available at website of Dr. Judith Reisman, www.drjudithreisman.com/archives/2005/12/senate_subcommi.html.

68. According to Layden, pornography also encourages the following improper views: "An example of Pornography Distortion would include beliefs such as 'Sex is not about intimacy, procreation or marriage. Sex is about predatory self-gratification, casual recreation, body parts, violence, feces, strangers, children, animals and using women as entertainment.'" See Dr. Mary Ann Layden, testimony before a hearing of the Senate Subcommittee on Science, Technology, and Space, November 18, 2004, available at: www.commerce.senate.gov/hearings/testimony.cfm?id= 1343&wit_id=3912 (accessed April 5, 2006); and Dr. Mary Ann Layden testimony, quoted in Gudrun Schultz, "Large Increase in Porn DVD Sales

Indicates Growing Pornography Addiction" (January 26, 2006), available at www.drjudithreisman.com/archives/2006/01/large_increase.html.

69. Pamela Paul, *Pornified: How Pornography Is Transforming Our Lives, Our Relationships, and Our Families* (New York: Henry Holt, 2005), pp. 3, 8, 39, 158, 192, 233, 239, 265, 267.

70. Naomi Wolf, "The Porn Myth," *New York*, October 20, 2003.

71. See the classics by Linda Williams, *Hard Core: Power, Pleasure, and the "Frenzy of the Visible"* (Berkeley: University of California Press, 1989); Feminist Anti-Censorship Task Force, ed., *Caught Looking: Feminism, Pornography, and Censorship* (East Haven, Conn.: LongRiver, 1992).

72. Kim Cattrall and Mark Levinson, *Satisfaction: The Art of the Female Orgasm* (New York: Warner Books, 2002), p. 81.

73. Frank Rich, "Naked Capitalists," *New York Times Magazine*, May 20, 2001, p. 51.

74. John Leo, "Romantic Porn in the Boudoir," *Time*, March 30, 1987, p. 63.

75. Williams, *Hard Core*, p. 231.

76. Carin Rubenstein and Carrol Tavris, "Survey Results," *Redbook*, September 1987, p. 214.

77. This Internet Filter Review finding is cited in Leslie Joseph, "Pornophobic No More" (review of Ayn Carrillo-Gailey, *Pornology* [2007]), PopMatters, June 27, 2007, available at: www.popmatters.com/pm/books/reviews/43172/pornology-by-ayn-carrillo-gailey/; and Mike Genung, "Statistics and Information on Pornography in the USA," available at: BlazingGrace, www.blazinggrace.org/pornstatistics.htm.

78. "Porn in the U.S.A.," CBSNews.com, September 5, 2004; Jane Lampman, "Churches Confront an 'Elephant in the Pews,'" *Christian Science Monitor*, August 25, 2005.

79. See, for example, the remarks of Tom Hynes, a spokesman for the porn industry's trade group, the Free Speech Coalition, quoted in Michael Scherer, "Debbie Does Washington," *Salon*, November 11, 2005, available at: dir.salon.com/story/news/feature/2005/11/11/porn_hearing/index.html. See also Terry M. Neal, "GOP Corporate Donors Cash in on Smut," *Washington Post*, December 21, 2004.

80. Duncan Campbell, "Pot and Porn Net More Than Corn," *The Guardian*, May 2, 2003.

81. Dr. Ruth K. Westheimer, *Sex for Dummies* (New York: Hungry Minds, 1995), pp. 357, 365.

82. Ellen Rapp, "Twenty-five Facts About Orgasms," *New Woman*, January 1996, p. 78.

83. Louanne Cole Weston, quoted in Bel Henderson, "Psyched for Sex," *New Woman*, May 1998. Similar advice could be found in the *Boston Globe*: "Letting your gaze roam, which at first might seem disloyal and forbidden, can actually be harnessed to a couple's advantage"; Betsy A. Lehman, "Is There Sex After Marriage?" *Boston Globe*, June 21, 1993.

84. Wendy Maltz and Suzie Boss, "The Sexiest Way to Relieve Stress and Boost Self-Esteem," *New Woman*, May 1997, pp. 136–38.

85. Harriet Lerner, "I Can't Stop Fantasizing About Other Men," *New Woman*, May 1999.

86. Alan Feuer, "Think a Boat Is Safe from Spying? Think Again, Experts Say," *New York Times*, October 1, 2006; Peter Applebome, "In a High-Powered Suburb, Not Your Average Rocky Marriage," *New York Times*, October 1, 2006; Nancy Keates, "One Tough Day for Two-Timers," *Wall Street Journal*, February 10, 2006.

87. Liz Brady, "You Got Nailed!" *O*, September 2006.

88. M. Gary Neuman, *Emotional Infidelity: How to Avoid It and 10 Other Secrets to a Great Marriage* (New York: Crown, 2001), p. 1.

89. Gail Saltz, "Emotional Cheating," *O*, May 2006, pp. 85–86.

90. Lynn Harris, "Emotional Affairs," *Ladies' Home Journal*, September 3, 2003, available at: www.lhj.com/lhj/story.jhtml?storyid=/templatedata/lhj/story/data/EmotionalAffairs_08012003.xml.

91. Vaughan, quoted in ibid.

92. Dr. Phil McGraw, "Advice, Etc.," *O*, February 2006, p. 61.

93. Thomas V. Hicks and Harold Leitenberg, "Sexual Fantasies About One's Partner Versus Someone Else: Gender Differences in Incidence and Frequency," *Journal of Sex Research* 38, no. 1 (February 2001); Russell Wild, "Mind over Mattress," *Men's Health*, October 1995, p. 98; Harold Leitenberg and Kris Henning, "Sexual Fantasy," *Psychological Bulletin* 117, no. 3 (1995): 469–95; Eileen L. Zurbriggen and Megan R. Yost, "Power, Desire, and Pleasure in Sexual Fantasies," *Journal of Sex Research* 41, no. 3 (August 2004).

94. Gabriel Rotello, "The Enemy Within—Homophobia," *The Advocate*, March 4, 1997. The research was conducted by Dr. Henry Adams, professor of clinical psychology at the University of Georgia.

95. Tristan Taormino, "Wanted: Bi Guy," *Village Voice*, November 2–8, 2005, p. 122.

96. Judy Kuriansky, "What Constitutes Emotional Cheating?" *New York Daily News*, August 8, 2005.

97. Donna L. Franklin, quoted in "When Does Flirting Become Cheating?" *Jet*, April 9, 2001.

98. Carrie Pierce, "Emotional Cheating?" *Maroon Weekly* (Texas A&M), 2005, available at: www.maroonweekly.com/index.php?u=17&ID=471 (accessed September 6, 2006).

99. Shirley P. Glass with Jean Coppock Staeheli, *Not "Just Friends": Rebuilding Trust and Recovering Your Sanity After Infidelity* (New York: Free Press, 2003), p. 8.

Chapter 2: Soulgasm

1. Joshua Harris, *Sex Is Not the Problem (Lust Is): Sexual Purity in a Lust-Saturated World* (Sisters, Oreg.: Multnomah Publishers, 2003), p. 11.

2. Tim Alan Gardner, *Sacred Sex: A Spiritual Celebration of Oneness in Marriage* (Colorado Springs, Colo.: WaterBrook Press, 2002), p. 54. Gardner adds: "The extreme intensity of the orgasmic experience is due to the fact that it is had *with* our God-given mate" (p. 55).

3. Clifford Penner and Joyce Penner, *The Gift of Sex: A Guide to Sexual Fulfillment* (Nashville: W Publishing, 1981), p. 31.

4. Timothy LaHaye and Beverly LaHaye, *The Act of Marriage: The Beauty of Sexual Love* (Grand Rapids, Mich.: Zondervan, 1976), pp. 30–31, 59, 61, 71.

5. Stephen Arterburn and Fred Stoeker, *Every Man's Battle: Winning the War on Sexual Temptation One Victory at a Time* (Colorado Springs, Colo.: WaterBrook Press, 2000), pp. 67, 137.

6. Ibid., pp. 68, 134.

7. See John Leland, "Sex and the Faithful Soldier," *New York Times*, October 30, 2005.

8. Ibid.; see also Dan Harris, "Soldiers Pray to Abstain, and to Save Their Marriages," ABCNews, May 12, 2006, available at: abcnews.go.com/WNT/story?id=1954936; and New Life Ministries, "Every Soldier's Battle," available at: www.everysoldiersbattle.com.

9. Stephen Arterburn and Fred Stoeker, with Mike Yorkey, *Preparing Your Son for Every Man's Battle: Honest Conversations About Sexual Integrity* (Colorado Springs, Colo.: WaterBrook Press, 2003), p. 9.

10. Stephen Arterburn and Fred Stoeker, with Mike Yorkey, *Every Young Man's Battle: Strategies for Victory in the Real World of Sexual Temptation* (Colorado Springs, Colo.: WaterBrook Press, 2002), pp. 65, 120, 123–25, 164, 173–74.

11. Shannon Ethridge, *Every Woman's Battle: Discovering God's Plan for Sexual and Emotional Fulfillment* (Colorado Springs, Colo.: WaterBrook Press, 2003), pp. 20–21, 154–55.

12. See Walter Kern, "Saving It for Jesus," *GQ*, April 2006, pp. 154, 157; Arterburn and Stoeker, *Every Man's Battle*, pp. 9–10.

13. Arterburn and Stoeker, *Every Man's Battle*, pp. 14, 98.

14. Teen Mania is an evangelical organization that contends that to-day's young people are reeling from despair and hopelessness and that they form "a generation without morality." The organization urges the millions of teens it reaches to become passionate crusaders for Christ.

15. Ethridge, *Every Woman's Battle*, pp. 3–7, 184.

16. Pamela Paul, *Pornified: How Pornography Is Transforming Our Lives, Our Relationships, and Our Families* (New York: Henry Holt, 2005); "Poll: Christians 'Addicted to Pornography,'" The Raw Story, August 14, 2006, available at: www.rawstory.com/news/2006/Poll_Christians_addicted_to_pornography_0814.html.

17. Marsha Means, *Living with Your Husband's Secret Wars* (Grand Rapids, Mich.: Fleming H. Revell, 1999), pp. 11–13.

18. See Eileen Finan, "Real Men Talk About God: A New Christian Movement Lets Guys Be Guys," *Newsweek*, October 30, 2006.

19. Arterburn and Stoeker, *Every Man's Battle*, pp. 25, 54, 58, 69, 89, 165, 191.

20. Stephen Arterburn and Fred Stoeker, with Mike Yorkey, *Every Heart Restored: A Wife's Guide to Healing in the Wake of a Husband's Sexual Sin* (Colorado Springs, Colo.: WaterBrook Press, 2004); Stephen Arterburn, *Addicted to "Love": Understanding Dependencies of the Heart: Romance, Relationships, and Sex* (Ann Arbor, Mich.: Vine Books, 1995); Arterburn and Stoeker, *Every Young Man's Battle.*

21. See Arterburn and Stoeker, *Preparing Your Son*, p. ix; Arterburn and Stoeker, *Every Young Man's Battle*, p. 105.

22. Linda Dillow and Lorraine Pintus, *Intimate Issues: Conversations Woman to Woman* (Colorado Springs, Colo.: WaterBrook Press, 1999), pp. 189–90.

23. Ibid., pp. 192–93.

24. Ibid., p. 197.

25. Ibid., pp. 207, 210, 216.

26. Ibid., p. 196.

27. Gardner, *Sacred Sex*, p. 52.

28. Dillow and Pintus, *Intimate Issues*, p. 247.

29. Louis McBurney and Melissa McBurney, "Christian Sex Rules," *Christianity Today*, Spring 2001, available at: www.christianitytoday.com/mp/2001/001/4.34.html.

30. Dillow and Pintus, *Intimate Issues*, p. 207.

31. Ibid., p. 209.

32. LaHaye and LaHaye, *The Act of Marriage*, p. 78.

33. Joseph C. Dillow, *Solomon on Sex* (Nashville: Thomas Nelson, 1982).

34. Joseph C. Dillow, quoted in Karin Brown, *The Power of Intimate Love: Experiencing Sexual Fulfillment in Marriage* (Tulsa: Harrison House, 2000), pp. 115–16.

35. Penner and Penner, *The Gift of Sex*, p. 212; Tommy Nelson, *The Book of Romance: What Solomon Says About Love, Sex, and Intimacy* (Nashville: Thomas Nelson, 1998), p. 99.

36. Brown, *The Power of Intimate Love*, p. 12.

37. Joe Beam, *Becoming One: Emotionally, Spiritually, Sexually* (West Monroe, La.: Howard Books, 1999), pp. 147, 152.

38. Gardner, *Sacred Sex*, p. 45.

39. Brown, *The Power of Intimate Love*, p. 118.

40. Ibid., pp. 126–27.

41. Dillow and Pintus, *Intimate Issues*, p. 204.

42. McBurney and McBurney, "Christian Sex Rules."

43. Brown, *The Power of Intimate Love*, p. 127.

44. Cited in Barbara Ehrenreich et al., *Re-Making Love: The Feminization of Sex* (New York: Anchor Books, 1986), pp. 148–49.

45. See Paul Byerly and Lori Byerly, "What's OK? What's Not?," The Marriage Bed, available at: www.themarriagebed.com/pages/sexuality/splay/whatisokay/shtml. The Byerlys' ministry is also discussed in JoAnn Wypijewski, "The Way of All Flesh," *Mother Jones*, July–August 2006, pp. 22–25.

46. Gardner, *Sacred Sex*, p. 148.

47. Dillow and Pintus, *Intimate Issues*, pp. 207, 214.

48. Ethridge, *Every Woman's Battle*, p. 50.

49. Stephen Arterburn, Fred Stoeker, and Mike Yorkey, *Every Man's Marriage: An Every Man's Guide to Winning the Heart of a Woman* (Colorado Springs, Colo.: WaterBrook Press, 2001).

50. Ethridge, *Every Woman's Battle*, p. 154.

51. Gary Rosberg and Barbara Rosberg, *Divorce-Proof Your Marriage: Six Secrets to a Forever Marriage* (Wheaton, Ill.: Tyndale House, 2003), p. 241.

52. Neil T. Anderson and Charles Mylander, *The Christ-Centered Marriage: Discovering and Enjoying Your Freedom in Christ Together* (Ventura, Calif.: Regal Books, 1996), p. 178.

53. Tim LaHaye, quoted in Mark Oppenheimer, "In the Biblical Sense," *Slate*, November 29, 1999.

54. James Dobson, *What Wives Wish Their Husbands Knew About Women* (Wheaton, Ill.: Tyndale House, 1975), p. 118.

55. See Ann Coulter, *Godless: The Church of Liberalism* (New York: Crown, 2006), pp. 14 and 283, n. 12; and Coulter on C-SPAN's *Booknotes* discussing *Godless* at the Clare Booth Luce Policy Institute, August 6, 2006.

56. Paul Coughlin, *No More Christian Nice Guy: Why Being Nice—Instead of Good—Hurts Men, Women, and Children* (Bloomington, Minn.: Bethany House, 2006), pp. 107–8, 115.

57. See Finan, "Real Men."

58. Rosberg and Rosberg, *Divorce-Proof Your Marriage*, pp. 141, 241.

59. Ethridge, *Every Woman's Battle*, pp. 26, 33.

60. Wypijewski, "The Way of All Flesh," p. 23.

61. Arterburn and Stoeker, *Every Man's Battle*, pp. 59, 108, 125, 136, 138, 153.

62. Ibid., p. 120.

63. Ibid., p. 79.

64. Ibid., p. 78.

65. This is truly an obsession for Arterburn. *Every Man's Challenge* also praises the wife who initiates sex "regularly" to help the husband "stay pure" (even as the book also takes the harsh view that "fantasizing over some buxom actress from *Baywatch* reruns is adultery," and *Every Heart Restored* has Fred's wife Brenda revealing that she makes herself available to Fred even when she knows she's not going to orgasm). Stephen Arterburn and Fred Stoeker, with Mike Yorkey, *Every Man's Challenge: How Far Are*

You Willing to Go for God? (Colorado Springs, Colo.: WaterBrook Press, 2004), pp. 102, 134; Arterburn and Stoeker, *Every Heart Restored*, p. 246.

66. James Dobson, *Straight Talk to Men and Their Wives* (Waco, Tex.: Word Books Publisher, 1980), pp. 114–15.

67. Beam, *Becoming One*, p. 155.

68. Arterburn and Stoeker, *Every Man's Battle*, p. 70.

69. Robert Bly, quoted in John Eldredge, *Wild at Heart: Discovering the Secret of a Man's Soul* (Nashville: Thomas Nelson, 1998), p. 8; see also p. 7, front flap.

70. Ibid., pp. 12, 175, back cover.

71. Arterburn and Stoeker, *Every Man's Battle*, p. 153.

72. Ibid., p. 155.

Chapter 3: Trial and Error

1. Peter Applebome, "Religious Right Intensifies Campaign for Bush," *New York Times*, October 31, 1992.

2. J. Warren Tompkins, quoted in Jeffrey Schmaltz, "Gay Politics Goes Mainstream," *New York Times Magazine*, October 11, 1992.

3. George Chauncey, *Why Marriage? The History Shaping Today's Debate over Gay Equality* (New York: Basic Books, 2004), p. 151.

4. Schmaltz, "Gay Politics Goes Mainstream."

5. Chauncey, *Why Marriage?* p. 150.

6. "Job Rights for Homosexuals Backed in Poll" (Reuters), *New York Times*, September 7, 1992.

7. Schmaltz, "Gay Politics Goes Mainstream." On the complexities of the sodomy laws, see Janet Halley, "Misreading Sodomy: A Critique of the Classification of 'Homosexuals' in Federal Equal Protection Law," in *Body/Guards: The Cultural Politics of Gender Ambiguity*, ed. Julia Epstein and Kristina Straub (New York: Routledge, 1991); Gay and Lesbian Alliance Against Defamation (GLAAD), "Supreme Court Sodomy Law Challenge: News Coverage Archive," available at: www.digitalalliance.org publications/archive_detail.php?id=3342&PHPSESSID=ac5517104a2ca5b 8f7178828a7bf9e90; and George Chauncey, "'What Gay Studies Taught the Court': The Historians' Amicus Brief in *Lawrence v. Texas*," *GLQ: A Journal of Lesbian and Gay Studies* 10, no. 3 (2004).

8. Schmaltz, "Gay Politics Goes Mainstream."

9. Molly Ivins, quoted in Philip A. Klinkner, "The Base Camp of Christendom," *The Nation*, March 11, 2002.

10. See Jeffrey Schmaltz, "Gay Rights and AIDS Emerging as Divisive Issues in Campaign," *New York Times*, August 20, 1992.

11. Timothy Egan, "Oregon Measure Asks State to Repress Homosexuality," *New York Times*, August 16, 1992.

12. Lon Mabon, quoted in Schmaltz, "Gay Politics Goes Mainstream."

13. Dirk Johnson, "Colorado Homosexuals Feel Betrayed," *New York Times*, November 8, 1992.

14. Urvashi Vaid, quoted in Schmaltz, "Gay Rights and AIDS." See also the remarks of Barney Frank (D-Mass.) several years later: "The right wing has seized on homosexuality because they think it's the last politically acceptable prejudice"; quoted in Susan Schindehette, "Straight Up," *People* 50, no. 20 (1998): 117–18.

15. See David Brock, *Blinded by the Right: The Conscience of an Ex-Conservative* (New York: Three Rivers, 2002), pp. 146–48; Peter Applebome, "Gay Issue Mobilizes Conservatives Against Clinton," *New York Times*, February 1, 1993; Robert Dreyfuss, "The Holy War on Gays," *Rolling Stone*, March 18, 1999. Dreyfuss notes that "the Republican takeover of Congress in 1994 was credited to the power of the Christian right, and many of the freshmen elected to Congress that year reinforced a loosely organized 'God squad' on issues like homosexuality, abortion and school prayer."

16. The account that follows of the Glen Eyrie conference is drawn from several sources, including Mel White, *Religion Gone Bad: The Hidden Dangers of the Christian Right* (New York: Tarcher, 2006), pp. 123–66; Skipp Porteous, "Glen Eyrie: The Organized Assault on Gay Rights," *Freedom Writer* (Institute for First Amendment Studies), August 1994, available at: http://www.publiceye.org/ifas/fw/9408/gleneyrie.html; Mike Shaver Citizens Project, "About the 'Colorado-for-Family-Values' Cult: Behind Closed Doors," *Freedom Watch* 3, no. 4 (July–August 1994), available at: http://www.holysmoke.org/hs00/cdoors.htm.

17. On Eldredge's life, see "The Dick Staub Interview: John Eldredge Is Wild at Heart," *Christianity Today*, November 1, 2003, available at: www.christianitytoday.com/ct/2003/novemberweb-only/11–10–21.0.html.

18. See Chris Hedges, *American Fascists: The Christian Right and the War on America* (New York: Free Press, 2006), pp. 22–26.

19. Robert Skolrood and John Eldredge, quoted in Mike Shaver Citizens Project, "About the 'Colorado-for-Family-Values' Cult: Behind Closed Doors."

20. Quoted in Mike Shaver, "Conference Speakers Bare Hidden Anti-Gay Agenda," *Freedom Writer* (Institute for First Amendment Studies), August 1994, available at: www.skepticfiles.org/fw/agenda.htm.

21. Presentation by Frank York, employee of Focus on the Family, tape 3 of the 1994 Glen Eyrie conference transcripts. I am deeply grateful to Mel White for sharing his copies of the transcripts of the Glen Eyrie tapes with me.

22. Robert Skolrood, quoted in Porteous, "Glen Eyrie"; and Shaver, "Conference Speakers"; Ron Ray, quoted in Shaver, "Conference Speakers."

23. Judith Reisman, quoted in Porteous, "Glen Eyrie."

24. John Eldredge, quoted in Mike Shaver Citizens Project, "About the 'Colorado-for-Family-Values' Cult."

25. John Eldredge, tape 1 of the 1994 Glen Eyrie transcripts.

26. John Eldredge, quoted in Mike Shaver Citizens Project, "About the 'Colorado-for-Family-Values' Cult"; and in Porteous, "Glen Eyrie."

27. This participant was distressed that conservative Christians did not own more media of their own, but also proposed that secular conservatives could prove helpful if properly prepped. "Even our friends like Rush Limbaugh aren't educated. We must educate them." Unnamed participant in the 1994 conference, tape 5 of the 1994 Glen Eyrie transcripts.

28. John Eldredge presentation, tape 1 of the 1994 Glen Eyrie transcripts.

29. Phil Burress, quoted in Dreyfuss, "The Holy War on Gays."

30. American Family Association Online, "General Information," available at: www.afa.net/about.asp.

31. Southern Poverty Law Center, "A Mighty Army," *Intelligence Report*, Spring 2005, available at: www.splcenter.org/intel/intelreport/article.jsp?pid=869.

32. Donald Wildmon, quoted in Robin Meyers, *Why the Christian Right Is Wrong: A Minister's Manifesto for Taking Back Your Faith, Your Flag, Your Future* (San Francisco: John Wiley and Sons, 2006), p. 95.

33. Trent Lott, quoted in Alison Mitchell, "Lott Says Homosexuality Is a Sin and Compares It to Alcoholism," *New York Times*, June 16, 1998.

34. Robert Wasinger, quoted in Jeff Sharlet, "God's Senator," *Rolling Stone*, January 25, 2006.

35. Robert Knight, quoted in Dreyfuss, "The Holy War on Gays."

36. Lou Sheldon, quoted in Julia Duin, "Gays' Critics Accused of 'Hate Speech': Killing's Backlash Brings Suppression," *Washington Times*, October 27, 1998.

37. Pat Robertson, *The 700 Club*, broadcasts of January 21, 1993, and January 18, 1995, quoted in People for the American Way, "Anti-Gay Politics and the Religious Right: Gays as Enemies of Faith," available at: www.pfaw.org/pfaw/general/default.aspx?oid=2046; Robertson on bombs and hurricanes, quoted in "America, Please Pray for Us," *Newsweek*, June 22, 1998.

38. See the website of Westboro Baptist Church, www.godhatesfags .com.

39. Beth Loffreda, *Losing Matt Shepard: Life and Politics in the Aftermath of Anti-Gay Murder* (New York: Columbia University Press, 2000), p. 92.

40. On Love in Action, see Tanya Erzen, *Straight to Jesus: Sexual and Christian Conversions in the Ex-Gay Movement* (Berkeley: University of California Press, 2006), p. 27. On Love Won Out, see Jyl Josephson, presentation at "The Religious Right's Obsession with Gay Sex," Princeton University, March 28, 2006; and the website of Love Won Out, www.lovewonout.com.

41. Erwin Lutzer, *The Truth About Same-Sex Marriage: Six Things You Need to Know About What's Really at Stake* (Chicago: Moody Publishers, 2004), pp. 9, 15, 41.

42. Hedges, *American Fascists*, p. 82.

43. David Van Biema et al., "Evangelicals in America," *Time*, February 7, 2005; Michael Crowley, "James Dobson," *Slate*, November 12, 2004.

44. James Dobson, *Bringing Up Boys: Practical Advice and Encouragement for Those Shaping the Next Generation of Men* (Wheaton, Ill.: Tyndale House, 2001), pp. 5–6, 113–15.

45. Ibid., p. 124.

46. The connections between abuse and homosexuality are theorized in a variety of ways. For example, see antigay activist Erwin Lutzer's speculation: "A boy recruited by an older homosexual may initially hate the experience, but because sex binds two people together, he may begin to feel a sense of security and fulfillment within this relationship. Soon he seeks out other partners, not because he was born a homosexual, but be-

cause his initial experiences were so stamped upon his soul that he now follows the lead of his newly awakened desires"; Lutzer, *The Truth About Same-Sex Marriage*, pp. 53–54. Another version is offered by evangelical ex-lesbian Melissa Fryrear: "For those who have been abused by a male, oftentimes that tremendous rage, that hurt, can go underground, if you will, and it can begin to emerge later in life, perhaps in rejecting your female identity or the fact that you look like a woman"; quoted in Hedges, *American Fascists*, p. 104.

47. Andrew Comiskey, *Strength in Weakness: Overcoming Sexual and Relational Brokenness* (Downers Grove, Ill.: InterVarsity Press, 2003), pp. 147–48.

48. Bob Davies and Lori Rentzel, *Coming Out of Homosexuality: New Freedom for Men and Women* (Downers Grove, Ill.: InterVarsity Press, 1993), pp. 26, 95–96, 123.

49. See Justin Chin, "Saved," *The Progressive*, December 1995; Wayne R. Besen, *Anything but Straight: Unmasking the Scandals and Lies Behind the Ex-Gay Myth* (Binghamton, N.Y.: Hayworth Press, 2003).

50. David A. Matheson, quoted in Michael Luo, "Reining in Desires Proves Complex, at Best: Some Tormented by Homosexuality Find Hope in Controversial Therapy," *New York Times*, February 12, 2007.

51. Mark Benjamin, "The 'Ex-Gay' Agenda," *Gay and Lesbian Review*, November–December 2005, p. 30.

52. Ibid., p. 28.

53. John Leland and Mark Miller, "Can Gays 'Convert'?" *Newsweek*, August 17, 1998. See also Margaret Carlson, "Praying Away the Gay," *Time*, July 27, 1998.

54. Erzen, *Straight to Jesus*, p. 185.

55. Among the many reports on this incident, see especially Joel Lawson, "Ex-Gay Leader Confronted in Gay Bar," *Southern Voice*, September 21, 2000.

56. Erzen, *Straight to Jesus*, pp. 213–14.

57. Dobson, *Bringing Up Boys*, p. 117.

58. Bob Davies, quoted in "Exodus Forgives John Paulk," *The Advocate*, May 8, 2001, p. 20.

59. Chin, "Saved," p. 35.

60. Leland and Miller, "Can Gays 'Convert'?"

61. Luo, "Reining in Desires."

62. Debra W. Haffner, "1992 Report Card on the States: Sexual Rights in America," and "Sample Incidents," both in *SIECUS Report* 20, no. 3 (February–March 1992).

63. "Silencing Voices: Waging War on LGBTQ Topics and Individuals in Schools," *SIECUS Report* 33, no. 4 (Fall 2005).

64. Benjamin, "The 'Ex-Gay' Agenda," p. 26; PFOX, "Parent Group Asks State to Halt Montgomery County's New Sex Ed Program" (press release), February 7, 2007, available at: pfox.org/blog/index.php?itemid=4.

65. More recently, PFOX has also argued that to be ex-gay is an expression of "self-determination." According to a 2007 PFOX press release, "Ex-gays and Americans who support the right to self-determination of same-sex attraction are routinely ridiculed by the very people who claim to be victims themselves. 'Gay activists lobby to be included in tolerance policies, hate crimes and employment non-discrimination legislation, but work hard to deny ex-gays the right to the same treatment,' said Regina Griggs, executive director of PFOX. 'This demonstrates how far the gay rights movement has moved from self-described victims to proactive perpetrators.'" In addition, Griggs has argued—again turning traditional antihomophobic rhetorical strategies against themselves—that "ex-gays should not have to be closeted for fear of others' negative reactions or disapproval. . . . They do not think something is wrong with them because they chose to fulfill their heterosexual potential. We need to ensure the safety, inclusion, and respect of former homosexuals in all realms of society, but especially by the medical and mental health communities starting at the highest levels"; see PFOX, "National Ex-Gay Group Defends Surgeon General Nominee: Holsinger and Ex-Gay Community Attacked by Gay Groups," June 11, 2007, available at: www.pfox.org/press.htm.

66. Richard Cohen, quoted in Benjamin, "The 'Ex-Gay' Agenda," p. 26.

67. Daniel de Vise, "Board of Education Approves New Sex-Ed Curriculum," *Washington Post*, January 10, 2007; PFOX, "Parent Group Asks State."

68. National Gay and Lesbian Task Force, "Youth in the Crosshairs: The Third Wave of Ex-Gay Activism," March 2, 2006, available at: www.thetaskforce.org/node/819.

69. See Jason Cianciotto, "State of the Union: Sea Change?" National Gay and Lesbian Task Force, January 24, 2007, available at: www.ouramericanvalues.org/press_release_article.php?id=37.

70. American Values, "Questions and Answers About Homosexual 'Marriage,'" July 23, 2004, available at: www.ouramericanvalues.org/press_release_article.php?id=37.

71. Tony Perkins, "All You Need Is Love?" *Washington Update*, Americans for Truth About Homosexuality, December 8, 2006, available at: americansfortruth.com/news/tony-perkins-all-you-need-is-love.html.

72. Tony Perkins, quoted in MediaMatters for America, "Perkins Claimed That 'Homosexual Men Are More Likely to Abuse Children Than Straight Men'; Experts Disagree," October 4, 2006, available at: mediamatters.org/items/printable/200610040014.

73. See the interview with Jennifer Terry, "Gay Brains?" *Gay Community News* 19, no. 14 (October 20–26, 1991) and 19, no. 15 (October 27–November 2, 1991); Natalie Angier, "Study of Sex Orientation Doesn't Neatly Fit Mold," *New York Times*, July 18, 1993; Neil McKenna, "From Limp Wrist to Long Finger," *New Statesman*, April 10, 2000; Nicholas D. Kristof, "Gay at Birth?" *New York Times*, October 25, 2003; "Underarm Odor May Send Very Specific Signals to Potential Mates," *Medical News Today*, May 10, 2005; Rebecca Young, "Hardwired Homos and Female Brains: Unpacking Narrative and Scientific Connections in the Biology of Gender and Sexuality," paper delivered at the Graduate Center, City University of New York, March 1, 2007; see also the sources collected in "'Gay Gene' Critique Links," QueerByChoice, available at: www.queerbychoice.com/gaygenelinks.html. For the historical background to the current preoccupation with biologically determined sources of homosexual orientation, see also Jennifer Terry, *An American Obsession: Science, Medicine, and Homosexuality in Modern Society* (Chicago: University of Chicago Press, 1999). For the finger-length study, see Qazi Rahman et al., "Sexual Orientation and the Second to Fourth Finger Length Ratio: Evidence for the Organizing Effects of Sex Hormones on Developmental Instability?" *Psychoneuroendocrinology* 28 (2003): 288–303.

74. Lutzer, *The Truth*, p. 6. Or, in James Dobson's inimitable phrasing: "'What if' it could be demonstrated beyond a shadow of a doubt that homosexuality is, as activists claim, genetic, biochemical, and neurological in origin? We would still want to know, 'So what?' As you [a concerned father who wrote to Dobson] said, the homosexual activist community would have us believe that because their behavior is genetically programmed and beyond their control, it is morally defensible. That is not supportable." In fact, this is the comparison that occurs to Dobson: "'What if' a pedophile

(child abuser) could claim that he inherited his lust for kids? He could make a good case for it. Certainly his sexual apparatus and the testosterone that drives it are creations of genetics. Even if his perversion resulted from early experiences, he could accurately claim not to have chosen to be what he is. But 'so what'? Does that make his abuse of children any less offensive? Should society accept, protect, and grant special civil rights to pedophiles?"; Dobson, *Bringing Up Boys*, p. 128.

75. Richard G. Howe, "Homosexuality in America: Exposing the Myths," American Family Association, 1994, available at: www.afa.net/homosexual_agenda/homosexuality.pdf.

76. R. Albert Mohler, "Is Your Baby Gay? What If You Could Know? What If You Could Do Something About It?" posted on Mohler's website, March 2, 2007, discussed in "Homosexuality May Be Based on Biology, Baptist Says," *New York Times*, March 16, 2007.

77. Paul Volle, quoted in "Christian Coalition of Maine's Paul Volle," Matthew Shepard Online Resources, available at: www.hatecrime.org/subpages/hatespeech/cc.html.

78. Ronnie Koenig, "Your Most Private Sex Questions—Answered," *Cosmopolitan*, January 2006, p. 84.

79. Eliza Marston, "Thirty Things Every Woman Should Know About Sex by Age Thirty," *Glamour*, January 2007, p. 151.

80. Dan Savage, *Savage Love: Straight Answers from America's Most Popular Sex Columnist* (New York: Plume, 1998), p. 159.

81. Barbara Ehrenreich, Elizabeth Hess, and Gloria Jacobs, *Re-Making Love: The Feminization of Sex* (New York: Anchor Books, 1986), p. 97.

82. Trey Walker, quoted in Kevin Sack, "Gay Rights Movement Meets Big Business in South Carolina," *New York Times*, July 7, 1998. In 1996 the Greenville County Council had adopted a resolution declaring homosexuality "incompatible with community standards."

Chapter 4: Saved from Sex

1. Elizabeth Bernstein, "Sex-Ed Class Becomes Latest School Battleground," *Wall Street Journal*, March 30, 2006.

2. Janice M. Irvine, *Talk About Sex: The Battles over Sex Education in the United States* (Berkeley: University of California Press, 2004), pp. xv–xvi.

3. Marty Klein, *America's War on Sex: The Attack on Law, Lust, and Liberty* (Westport, Conn.: Praeger, 2006), pp. 6, 16. See also Barry Lynn, "Faith-Based Initiatives: Paying for Piety," in *Piety and Politics: The Right-Wing Assault on Religious Freedom* (New York: Harmony Books, 2006), pp. 117–47; *New York Times*, "Religious Earmarks," NYTimes.com, available at: www.nytimes.com/2007/05/12/us/20070513_LOBBY_GRAPHIC.html ?ex=1180324800&en=690ff494899f3f1e&ei=5070; Diana B. Henriques and Andrew Lehren, "Religious Groups Granted Millions for Pet Projects," *New York Times*, May 13, 2007. The Abstinence Clearinghouse provides on-line advice on how to access government funding for abstinence projects. (The clearinghouse itself landed a $2.7 million contract with the Department of Health and Human Services in 2002; see Russell Cobb, "Cracks in the Christian Ascendancy," *Slate*, June 27, 2006.) On how the organizations manage to avoid being charged with violating the constitutional guarantee of separation of church and state, see also Zoe Williams, "Just Say No to Abstinence," *The Guardian*, September 9, 2003. And for the recent attempts by the American Civil Liberties Union and sexual health–focused organizations to challenge in court the erosion of the boundary between church and state and the "evidence of injury" to public health demonstrated by the abstinence programs (as well as the difficulties encountered by these efforts), see Julie Sternberg, "Fighting Abstinence-Only-Until-Marriage Programs in the Courts," presentation at Columbia University, February 5, 2007.

4. See Arthur Caplan, "Abstinence-Only Sex Ed Defies Common Sense," MSNBC.com, October 13, 2005, available at: www.msnbc .msn.com/id/9504871/print/1/displaymode/1098/.

5. This is certainly my memory from growing up in the Bible Belt. But a 1994 survey of teens from thirteen evangelical denominations also confirms these points. See Terry Wier, with Mark Carruth, *Holy Sex: God's Purpose and Plan for Our Sexuality* (New Kensington, Penn.: Whitaker House, 1999), pp. 156–57. See also the summary of a 1987 study of "young, active church members at eight conservative Christian evangelical denominations in the Midwest and South. Of those surveyed, 43 percent had had intercourse by the age of 18, and an almost equal number had experimented with sexual behaviors that stopped short of intercourse while in their teens"; Kathleen McCoy, "It's 4 P.M.: Do You Know What Your Teens Are Doing?" *Family Circle*, May 14, 1991, p. 52.

6. Doug Herman, quoted in Jane Dunford, "Heard About the Latest Craze? Nope, It's Not Drugs or Alcopops—It's Born-Again Virgins: Abstinence Makes the Heart Grow Fonder," *The Mirror*, May 17, 2003, pp. 18–20.

7. Silver Ring Thing's founder, Denny Pattyn, quoted in Stephanie Rosenbloom, "A Ring That Says No, Not Yet," *New York Times*, December 8, 2005.

8. Republican New Jersey state senator Gerald Cardinale, quoted approvingly in Oliver North, "Animosity for Abstinence," Townhall.com, October 25, 2002, available at: www.townhall.com/columnists/OliverNorth/2002/10/25/animosity_for_abstinence.

9. James Dobson, *Bringing Up Boys: Practical Advice and Encouragement for Those Shaping the Next Generation of Men* (Wheaton, Ill.: Tyndale House, 2001), pp. 76–77.

10. See Silver Ring Thing, "SRT 434 Program," available at: srt .hostcentric.com/store/page2.html.

11. BarlowGirl, quoted in *The HCSB {Holman Christian Standard Bible} Student Bible* (Nashville: Holman Bible Publishers, 2007), p. 1583.

12. Linda Dillow and Lorraine Pintus, *Gift-Wrapped by God: Secret Answers to the Question "Why Wait?"* (Colorado Springs, Colo.: WaterBrook Press, 2004), p. 93.

13. Ibid., pp. 14, 26.

14. Joe Beam, *Becoming One: Emotionally, Spiritually, Sexually* (West Monroe, La.: Howard Publishing, 1999), p. 135.

15. Dunford, "Heard About the Latest Craze?" pp. 18–20; Motoko Rich, "A Writer's Search for the Sex in Abstinence," *New York Times*, October 14, 2007.

16. Tom Lickona, "Sex Is Awesome! (Unless You Are . . .)," adapted from Lickona, *Sex, Love, and You*, available at: www.lovematters.com/awesome.htm. LoveMatters.com is based in Redondo Beach, Calif.

17. Heather Jamison, *Reclaiming Intimacy: Overcoming the Consequences of Premarital Relationships* (Grand Rapids, Mich.: Kregel, 2001), pp. 100–101.

18. Ibid., pp. 33, 78–79; see also p. 83.

19. Dillow and Pintus, *Gift-Wrapped by God,* pp. 47–48.

20. Lisa Bevere, *Kissed the Girls and Made Them Cry: Why We Lose When We Give In* (Nashville: Thomas Nelson, 2002), p. 5.

21. Dunford, "Heard About the Latest Craze?"

22. Florida Department of Health, "It's Great to Wait: Secondary Virginity," available at: www.greattowait.com/secondary_virginity.html.

23. Leslee Unruh, quoted in Michelle Goldberg, *Kingdom Coming: The Rise of Christian Nationalism* (New York: Norton, 2006), p. 144.

24. Joe White, *Pure Excitement* (Colorado Springs, Colo.: Focus on the Family Publishing, 1996), pp. 20–21.

25. Ibid.

26. Ibid., pp. 8–10.

27. Campaign for Our Children, "Abstinence," available at: www.cfoc.org/teenguide/abstinence.

28. Dunford, "Heard About the Latest Craze?" pp. 18–20.

29. Leslee Unruh, quoted in Goldberg, *Kingdom Coming*, p. 144.

30. Dillow and Pintus, *Gift-Wrapped by God*, pp. 10–11, 45–46, 60–63.

31. Ken Abraham, *Don't Bite the Apple Till You Check for Worms* (Old Tappan, N.J.: Fleming H. Revell, 1985).

32. Michelle Ingrassia, "Virgin Cool," *Newsweek*, October 14, 1994.

33. See, for example, William Mattox, "The Next Hip Trend: Saving Sex for Marriage," *Washington Times* (national weekly edition), February 22–28, 1999. On the "Revolutionary Purity" project that was launched by True Love Waits in order to bring its message to an international audience, see True Love Waits, "LifeWay Student Ministry: True Love Waits," available at: www.lifeway.com/tlw.

34. Williams, "Just Say No to Abstinence."

35. See True Love Waits, "LifeWay Student Ministry" and "U.S. True Love Waits History," available at: www.truelovewaits.org.za/page_11.html.

36. Others include Julie Laipply, Rashida Jolley, and Tara Dawn Christensen.

37. Emily Weinstein, "Salvation Army" (review of *Believers* by Jeffrey L. Sheler and *Righteous* by Lauren Sandler), *Village Voice*, September 21, 2006.

38. See the website of Abstinence Clearinghouse Online Store, http://www.abstinence.net/store/00632.html.

39. See the website of WaitWear, www.waitwear.com/waitwear/faq.html.

40. See the website of Little Way Design, www.littlewaydesign.com/custom_page.cfm?category=1&page=36.

41. Dillow and Pintus, *Gift-Wrapped by God*, p. 26.

42. Lickona, "Sex Is Awesome! (Unless You Are . . .)."

43. See Lynn, *Piety and Politics*, pp. 187–88.

44. Lorraine Ali and Julie Scelfo, "Choosing Virginity," *Newsweek*, December 9, 2002.

45. Lakita Garth, quoted in "U.S. Celebration Caps Year of True Love Waits," *Lifeway*, July 1994, available at: www.lifeway.com/tlw/media/news_capsyear.asp.

46. Abstinence advocates summarized by Wendi Williams, "True Love Waits for Marriage; Most Still Don't," *College Press Service*, www.thedailycougar.com/static/vol61/950914/5a.html.

47. For one of many examples, see Ed Vitagliano, "Sex . . . To Whom Are Teens Listening?" *American Family Association Journal*, June 2003. Or see the sarcastic comment of Terry Wier, who compares safer sex campaigns with an imaginary ad campaign: "Practice safer Russian roulette. Never load the gun with more than one bullet"; Wier, *Holy Sex*, p. 138. Even more extreme, again, is the abstinence curriculum "Choosing the Best," which states that "there is a greater risk of a condom failure than the bullet being in the chamber"; see Goldberg, *Kingdom Coming*, p. 147.

48. Kaye Wellings, quoted in Simon Watney, *Policing Desire: Pornography, AIDS, and the Media*, 2nd ed. (Minneapolis: University of Minnesota Press, 1989), p. 127.

49. See, for example, the story told (with the opposite intent) in Ann Coulter, *Godless: The Church of Liberalism* (New York: Crown, 2006), pp. 12–14.

50. Gravity Teen, "Stack It Up!," available at: www.gravityteen.com/abstinence/stackit.cfm.

51. Raymond G. Bolin, "Safe Sex and the Facts," Probe Ministries, July 14, 2002, available at: www.leaderu.com/orgs/probe/docs/safesex.html. For a similar kind of alarmism, see Goldberg, *Kingdom Coming* (p. 147): "During her talk at Reclaiming America for Christ, [Pam] Stenzel announced, 'There is no way statistically that you can have sex with someone who is not a virgin and not get a disease.'"

52. Bolin, "Safe Sex and the Facts."

53. Peter Bearman and Hannah Brückner, "Promising the Future: Virginity Pledges and the Transition to First Intercourse," *American Journal of Sociology* 106, no. 4 (2001): 859–912; Hannah Brückner and Peter Bearman, "After the Promise: The STD Consequences of Adolescent Virginity Pledges," *Journal of Adolescent Health* 36, no. 4 (2005): 271–78.

54. Klein, *America's War on Sex*, p. 20.

55. Gravity Teen, "Virgin . . . Who Me?" available at: www.gravity teen.com/abstinence/virgin.cfm.

56. "True Love Waits Pledges Shown Highly Effective, Other Studies," Physicians for Life, http://www.physiciansforlife.org/content/view/160/56. Also see another Physicians for Life statement, which accuses Bearman and Brückner of "junk science": "Virginity Pledgers Engage in Less Sex and Have Less STDs (6/05)," http:www.physiciansforlife.org/content/view/734/2/.

57. "Forget Sex? Virginity Pledgers Lie About Past," MSNBC.com (Reuters), June 1, 2006, available at: www.msnbc.msn.com/id/13088669/print/1/displaymode/1098/; see also "I Used to Sleep Around, but Now I'm a Virgin," *Rolling Stone,* December 2006, p. 82.

58. Abstinence Clearinghouse, "Much Ado About Nothing: New Student 'Study' Shows Old Data on Virginity Pledges Needs a Rest from Scrutiny," May 2, 2006, available at: www.abstinence.net/library/index.php?entryid=2620.

59. David Baltimore, quoted in Michael Specter, "Political Science: The Bush Administration's War on the Laboratory," *The New Yorker,* March 13, 2006.

60. Reginald Finger, quoted in ibid.

61. Silver Ring Thing, "Teen STDs—Just the Facts," available at: www.silverringthing.com/statistics.asp.

62. Abstinence Clearinghouse, "Condoms Don't Protect the Heart," *News and Current Events: Advice,* the Care Center, www.teencarecenter.org/index.php?s=news&p+news01 (accessed December 20, 2006).

63. Abstinence Clearinghouse, "Abstinence Supporters Write Back: Sample Letter to Superintendents/School Administrators," October 5, 2005, available at: www.abstinence.net/blog/index.php?postid=85.

64. Guidelines quoted in Bernstein, "Sex-Ed Class."

65. John Diggs and Eric Keroack, quoted in Tild, "Keroack to Kids: Keep Your Tape Sticky," November 27, 2006, available at: tildology.com/category/eric-kerouack.

66. National Organization for Women, "Sack Keroack!," November 18, 2006, available at: www.now.org/lists/now-action-list/msg00272.html.

67. Lindsay Beyerstein and Larisa Alexandrovna, "Heckuva Job? Bush Administration Vaunted Bogus Credentials for Birth Control Czar, Records Show," *The Raw Story,* May 15, 2007.

68. Think Progress, "Bush Family Planning Appointee Called Contraceptives Part of the 'Culture of Death,'" October 17, 2007, available at: thinkprogress.org/2007/10/17/susan-orr.

69. Robin Toner, "Welfare Chief Is Hoping to Promote Marriage," *New York Times*, February 19, 2002.

70. See Brian Hartman, "Government Tells Singles No Sex Till You're Thirty," ABCNews.com, October 31, 2006, available at: abcnews .go.com/Health/print?id=2619061; Sharon Jayson, "Abstinence Message Goes Beyond Teens," *USA Today*, October 31, 2006; Associated Press, "Even Grandma Had Premarital Sex, Survey Finds," MSNBC.com, available at: www.msnbc.msn.com/id/16287113/ .

71. Cris Mayo, "Gagged and Bound: Sex Education, Secondary Virginity, and the Welfare Reform Act," *Philosophy of Education/PES Yearbook* (1998), available at: www.ed.uiuc.edu/eps/PES-Yearbook/1998/mayo .html.

72. See Randall Balmer, *Thy Kingdom Come—An Evangelical's Lament: How the Religious Right Distorts the Faith and Threatens America* (New York: Basic Books, 2006), pp. 8–17; Susan Friend Harding, "The Pro-Life Gospel," in *The Book of Jerry Falwell: Fundamentalist Language and Politics* (Princeton, N.J.: Princeton University Press, 2000).

73. Dillow and Pintus, *Gift-Wrapped by God*, pp. 10–11.

Chapter 5: Missionary Positions

1. U.S. Department of State, Bureau of Public Affairs, "The President's Emergency Plan for AIDS Relief: Five-Year Strategy," September 10, 2004.

2. "President Delivers 'State of the Union'" (press release), January 28, 2003, available at: www.whitehouse.gov/news/releases/2003/01/2003 0128-19.html.

3. See The United States President's Emergency Plan for AIDS Relief, "Country Profile: Uganda," available at: www.pepfar.gov/press/ 75891.htm.

4. U.S. Department of State, Bureau of Public Affairs, "The President's Emergency Plan for AIDS Relief: Five-Year Strategy."

5. See the discussion of the controversy by CNN correspondent Bill Schneider, CNN.com, April 29, 2003, available at transcripts.cnn.com/ TRANSCRIPTS/0304/29/se.06.html.

6. For excellent summaries of the crucial differences between prostitution and other kinds of consensual sex work, on the one hand, and coercive and exploitative sex trafficking, on the other, see Central and Eastern European Harm Reduction Network, *Sex Work, HIV/AIDS, and Human Rights in Central and Eastern Europe and Central Asia* (Lithuania: Ex Arte UAB, 2005); Kate Butcher, "Confusion Between Prostitution and Sex Trafficking," *The Lancet* 361 (June 7, 2003): 1983; Joanna Busza, Sarah Castle, and Aisse Diarra, "Trafficking and Health," *British Medical Journal* 328 (June 2004): 369–71; Amy Kazmin, "Deliver Them from Evil," *Financial Times*, July 10, 2004.

7. Statement of Rep. Chris Smith, April 2, 2003, reprinted in Republican Study Committee, "Background on the Prostitution/Sex Trafficking Provision in International HIV/AIDS Funding" (policy brief), September 2005.

8. The news was first leaked to the *Baltimore Sun*: "More HIV Funds to Promote Abstinence," *Baltimore Sun*, December 10, 2005. See also Annabel Kanabus and Rob Noble, "President's Emergency Plan for AIDS Relief (PEPFAR)," available at the website of the international AIDS charity Avert, www.avert.org/pepfar.htm.

9. Ozge Tuncalp, "U.S. Is Accused of Jeopardizing HIV Prevention in Uganda," *British Medical Journal* (October 1, 2005); Population Action International in Washington, D.C., confirmed that this restriction remained in place in 2007.

10. Prohibition on the Promotion or Advocacy of the Legalization or Practice of Prostitution or Sex Trafficking, June 9, 2005, quoted in *DKT International, Inc. v. United States Agency for International Development*, U.S. District Court for the District of Columbia, memorandum opinion by U.S. District Court Judge Emmet G. Sullivan, May 18, 2006, p. 5.

11. Richard Parker, "Administering the Epidemic: HIV/AIDS Policy, Models of Development, and International Health," in *Global Health Policy, Local Realities: The Fallacy of a Level Playing Field*, ed. Linda M. Whiteford and Lenore Manderson (Boulder, Colo.: Lynne Rienner Publishers, 2000); Paul Mosley et al., *Aid and Power: The World Bank and Policy-Based Lending in the 1980s: Case Studies*, vol. 2 (London: Routledge,

1991); Yifat Susskind, "Death, Politics, and the Condom: African Women Confront Bush's AIDS Policy," *CounterPunch*, December 6, 2005.

12. "One Person Making a Difference: Dr. Mardge Cohen Speaks About Her Experiences in Rwanda," *Latin Today*, January 30, 2006, available at: www.latinschool.org/latintoday/article_196.shtml.

13. Donald G. McNeil Jr., "UN Agency to Say It Overestimated Extent of HIV Cases by Millions," *New York Times*, November 20, 2007.

14. Haider Rizvi, "Challenging the 'Luxury' of Abstinence," Inter Press Service, December 1, 2006, available at: www.commondreams.org/headlines06/1201–06.htm.

15. On the drop in U.S. condom donations between 1993 and 2003, see Nicholas D. Kristof, "The Secret War on Condoms," *New York Times*, January 10, 2003.

16. The situation is particularly pressing in nations that continue to criminalize same-sex behaviors (Uganda is one of these). See Cary Alan Johnson, *Off the Map: How HIV/AIDS Programming Is Failing Same-Sex Practicing People in Africa* (International Gay and Lesbian Human Rights Commission, 2007), available at: www.iglhrc.org/files/iglhrc/otm/Off%20The%20Map.pdf; as well as the letter sent by the International Gay and Lesbian Rights Commission to Mark Dybul, the global AIDS coordinator for the Bush administration, on September 18, 2007; and the press release of the International Gay and Lesbian Rights Commission, October 10, 2007. Both of the latter documents note that Christian and Muslim organizations in Uganda funded by PEPFAR were openly homophobic, while the needs of same-sex-desiring individuals were to a considerable extent being ignored in PEPFAR programming.

17. See, for example, Vanessa Brocato, introduction to "PEPFAR Country Profiles: Focusing in on Prevention and Youth," 2005, p. 6, SIECUS, available at: www.siecus.org/inter/pepfar. As of 2006, more than 20 percent of the adult population was said to be infected in Botswana, Lesotho, Swaziland, and Zimbabwe.

18. President's Emergency Plan for AIDS Relief, Office of the U.S. Global AIDS Coordinator, "ABC Guidance #1 for United States Government In-Country Staff and Implementing Partners Applying the ABC Approach to Preventing Sexually-Transmitted HIV Infections Within the President's Emergency Plan for AIDS Relief," available at: www.state.gov/documents/organization/57241.pdf.

19. Quoted in Wendy Turnbull, "Uncharted Waters: The Impact of U.S. Policy in Vietnam," *Population Action International*, December 2006, available at: www.populationaction.org/resources/CaseStudies/Vietnam/VietnamCS2.htm (accessed March 2, 2007).

20. David Veazey, quoted in Sarah Fort, "Bush's Failed Global AIDS Plan," *Ms.*, November 30, 2006, available at: www.alternet.org/story/44852.

21. EU declaration and Hilary Benn, both quoted in Sarah Boseley, "Europeans Reject Abstinence Message in Split with U.S. on AIDS: EU Urges African Nations Not to Heed Bush Agenda; Condoms 'Most Effective' Weapon Against Epidemic," *The Guardian*, December 1, 2005.

22. Turnbull, "Uncharted Waters." The eleven countries exempted from the 66 percent abstinence/fidelity earmark for 2006 were Cambodia, Côte d'Ivoire, Ethiopia, Guyana, Haiti, India, Mozambique, Russia, Rwanda, Tanzania, and Vietnam. On the non-exempted countries' need to compensate for the exempted ones, as well as the requirement's negative impact on countries' ability to promote and finance condom use, see also SIECUS, "GAO Report Finds Frustration and Confusion in Countries Receiving U.S. Assistance for HIV/AIDS" (policy update), April 4, 2006, available at: www.siecus.org/policy/PUpdates/pdate0242.html.

23. U.S. Government Accountability Office, "Global Health: Spending Requirement Presents Challenges for Allocating Prevention Funding Under the President's Emergency Plan for AIDS Relief," April 2006, available at: www.gao.gov/new.items/d06395.pdf.

24. "Abstinence and AIDS" (editorial), *Boston Globe*, December 1, 2006.

25. Steve Stecklow, "U.S. Abstinence Tack in AIDS Prevention Is Criticized by GAO," *Wall Street Journal*, April 5, 2006.

26. See David Brown, "Africa Gives 'ABC' Mixed Grades," *Washington Post*, August 15, 2006.

27. Andrew Quinn, "Low Condom Use Blamed in Southern Africa AIDS Crisis," *Reuters NewMedia*, August 14, 2006, available at: www.aegis.org/news/re/2006/RE060840.html. One of the reports was conducted by the Southern African Development Community (SADC).

28. Keith E. Hansen, (review of Catherine Campbell, *Letting Them Die: Why HIV/AIDS Prevention Programs Fail*), *New England Journal of Medicine* (May 13, 2004).

29. See Tuncalp, "U.S. Is Accused"; and Helen Epstein, "God and the Fight Against AIDS," *New York Review of Books*, April 28, 2005.

30. Lawrence K. Altman, "U.S. Blamed for Condom Shortage in Fighting AIDS in Uganda," *New York Times*, August 30, 2005.

31. Bridget Maher, "Why Wait: The Benefits of Abstinence Until Marriage," Family Research Council, April 12, 2007, available at: www.frc.org/get.cfm?i=IS06B01.

32. John S. Gardner, "Condomania," *National Review Online*, April 12, 2006.

33. This is one of the most important points made in Helen Epstein, *The Invisible Cure: Africa, the West, and the Fight Against AIDS* (New York: Farrar, Straus and Giroux, 2007).

34. Edward C. Green, "HIV/AIDS, TB, and Malaria: Combating a Global Pandemic," testimony before the House Subcommittee on Health, March 20, 2003, available at: republicans.energycommerce.house.gov/108/Hearings/03202003hearing832/Green1379.htm.

35. Edward C. Green, *Rethinking AIDS Prevention: Learning from Successes in Developing Countries* (Westport, Conn.: Praeger Press, 2003), pp. 93–124.

36. Arthur Allen, "Sex Change: Uganda v. Condoms," *The New Republic*, May 27, 2002; Epstein, *The Invisible Cure*, p. 187.

37. Edward C. Green, testimony before the Senate Subcommittee on African Affairs, May 19, 2003.

38. Elisabeth Bumiller, "Ugandan's Key to White House: AIDS," *New York Times*, June 11, 2003.

39. See James Putzel, "The Politics of Action on AIDS: A Case Study of Uganda," *Public Administration and Development* 24 (2004): 19–30; Tim Allen, "AIDS and Evidence: Some Ugandan Myths," *Journal of Biosocial Science* (2005): 14–16.

40. Epstein, "God and the Fight Against AIDS."

41. Population Action International, "Why the ABCs Are Essential to HIV/AIDS Prevention" (fact sheet), available at: www.populationaction.org/resources/factsheets/factsheet_22.htm (accessed April 17, 2007).

42. See Maria J. Wawer et al., "Uganda's HIV Prevention Success: The Role of Sexual Behavior Change and the National Response: Commentary on Green et al.," *AIDS and Behavior* 10, no. 4 (July 2006); see also the discussion of the early findings of this study discussed in Allen, "AIDS and Evidence," pp. 15–16.

43. Chris Beyrer, quoted in Lawrence K. Altman, "Study Challenges Abstinence as Crucial to AIDS Strategy," *New York Times*, February 24, 2005.

44. "The Missing Condoms" (editorial), *New York Times*, September 4, 2005.

45. Human Rights Watch, "The Less They Know, the Better: Abstinence-Only HIV/AIDS Programs in Uganda," available at: hrw.org/reports/2005/uganda0305/8.htm.

46. Fred de Sam Lazaro, "Uganda, Abstinence, and the Spread of HIV," NPR, August 14, 2006, available at: www.npr.org/templates/story/story.php?storyId=5644177.

47. UNAIDS, "AIDS Epidemic Update," December 6, 2006, p. 18, summarized in SIECUS, "UNAIDS Report: Lack of Comprehensive Prevention Knowledge Among Young People Contributes to Increase in HIV in PEPFAR Focus Countries" (policy update), November 2006, available at: www.siecus.org/policy/PUpdates/pdate0288.html.

48. Lazaro, "Uganda, Abstinence, and the Spread of HIV."

49. Fort, "Bush's Failed Global AIDS Plan."

50. Yifat Susskind, "Greed, Dogma, and AIDS," *CounterPunch*, December 2–3, 2006, available at: www.counterpunch.org/susskind12022006.html.

51. Shawn Hendricks, "Ugandan First Lady Honored for Support of Abstinence Promotion," Baptist Press, June 23, 2004, available at: www.bpnews.net/bpnews.asp?ID=18556.

52. Janet Museveni in a 2004 speech, quoted in Epstein, "God and the Fight Against AIDS."

53. "Call for Ugandan Virgin Census," BBC News, December 2, 2004, available at: news.bbc.co.uk/1/hi/world/africa/4061779.stm.

54. Hendricks, "Ugandan First Lady Honored."

55. "AIDS Workers: USAID Starting to See Value of Abstinence," *Baptist Press News*, March 14, 2005, available at: www.bpnews.net/bpcollectionnews.asp?ID=58.

56. Emily Chambers, quoted in Epstein, "God and the Fight Against AIDS."

57. *New York Times*, "The Missing Condoms."

58. Sarah Boseley, "Gates Criticizes HIV Abstinence Policies," *The Guardian*, August 14, 2006.

59. "HIV Prevention Policy Needs an Urgent Cure," *The Lancet* (April 15–21, 2006).

60. Paul Zeitz, quoted in David Brown, "GAO Criticizes Bush's AIDS Plan: Abstinence-and-Fidelity Provision Sowing Confusion, Report Says," *Washington Post*, April 5, 2006.

61. Health Gap Global Access Project, quoted in Anne Farris, "Government Report Faults Limiting AIDS Strategies to Abstinence and Fidelity," Roundtable on Religion and Social Welfare Policy, April 11, 2006, available at: www.religionandsocialpolicy.org/news/article.cfm?id=4060.

62. Richard Holbrooke, quoted in Chris Tomlinson, "U.S. AIDS Program Revolutionizes Kenya," Associated Press, December 1, 2006, available at: www.sfgate.com/cgi-bin/article.cgi?file=/n/a/2006/12/01/international/i043759S09.DTL&type=printable.

63. Stephen Lewis, keynote address at the closing session of the sixteenth International AIDS Conference, August 18, 2006, available at: www.stephenlewisfoundation.org/news_item.cfm?news=1338.

64. Stephen Lewis, quoted in Altman, "U.S. Blamed for Condom Shortage."

65. Population Action International, "Why the ABCs Are Essential to HIV/AIDS Prevention."

66. *Boston Globe*, "Abstinence and AIDS."

67. Sarah Boseley, "UN Highlights Spread of Disease Across the World," *The Guardian*, December 1, 2006.

68. *Boston Globe*, "Abstinence and AIDS"; McNeil, "U.N. Agency to Say It Overestimated Extent of HIV Cases."

69. Barbara Crossette, "Hurting the World's Poor in Morality's Name," *World Policy Journal* 21, no. 4 (Winter 2004–2005). Crossette was chief correspondent for the *New York Times* in Southeast Asia and South Asia and then the *Times'* UN bureau chief from 1994 to 2001.

70. Dean Jamison and Nancy Padian, "Where AIDS Funding Should Go," *Washington Post*, May 20, 2006, summarizing the conclusions on HIV prevention put forward in the book resulting from the Beijing meeting, *Disease Control Priorities in Developing Countries* (2nd ed.). Jamison is an economist and Padian an epidemiologist.

71. Sarah Boseley, "UN Calls for Male Circumcision to Tackle AIDS," *The Guardian*, April 13–19, 2007.

72. Population Action International, "Why the ABCs Are Essential to HIV/AIDS Prevention."

73. E. J. Dionne Jr., "Message from a Megachurch," *Washington Post*, December 5, 2006.

74. Malcolm Gladwell, "The Cellular Church," *The New Yorker*, September 12, 2005.

75. Robert Lanham, *The Sinner's Guide to the Evangelical Right* (New York: New American Library, 2006), pp. 54, 56.

76. Rick Warren, "Use Your Influence to Tackle HIV/AIDS," *Rick Warren's Ministry ToolBox* no. 149, April 7, 2004, available at www. pastors.com/RWMT/?ID=149.

77. David Van Biema, "Warren of Rwanda," *Time*, August 15, 2005; Marc Gunther, "Will Success Spoil Rick Warren?" *Fortune*, October 31, 2005. Kagame's own main argument is that the battle against HIV/AIDS must be embedded in a larger battle to reduce poverty and encourage the development of a sound infrastructure and health care system; trade, he says, is as important as aid; see Henry J. Kaiser Family Foundation, "HIV/AIDS Threatens to Undo Social, Economic Achievements in Africa, Rwandan President Paul Kagame Says," March 7, 2003, available at www.kaisernetwork.org/daily_reports/rep_hiv_recent_rep.cfm?dr_cat=1& show=yes&dr_DateTime=03–07–03#16441.

78. See the website for the PEACE Plan, www.thepeaceplan.com.

79. Warren spoke about CHURCH at the Ecumenical and Interfaith Pre-Conference held before the sixteenth International AIDS Conference in Toronto; see "Rick Warren Tells AIDS Conference: 'When You Love People, You Use Money,'" Assist News Service, August 14, 2006, available at: www.streamingfaith.com/community/news/news.aspx?NewsId= 353&bhcp=1.

80. Elizabeth Kwon, "Rick Warren: Church Can S.T.O.P. HIV/AIDS," *Christian Post*, December 31, 2006, available at: www.christianpost.com/ article/20061231/24610.htm.

81. TIME Global Health Summit, press conference, New York, November 1, 2005, transcript available at: www.time.com/time/2005/ globalhealth/transcripts/110105warrenpc.pdf.

82. James Pinkerton, "The Coming AIDS Reformation," *Huffington Post*, August 16, 2006, available at: www.huffingtonpost.com/james-pinkerton/the-coming-aids-reformati_b_27388.html.

83. Sue Sprenkle, "Jesus Only Answer to HIV/AIDS Crisis, Missionary Tells Youth," International Mission Board, November 30, 2001, available at: www.imb.org/core/story.asp?storyID=733; also available as a

link under "Pastors.com Ministry Library" at *Rick Warren's Ministry Tool-Box* no. 149, April 7, 2004, www.pastors.com/RWMT/?ID=149.

84. Traci Gross, "Right Message for Teenagers Is Abstinence," *News and Observer* (Raleigh, N.C.), December 4, 2007.

85. Edward C. Green, quoted in Priya Abraham, "Hooked on Failure," *World*, November 6, 2004.

86. Kathryn Jean Lopez, "ABC, Sir Elton," National Review Online, June 22, 2005, available at: www.nationalreview.com/lopez/lopez2005 06220752.asp.

87. "FRC: Africans May Be in Danger if President's AIDS Proposal Passes," OneNewsNow.com, June 5, 2007, available at: www.one newsnow.com/2007/06/frc_africans_may_be_in_danger_.php (accessed June 6, 2007).

88. Mike Huckabee, quoted in Peter Hamby, "Huckabee Skeptical of Condom Use to Fight AIDS in Africa," CNN.com, September 20, 2007, available at: politicalticker.blogs.cnn.com/2007/09/20/huckabee-skeptical-of-condom-use-to-fight-aids-in-africa.

89. Adam Nagourney, "McCain Stumbles on HIV Prevention," *New York Times*, March 16, 2007.

90. *DKT International, Inc. v. United States Agency for International Development*, memorandum opinion, p. 4, available at: hrw.org/pub/amicusbriefs/DKTdecision.pdf.

91. *DKT International, Inc. v. United States Agency for International Development*, complaint filed in U.S. District Court for the District of Columbia, available at: www.dktinternational.org/pdf/DKT_Complaint.pdf.

92. *DKT International, Inc. v. USAID*, memorandum opinion, p. 8.

93. Turnbull, "Uncharted Waters."

94. DKT International, "Vietnam," available at: www.dktinternational .org/vietnam.htm.

95. Beth Schnayerson, "AIDS in Asia: The Continent's Growing Crisis," *San Francisco Chronicle*, November 24, 2002.

96. *DKT International, Inc. v. USAID*, complaint.

97. Helene Cooper, "What? Condoms Can Prevent AIDS? No Way!" *New York Times*, August 26, 2005.

98. "Social marketing" is neutrally described in DKT's complaint as making "products and services affordable to poor populations by subsidizing the price and by making effective use of marketing techniques and

private sector networks to deliver products and services." *DKT International, Inc. v. USAID,* complaint.

99. Philip D. Harvey, quoted in Jay Cheshes, "Hard-Core Philanthropist," *Mother Jones,* November–December 2002.

100. Anne Philpott, Wendy Knerr, and Dermot Maher, "Promoting Protection and Pleasure: Amplifying the Effectiveness of Barriers Against Sexually Transmitted Infections and Pregnancy," *The Lancet* (December 2–8, 2006): 2028–31.

101. DKT International, "Vietnam."

102. Turnbull, "Uncharted Waters."

103. Community Action for Preventing HIV/AIDS: Responding to HIV/AIDS in the Greater Mekong Subregion, "Vietnam—Social Marketing of Condoms," available at: www.jfpr-hiv.org/VNSocialMktofCondoms.htm.

104. See *DKT International, Inc. v. USAID,* memorandum opinion.

105. "Federal Appeals Court Rules in Favor of U.S. Policy Requiring Groups That Receive HIV/AIDS Funding to Condemn Commercial Sex Work," *Medical News Today,* March 2, 2007, available at: www.medical newstoday.com/articles/64200.php; see also Kaiser Daily HIV/AIDS Report, October 11, 2006.

106. Andrew S. Natsios, quoted in Bob Herbert, "In America; Refusing to Save Africans," *New York Times,* June 11, 2001; see also Africa Action, www.africaaction.org/docs01/nat0106.htm (originally from *Boston Globe,* June 7, 2001).

107. "The Global Battle Against AIDS; Opposition to Condoms," *New York Times,* May 18, 2004.

108. Randall Tobias, quoted at "Ask the White House," December 1, 2004, available at: www.whitehouse.gov/ask/20041201.html.

109. Brian Ross and Justin Rood, "The Blotter: Senior Official Linked to Escort Service Resigns," ABCNews.com, April 27, 2007, available at: blogs.abcnews.com/theblotter/2007/04/senior_official.html.

110. Anne Gearan, "Foreign Aid Coordinator Resigns," Associated Press, April 27, 2007, available at: abcnews.go.com/Politics/wireStory ?id=3092819.

111. Guttmacher Institute Media Center, "Earlier and More Detailed Sex Education Needed in Africa: Critical to Preventing HIV and Teen Pregnancy," December 12, 2007, available at: www.guttmacher.org/media/nr/2007/12/12/index.html.

112. "Tanzania Implements HIV Prevention Measures as World Marks AIDS Day," Online NewsHour, November 30, 2007, available at: www.pbs.org/newshour/bb/africa/july-dec07/aids_11-30.html.

113. "Barbara Lee Introduces Bill to Reduce Women and Girls' Vulnerability to HIV/AIDS," *Medical News Today*, March 28, 2007, available at: www.medicalnewstoday.com/articles/66480.php.

114. Bill Frist, speaking at Princeton University's Woodrow Wilson Center, December 3, 2007.

115. See Esther Kaplan, "Lantos' Last Act for AIDS," *The Nation*, March 3, 2008.

Chapter 6: In Pursuit of Happiness

1. Ralph Blumenthal, "Joel Osteen's Credo: Eliminate the Negative, Accentuate Prosperity," *New York Times*, March 30, 2006; see also the website for Benny Hinn Ministries, www.bennyhinn.org/default.cfm.

2. Melani McAlister, "An Empire of Their Own," *The Nation*, September 22, 2003; Chris Hedges, *American Fascists: The Christian Right and the War on America* (New York: Free Press, 2006); Nicholas Guyatt, *Have a Nice Doomsday: Why Americans Are Looking Forward to the End of the World* (New York: Harper Perennial, 2007).

3. Susan Friend Harding, *The Book of Jerry Falwell: Fundamentalist Language and Politics* (Princeton, N.J.: Princeton University Press, 2000); Thomas Frank, *What's the Matter with Kansas? How Conservatives Won the Heart of America* (New York: Metropolitan, 2004); Chris Mooney, *The Republican War on Science* (New York: Basic Books, 2006); Bryan F. Le Beau, "Science and Religion: A Historical Perspective on the Conflict over Teaching Evolution in the Schools," and Melanie A. Bailey, "From Spontaneous Generation to Intelligent Design: Conservative Challenges to Science and to Radicalism," both in *Radical History Review* 99 (Fall 2007).

4. D. Michael Lindsay, *Faith in the Halls of Power: How Evangelicals Joined the American Elite* (New York: Oxford University Press, 2007); Hanna Rosin, *God's Harvard: A Christian College on a Mission to Serve America* (New York: Harcourt, 2007); Monique El-Faizy, *God and Country: How Evangelicals Have Become America's New Mainstream* (New York: Bloomsbury, 2006); Dan Gilgoff, *The Jesus Machine: How James Dobson, Focus on the Family, and Evangelical America Are Winning the Culture War*

(New York: St. Martin's, 2007); Michelle Goldberg, *Kingdom Coming: The Rise of Christian Nationalism* (New York: Norton, 2006).

5. Beliefnet.com, "Evangelical Views of Islam," April 7, 2003, available at: www.beliefnet.com/story/124/story_12447_1.html; see critiques in Muqtedar Khan, "The Public Face of Christian Evangelical Bigotry," altmuslim comment, June 25, 2003, available at: www.altmuslim.com/a/a/a/2102/; Charles Marsh, "Wayward Christian Soldiers," *New York Times*, January 20, 2006.

6. See the ad "Christians Call for a United Jerusalem," *New York Times*, April 18, 1997; "The Rebirth of Ralph Reed," *Atlanta Jewish Times*, July 23, 1999; the ad of the Anti-Defamation League with text by Ralph Reed, *New York Times*, May 2, 2002; Abraham H. Foxman, "Why Evangelical Support for Israel Is a Good Thing," Anti-Defamation League, July 16, 2002, available at www.adl.org/Israel/evangelical.asp; Maureen Dowd, "Rapture and Power," *New York Times*, October 6, 2002; Donald Wagner, "The Evangelical-Jewish Alliance," *The Christian Century*, June 28, 2003; Joan Didion, "Mr. Bush and the Divine," *New York Review of Books*, November 6, 2003; Rick Perlstein, "The Jesus Landing Pad," *Village Voice*, May 18, 2004; Max Blumenthal, "Born-Agains for Sharon," *Salon*, October 30, 2004; Karen Armstrong, "Root Out This Sinister Cultural Flaw," *The Guardian*, April 6, 2005; E. J. Kessler, "Right-Wing Jews Rally to Defense of Embattled DeLay," *The Forward*, April 15, 2005; Esther Kaplan, *With God on Their Side: George W. Bush and the Christian Right* (New York: New Press, 2005), esp. pp. 23–29; Melani McAlister, *Epic Encounters: Culture, Media, and U.S. Interests in the Middle East Since 1945* (Berkeley: University of California Press, 2005).

7. See, for instance, sample web pages for Pure Intimacy, a subgroup of Focus on the Family run by Daniel L. Weiss, www.pureintimacy.org/gr/theology/a0000077.cfm and www.pureintimacy.org/gr/getting_started/a0000149.cfm.

8. On sexual abuse, domestic violence, and addiction and substance abuse recovery, see the Pure Intimacy web page, www.pureintimacy.org/gr/intimacy/, the Focus on the Family–endorsed book by Donald Stewart, *Refuge: A Pathway Out of Domestic Violence and Abuse* (Birmingham, Ala.: New Hope, 2004), and the websites for Christian Recovery International, www.christianrecovery.com/, and Missing Link, Inc., misslink.org/practicl.html. Also relevant in this context is the popular self-help series by Liz Curtis Higgs, *Bad Girls of the Bible and What We Can Learn from*

Them (Colorado Springs, Colo.: WaterBrook Press, 2000), and its sequels. On Christian dieting, see Grant Wacker, "Slim for Him: Christian Dieting and American Culture," *Christianity Today*, November 1, 2005; R. Marie Griffith, *Born Again Bodies: Flesh and Spirit in American Christianity* (Berkeley: University of California Press, 2004). For examples of these texts, see Gwen Shamblin, *The Weigh Down Diet* (New York: Galilee/Doubleday, 1997); and Ted Haggard, *The Jerusalem Diet: The "One-Day" Approach to Reach Your Ideal Weight—and Stay There* (Colorado Springs, Colo.: WaterBrook Press, 2005). Anti-masturbation guru Stephen Arterburn's New Life Ministries also offers chemical dependency treatment (cd.newlife.com/) and eating disorder treatment (remuda.newlife.com/) at New Life's Recovery Place, and New Life is in the dieting business as well, mixing biblical guidance with such helpful pointers as the information that darker greens such as spinach are healthier than iceberg lettuce. See Stephen Arterburn and Linda Mintle, *Lose It for Life: The Total Solution—Spiritual, Emotional, Physical—For Permanent Weight Loss* (Brentwood, Tenn.: Integrity Publishers, 2004).

9. Emily Weinstein, "Salvation Army," *Village Voice*, September 27–October 3, 2006; Lauren Sandler, *Righteous: Dispatches from the Evangelical Youth Movement* (New York: Viking, 2006); Andrew Beaujon, *Body Piercing Saved My Life: Inside the Phenomenon of Christian Rock* (New York: Da Capo Press, 2006); John Leland, "Rebels with a Cross," *New York Times*, March 2, 2006.

10. Two classic texts are John Eldredge, *Wild at Heart: Discovering the Secret of a Man's Soul* (Nashville: Thomas Nelson, 1998); and Paul Coughlin, *No More Christian Nice Guy: Why Being Nice—Instead of Good—Hurts Men, Women, and Children* (Bloomington, Minn.: Bethany House, 2006). See also Eileen Finan, "Real Men Talk About God: A New Christian Movement Lets Guys Be Guys," *Newsweek*, October 30, 2006; for a different take on how masculinity functions in Religious Right culture, see Chris Hedges, "The Cult of Masculinity," in *American Fascists*.

11. Randall Balmer, "Strange Bedfellows: The Abortion Myth, Homosexuality, and the Ruse of Selective Literalism," in *Thy Kingdom Come—An Evangelical's Lament: How the Religious Right Distorts the Faith and Threatens America* (New York: Basic Books, 2006); Harding, "The Pro-Life Gospel," in *The Book of Jerry Falwell*; Nicholas Ray, *False Promises: How the Right Deploys Homophobia to Win Support from African-*

Americans, National Gay and Lesbian Task Force, 2006, available at: www.thetaskforce.org/downloads/reports/reports/FalsePromises.pdf.

12. Janice Irvine, *Talk About Sex: The Battles over Sex Education in the United States*, 2nd ed. (Berkeley: University of California Press, 2004).

13. Eyal Press, *Absolute Convictions: My Father, a City, and the Conflict That Divided America* (New York: Picador, 2007).

14. See, however, the recent critique of the sincerity of Bush's religious convictions in Jacob Weisberg, "He'd Rather Talk About Sex Than God," *The Sunday Times* (London), January 27, 2008.

15. Barry W. Lynn, *Piety and Politics: The Right-Wing Assault on Religious Freedom* (New York: Harmony Books, 2006); R. Marie Griffith and Melani McAlister, "Introduction: Is the Public Square Still Naked?" *American Quarterly* 59, no. 3 (September 2007), special issue on "Religion and Politics in the Contemporary United States"; Neil A. Lewis, "Justice Department Reshapes Its Civil Rights Mission," *New York Times*, June 14, 2007; Diana B. Henriques and Andrew Lehren, "Religious Groups Granted Millions for Pet Projects," *New York Times*, May 13, 2007; Stephen Lendman, "Apocalyptic Imperialists," *CounterPunch*, April 23, 2007.

16. For a good glimpse of what was at the end of the 1990s still a rather more evenly balanced stand-off, see Ron Stodghill, "Where'd You Learn That?" *Time*, June 15, 1998. See also the overviews of the state of debate in Debra W. Haffner and James Wagoner, "Vast Majority of Americans Support Sexuality Education," *SIECUS Report* 27, no. 6 (August–September 1999); Cynthia Dailard, "Sex Education: Politicians, Parents, Teachers, and Teens," *Guttmacher Report on Public Policy* 4, no. 1 (February 2001); and "Sex Education in the U.S.: Policy and Politics," *Kaiser Family Foundation Update* (October 2002); as well as the information in Christopher Healy, "No Sex, Please—Or We'll Audit You," *Salon*, October 28, 2003, that as of 1999 all the sex education curricula endorsed officially by the Centers for Disease Control were comprehensive curricula.

17. Mooney, *The Republican War on Science*.

18. Deborah Arindell, quoted in Brian Alexander, "The New Lies About Women's Health Update," *Glamour*, October 2, 2006, available at: www.glamour.com/health/feature/articles/2006/10/02/liesaboutwomens healthupdate; Sen. Frank Lautenberg, press release; Lynn Neary, "Maine Sparks Debate over Pre-Teens, Birth Control," NPR, *Talk of the Nation*,

October 22, 2007, available at: www.encyclopedia.com/doc/1P1–14521 1335.html?Q="birth%20control."

19. Atul Gawande, "Let's Talk About Sex," *New York Times*, May 19, 2007. Each year in the United States, 3 million women face an unwanted pregnancy, and half of those pregnancies end in abortion. See the information at the website of Louise M. Slaughter, congresswoman for New York's Twenty-eighth District, on the Emergency Contraception Education Act, HR 3326, available at: www.louise.house.gov/index .php?option=com_content&task=view&id=476&Itemid=.

20. Christine Stansell, "Partial Law: A Lost History of Abortion," *The New Republic*, May 21, 2007; Ronald Dworkin, "The Court and Abortion: It's Worse Than You Think," *New York Review of Books*, May 31, 2007.

21. Janelle Nanos, "Abortion Ruling Causes Worries, Confusion for Angry City Docs," *New York*, April 23, 2007.

22. Joerg Dreweke and Rebecca Wind, "Abortion Counseling Requirements Often Violate Core Principles of Informed Consent," Guttmacher Institute Media Center, November 13, 2007, available at: www.guttmacher.org/media/nr/2007/11/13/index.html.

23. Wanda Franz, quoted in Robin Toner, "Abortion Foes See Validation for New Tactic," *New York Times*, May 22, 2007.

24. "Rep. Nadler, Sen. Boxer Reintroduce the Freedom of Choice Act: Legislation Would Codify *Roe v. Wade* Decision," April 19, 2007, available at the website of Representative Nadler, www.house.gov/list/ press/ny08_nadler/IntroFOCA041907.html.

25. Justice Anthony Kennedy's April 18, 2007, majority opinion in the case of *Gonzales v. Carhart* can be found at the website of Cornell University Law School, www.law.cornell.edu/supct/html/05–380.ZO.html.

26. This quotation appears on the website of Operation Outcry (www.operationoutcry.org/pages.asp?pageid=48047), a 2007 project of the Justice Foundation, and was included in the foundation's friend-of-the-court brief.

27. House Committee on Oversight and Government Reform, "Federally Funded Pregnancy Resource Centers Mislead Teens About Abortion Risks," *Public Health*, July 17, 2006, available at: reform.democrats .house.gov/story.asp?ID=1080.

28. Gary Langer, "Support for Legal Abortion Wobbles; Religion Informs Much Opposition," ABCNews.com, July 2, 2001, available at: abcnews.go.com/us/DailyNews/p011010702.html; "Abortion Access:

U.S. Public Opinion Polls: Year 2005," ReligiousTolerance.org, available at: www.religioustolerance.org/abopoll05.htm; Celinda Lake, "The Polls Speak: Americans Support Abortion," *Ms.*, Summer 2005, available at: www.msmagazine.com/summer2005/polls.asp.

29. PERVERS IST NUR, WER KEIN KONDOM BENUTZT; see the Michael Stich campaign in "Drastische Kampagne gegen AIDS," *Spiegel Online*, March 29, 2007, available at: www.spiegel.de/panorama/0,1518,474758 ,00.html. The poster shows silhouettes of numerous sex toys and S&M paraphernalia.

30. SEITENSPRUNG? ICH KOMM MIT!, 2001 condom campaign of the Bundeszentrale für gesundheitliche Aufklärung, available at: www.bzga.de.

31. From the condom campaign of the Lega Italiana per la Lotta contro L'Aids, available at: www.lila.it/galleria_camp_nazionali.htm.

32. PARIS PROTÈGE L'AMOUR, 2004 condom campaign in Paris.

33. See SuperFrenchie, "Abstinence Vs. 20-Cent Condoms," Culture Wars, December 5, 2005, available at: superfrenchie.com/?m= 20051205.

34. Ongoing debate concerns how best to ensure prostitutes' safety (decriminalizing brothels as well in the hopes that this will give prostitutes more control over their working conditions has been one approach)—and also how best to give prostitutes the ability to leave the profession should they choose. Some have hoped that regularizing work conditions would also encourage prostitutes to pay taxes; this goal has proved more elusive. For a useful discussion of the mixed results of the new prostitution law passed in Germany in 2002 with all these goals in mind, see Bundesministerium für Familie, Senioren, Frauen, und Jugend, "Prostitutionsgesetz," March 15, 2006, available at: www.bmfsfj.de/ Politikbereiche/gleichstellung,did=72948.html.

35. On the legalization process in Portugal, see Elaine Sciolino, "Portugal's Vote on Abortion Ban Stirs Emotions," *New York Times*, February 11, 2007; SIECUS, "Portugal Set to Legalize Abortions" (policy updates), February 2007, available at: www.siecus.org/policy/PUpdates/pdate 0311.html; "World Briefing/Europe: Portugal: Legal Abortion Comes into Effect," *New York Times*, April 11, 2007. On the Portuguese Catholic church's reluctance to intervene, see Luis Sérgio Solimeo, "Why Did Catholic Portugal Legalize Abortion?" American Society for the Defense of Tradition, Family, and Property, 2007, available at: www.tfp.org/ TFPForum/catholic_perspective/why_did_catholic_portugal.htm. On

the liberalizations in France (2001) and Switzerland (2002), see Center for Reproductive Rights, "Abortion Worldwide: Twelve Years of Reform" (briefing paper), July 2007, available at: www.reproductiverights .org/pdf/pub_bp_abortionlaws10.pdf.

36. See the remarks of BPAS (formerly British Pregnancy Advisory Service) executive director Ann Furedi, quoted in Lucy Ward and Riazat Butt, "Too Many Abortions: Lord Steel," *The Guardian*, October 24, 2007.

37. John Santelli et al., "Contraceptive Use and Pregnancy Risk Among U.S. High School Students, 1991–2003," *Perspectives on Sexual and Reproductive Health* 38 (2006): 106–11; Bundeszentrale für gesundheitliche Aufklärung, ed., *Jugendsexualität: Repräsentative Wiederholungsbefragung von 14- bis 17-Jährigen und ihrer Eltern* (Cologne: BZgA, 2006).

38. See the Charter of Fundamental Rights of the European Union, promulgated in 2000, available at: www.europarl.europa.eu/charter/ pdf/text_en.pdf; "Homo-Ehe ohne Grenzen: Signal aus Brüssel," *EuroGay*, February 13, 2003, available at: www.eurogay.de/8420.html; Stephanie Holmes, "Profile: Rocco Buttiglione," BBC News.com, October 21, 2004, available at: news.bbc.co.uk/2/hi/europe/3718210.stm; Peter Popham, "Rocco Buttiglione," *The Independent*, November 8, 2004, available at: news.independent.co.uk/people/profiles/article19208.ece; Matti Bunzl, "Queering Austria for the New Europe," *Contemporary Austrian Studies* 15 (2007), special issue on "Sexuality in Austria," ed. Gunter Bischof et al.

39. Mubarak Dahir, "Bertrand Delanoe—Gay Mayor of Paris, France," *The Advocate*, August 14, 2001; Jan Feddersen, "'Und das ist gut so': Klaus Wowereit bekennt als erster Spitzenpolitiker selbstbewusst seine Homosexualität," *die tageszeitung*, June 12, 2001.

40. Jennifer Green, "Spain Legalizes Same-Sex Marriage," *Washington Post*, July 1, 2005. On the Netherlands and Belgium, see "Expanding Rights in Europe," *International Herald Tribune*, July 3, 2003.

41. "'Gay' Baby Triggers Row," *Sydney Morning Herald*, October 24, 2007, available at: www.smh.com.au/news/World/Gay-baby-triggers-row/2007/10/24/1192941155033.html.

42. Michele Grigolo, "Sexualities and the ECHR: Introducing the Universal Sexual Legal Subject," *European Journal of International Law* (November 2003); Helmut Graupner, "Das späte Menschenrecht," *Sexuologie* 11, nos. 3–4 (2004) and 12, nos. 1–2 (2005).

43. Graupner, "Das späte Menschenrecht," p. 71.

44. Liesbet Stevens and Marc Hooghe, "The Swing of the Pendulum: The Detraditionalization of the Regulation of Sexuality and Intimacy in Belgium (1973–2003)," *International Journal of the Sociology of Law* 31 (2003): 131–51; Janine Mossuz-Lavau, *Women of Europe: 10 Years*, no. 27 (June 1988): 9–13; Alastair Mowbray, "European Convention on Human Rights: The Issuing of Practice Directions and Recent Cases," *Human Rights Law Review* 4, no. 1 (2004): 169–74; Martin Scheinin, "Sexual Rights as Human Rights—Protected Under Existing Human Rights Treaties?" *Nordic Journal of International Law* 67 (1998).

45. "Nur wenn beide es wollen," From "Sexualität—Was sind unsere Rechte?," Pro Familia flyer, 2005.

46. Lynn Harris, "What Happens When Your Country's Not Weird About Sex? European Teens Are Far from Abstinent, but Their Rates of Pregnancy and STDs Are Much Lower Than Ours. Hmm." *Salon*, May 17, 2006.

47. See the French teen magazines *Girls!* (especially the column "Questions Sexo") and *Muteen* (the October 2007 issue, for instance, explains tantric sex to teens), as well as the nudes and detailed sex advice in the German *Bravo*, also available in part at: www.bravo.de/online/. And although there is no nudity in the best-selling Italian teen girl magazine *Top Girl*, there are certainly open discussions of teen sex. (On the other hand, the mainstream TV channels in Italy have offered not just nudity but also pornography—generally naked women pleasuring themselves or each other.) See topgirl.tiscali.it/default.aspx.

48. Elisabeth Pott, "Macht's mit der BZgA zusammen," *Pro Familia Magazin*, no. 4 (2006): 21–22.

49. Elizabeth Agnvall, "In Western Europe," *Washington Post*, May 16, 2006.

50. John Santelli et al., "Exploring Recent Declines in Adolescent Pregnancy in the United States: The Contribution of Abstinence and Increased Contraceptive Use," *American Journal of Public Health* 97 (2007): 150–56.

51. Susheela Singh and Jacqueline E. Darroch, "Adolescent Pregnancy and Childbearing: Levels and Trends in Developed Countries," *Family Planning Perspectives* 32, no. 1 (2000): 14–23, also summarized in Elizabeth Agnvall, "Run the Numbers," *Washington Post*, May 16, 2006.

52. "Senator Lautenberg, Representatives Lee and Shays Say It's Time to Provide 'REAL' Comprehensive Sex Education" (press release), March 22, 2007, available at the website of Senator Lautenberg, lautenberg .senate.gov/newsroom/record.cfm?id=271129.

53. Nicholas D. Kristof, "Bush's Sex Scandal," *New York Times*, February 16, 2005.

54. Pierre-André Michaud, "Adolescents and Risks: Why Not Change Our Paradigm?" *Journal of Adolescent Health* 38, no. 5 (May 2006): 481–83.

55. Joan-Carles Surís, head of the Research Group on Adolescent Medicine, University of Lausanne, Switzerland, quoted in Agnvall, "In Western Europe."

56. For example, see *Transformations, Butterflies, Passions . . . and All Sorts of Questions: Parents' Guide for Discussing Sexuality with Their Teens* (Quebec City: Government of Quebec, 2007), available at: publications .msss.gouv.qc.ca/acrobat/f/documentation/2006/06–307–01A.pdf.

57. National Sexuality Research Center, "A Message from NSRC Director Gilbert Herdt," SexLiteracy.org, available at: nsrc.sfsu.edu/ SexLiteracyAbout.cfm.

58. Alan Guttmacher Institute, "Can More Progress Be Made? Teenage Sexual and Reproductive Behavior in Developed Countries," 2001, available at: www.guttmacher.org/pubs/euroteens_summ.pdf.

59. See John Gagnon, Alain Giami, Stuart Michaels, and Patrick Colomby, "A Comparative Study of the Couple in the Social Organization of Sexuality in France and the United States," *Journal of Sex Research* (February 2001); Gunter Schmidt, Silja Matthiesen, Arne Dekker, and Kurt Starke, *Spätmoderne Beziehungswelten* (Wiesbaden: VS Verlag für Sozialwissenschaften, 2006); A. Tonks, "British Sex Survey Shows Popularity of Monogamy," *British Medical Journal* 308 (January 29, 1994): 289.

60. See especially Joan W. Scott, *The Politics of the Veil* (Princeton, N.J.: Princeton University Press, 2007); Ian Buruma, *Murder in Amsterdam: The Death of Theo van Gogh and the Limits of Tolerance* (London: Penguin, 2006).

61. See "Integration auf Niederländisch: Der Holland-Test der eisernen Rita," *Spiegel Online*, March 14, 2006; "Die Gesinnungsprüfung," *die tageszeitung*, January 4, 2006.

62. See Maxwell Ciardullo, "Advocates on Both Sides Are Passionate as Ever: SIECUS Controversy Report 2004–2005 School Year," *SIECUS Report* 33, no. 4 (Fall 2005).

63. Alexander, "The New Lies About Women's Health Update."

64. National Conference of State Legislatures, "Pharmacist Conscience Clauses: Laws and Legislation," November 2007, available at: www.ncsl.org/programs/health/conscienceclauses.htm.

65. See Lisa Stokes, "EC Ban on Campuses," Planned Parenthood, 2005, available at: www.plannedparenthood.org/issues-action/birth-control/ec-ban-6521.htm.

66. "Massachusetts Pharmacy Board Rules Wal-Mart Must Stock EC," Pharmacist.com, February 23, 2006, available at: www.pharmacist.com/AM/Template.cfm?Section=Pharmacy_News&template=/CM/ContentDisplay.cfm&ContentID=9473.

67. William Smith and John Wagoner, quoted in Rob Stein, "Abstinence Programs Face Rejection," *Washington Post*, December 16, 2007.

68. Gary Langer, "Poll: Support for Civil Unions Rises, yet Sharp Divisions Remain," ABCNews.com, November 8, 2007, available at: abcnews.go.com/PollingUnit/story?id=3834625&page=1; see also "Relationship Recognition for Same-Sex Couples in the U.S.," National Gay and Lesbian Task Force, February 22, 2008, available at: www.thetask force.org/downloads/reports/issue_maps/relationship_recognition _2_08.pdf.

69. Santelli et al., "Exploring Recent Declines."

70. Henry J. Kaiser Family Foundation, *Safer Sex, Condoms, and "The Pill": A Series of National Surveys of Teens About Sex* (Menlo Park, Calif.: Henry J. Kaiser Family Foundation, 2000).

71. D. K. Eaton et al., "Youth Risk Behavior Surveillance, United States, 2005," *Morbidity and Mortality Weekly Report 2006* 55 (SS-5).

72. "Adolescent Protective Behaviors: Abstinence and Contraceptive Use," Advocates for Youth, December 21, 2007, available at: www .advocatesforyouth.org/publications/factsheet/fsprotective.htm.

73. Monica Davey, "Big Rise in Cost of Birth Control on Campuses," *New York Times*, November 22, 2007; Sara Rimer, "TV's Perfect Girl Is Pregnant; Real Families Talk," *New York Times*, December 21, 2007.

74. About.com, "Faye Wattleton (1943–)," available at: womenshistory .about.com/od/quotes/a/faye_wattleton.htm.

INDEX